DEVELOPING BUSINESS ETHICS IN CHINA

D1367659

DEVELOPING BUSINESS ETHICS IN CHINA

Edited by

Xiaohe Lu and Georges Enderle

With the Linguistic Assistance of

Jonathan Noble

DEVELOPING BUSINESS ETHICS IN CHINA

First published in 2006 by
PALGRAVE MACMILLAN™
175 Fifth Avenue, New York, N.Y. 10010 and
Houndmills, Basingstoke, Hampshire, England RG21 6XS
Companies and representatives throughout the world.

PALGRAVE MACMILLAN is the global academic imprint of the Palgrave Macmillan division of St. Martin's Press, LLC and of Palgrave Macmillan Ltd. Macmillan® is a registered trademark in the United States, United Kingdom and other countries. Palgrave is a registered trademark in the European Union and other countries.

ISBN 1–4039–7253–2

Library of Congress Cataloging-in-Publication Data

International Conference on Developing Business Ethics in China
    (2002: Shanghai, China)
        Developing business ethics in China / edited by Xiaohe Lu
    and Georges Enderle.
            p. cm.
        Selected papers from the International Conference on Developing
    Business Ethics in China, held in Shanghai on May 29–31, 2002.
        Includes bibliographical references and index.
        ISBN 1–4039–7253–2
            1. Business ethics—China—Congresses. I. Lu, Xiaohe.
    II. Enderle, Georges. III. Title.

HF5387.5.C6I58 2002
174'.4'0951—dc22   2005049306

A catalogue record for this book is available from the British Library.

Design by Newgen Imaging Systems (P) Ltd., Chennai, India.

First edition: March 2006

10 9 8 7 6 5 4 3 2 1

Printed in the United States of America.

Transferred to digital printing in 2007.

CONTENTS

ACKNOWLEDGMENTS

In preparing this book on *Developing Business Ethics in China*, we could draw on the expertise and commitment of many scholars and business practitioners in China and around the world. We are particularly grateful to all the contributors of this volume, who provided a firm and inspiring basis for addressing the vital challenges of business ethics in China. From the very beginning of this exciting undertaking, we had steadfast support by the Shanghai Academy of Social Sciences with its former President Yin Jizuo and its Centre for Business Ethics, along with the aid of the Shanghai Municipal Office for Spiritualization, in hosting the International Business Ethics Conference 2002 in Shanghai and publishing the proceedings in Chinese. We also acknowledge the professional collaboration with the International Society of Business, Economics, and Ethics (ISBEE). Moreover, we would like to thank Novartis and the Mendoza College of Business at the University of Notre Dame for their moral and financial assistance. Our sincere thanks also goes to Toby Wahl, Senior Editor, and Palgrave Macmillan for their great encouragement and very helpful suggestions.

We hope all these efforts of developing business ethics in China will provide a platform for further dialogue.

Xiaohe Lu and Georges Enderle

Introduction

An Overview of the Essays as a Platform for Further Dialogue

Georges Enderle

Developing business ethics in China is a long-term undertaking, full of complex issues, uncertain prospects, and urgent tasks. Nobody can reliably predict how China will look like in ten years. Through the economic reform and the opening up to the world, the last 20 plus years have brought about tremendous changes to the country; undoubtedly it deserves to be called, over all, an impressive success. But it is also undeniable that enormous challenges lie ahead: to build up not only a competitive and prosperous, but also an equitable and sustainable economy; to establish not only an effective, but also a democratic and stable rule of law; to foster a vibrant civil society; and to play a constructive and responsible part in international affairs.

While it goes far beyond business ethics to address all these challenges, its limited scope is still very large. To develop business ethics in China is vital for the country as well as for the world community. This development requires thorough investigations, courageous actions, and lasting commitments on the side of researchers and academic institutions on one hand and of business people, companies, and policy makers on the other. The aim of this book is to encourage and advance this multifaceted development of business ethics. The intention is to engage both Chinese and non-Chinese scholars and business leaders in a dialogue to explore the concerns and views of each other and thus learn from each other. Although this collection of essays is only a modest step in this long-term undertaking, it already makes several important points unmistakably clear.

Four Essentials

1. Contrary to a belief widely held in Western countries, there is no "ethical vacuum" in China. Confucian ethics, with its history of

2,500 years, socialist ethics promulgated since 1949, and many Western and other influences have combined to create a kind of ethical awareness that sharply contrasts with a "value-free" view of business. This does not mean that China has a unified and consistent ethical understanding. Indeed, one can observe not only moral pluralism but also much moral confusion (which, by the way, also characterizes other countries in varying degrees). To put it simply, *the question is less whether or not ethics matters and more what kind of ethics should be applied.*

2. Given the extremely complex and dynamic transformation process of the country, there is *an urgent need to build up formal institutions that are effective, stable, and fair.* Of course, institution building is a difficult and lengthy process and cannot succeed without numerous trials and errors. Yet, it is essential from the ethical perspective because institutions and the lack thereof shape, for better or worse, the behavior of individuals and organizations. Those who conceive ethics only in personal terms, be they influenced by a widespread view in the United States or an exclusive notion of virtue ethics, have difficulty recognizing the crucial importance of institutional ethics. Well understood, it does not diminish in any way the indispensability of personal ethics.

3. With the national economic reform, the world of enterprises in China has changed dramatically. Not only have business organizations multiplied in number and taken on a wide variety of forms, but more importantly they have gradually gained more autonomy and bigger spaces of freedom. Accordingly, the presuppositions for corporate ethics have been established. There is no doubt that, for the development of business ethics in China, *the roles and responsibilities of business organizations, be they Chinese, joint-ventures, or foreign companies, are becoming increasingly important.* If, as stated earlier, a kind of ethical awareness exists in China today, it will be interesting to observe how this drives and impacts the shape of business organizations.

4. Talking about business ethics in China evokes many questions in the West as to whether or not the cultural differences between the two prevent a genuine mutual understanding. Such questioning is part of a necessary and healthy process to neutralize naive assumptions about Chinese attitudes and behavior, and to identify real cultural differences. At the same time, to consider all cultural differences as insurmountable seems to me equally naive and unacceptable. Continuous and open communication can certainly reduce the "cultural obstacles" significantly and cultural diversity does not necessarily mean ethical relativism. The development of business ethics in China *needs to*

address cultural differences and to find a common ethical ground supported by a majority of Chinese and in accordance with international standards.

These four major insights emerged from the International Conference, *Developing Business Ethics in China*, held on May 29–31, 2002 in Shanghai and supported by the Shanghai Academy of Social Sciences and the International Society of Business, Economics, and Ethics (ISBEE). They also form the context that may help to ground the various chapters of this book that were selected from this rich conference program. (For more about this meeting, see Xiaohe Lu's review in the following chapter.)

Overview

This book includes three parts, each dedicated to a crucial area of research and discussed by both Chinese and non-Chinese authors. Some contributors address their particular topics from their own country's perspective, be it Chinese, Japanese, American, German, or South African, offering their ideas and experiences without drawing direct links to another country's situation. These contributions are like bridgeheads, well positioned and carefully constructed, which constitute an important first step for a real dialogue, helping to clearly identify the concerns and questions for a fruitful dialogue. Other writers adopt a very global point of view that sets out the broad context that should be taken seriously in any encounter between China and other countries in the twenty-first century. A third group of authors go further in the bridge building by directly dealing with how international exchange may contribute to the development of business ethics in China. Crucial issues are: the importance of a systemic perspective for developing appropriate institutions that support "good business" in China; similar conceptions of the market economy between different ethical traditions, for instance Confucian ethics and Christian ethics; the shift away from the corporate amorality doctrine toward an understanding of the corporation as a moral personality; and the indispensable roles and responsibilities individuals have to assume in business and economic life. While these systemic, organizational, and individual perspectives are distinct, they are also closely interconnected. China's pursuit of a "socialist market economy," defined by a prominent role of public ownership and free market institutions, cannot be understood without the far-reaching implications for the types of Chinese companies, particularly for state-owned enterprises (SOEs). On the other hand, individual and organizational decision makers matter as well. In an economic system that is essentially "in transition," individuals and organizations cannot just execute orders and follow "mechanisms" but are forced to make decisions without the guidance of a firmly established order. In a nutshell, systemic, organizational, and individual perspectives have to be treated as being interrelated, all of which, by the way, are embraced in the now common Chinese term "*jingji lunli/xue*" for business ethics that includes, but does not limit itself to "*shangye lunli/xue*" (ethics of commerce) and "*gongsi lunli/xue*" (corporate ethics). The Index by name and subject at the end of this book may help to better grasp the immensely rich variety of interrelations.

Part I: Foundational Questions

Part I "Foundational Questions" ranges from a historical exploration by Yiting Zhu (chapter 1) to the prospects for business ethics in the era of globalization and information age by Richard De George (chapter 9). The first essay is not only of historical interest but it also makes clear that the tradition is part of the present, which needs to be clearly confronted, if one wants to choose the right opportunities for tomorrow. Many topics introduced in this chapter will be taken up by other chapters later in the book, in particular, the ethics of property rights, ethical principles of income and wealth distribution, the relevance of credibility and trust in modern markets, and the influence of the "ideology of the household" (familism) on the shaping of corporate culture. De George (chapter 9), reflecting on the indispensable role of legislation for business ethics at the national level, extends his considerations to the countries that still have to build up many institutions for preventing abuses such as bribery, child labor, and environmental harm. He then turns to the future and the global level, calling for new ethical requirements of business relating to information such as truthfulness, accuracy, and trust, for international background institutions, and for the still central role of countries, easily exemplified by the case of China.

Within this wide range from the historical perspective to the future outlook, the chapters address a number of crucial issues for developing business ethics in China. Zeying Wang (chapter 2) outlines a grand vision of "eco-economic ethics" that integrates economics, ecology, and ethics as three equally important dimensions. Instead of restricting each other, they are rather designed to reinforce each other and become a powerful moral force to push forward sustainable development. With a comparative view, Kit-Chun

Joanna Lam (chapter 3) investigates the historical developments of Confucian and Christian ethics with regard to market exchange and distribution of wealth. She discovers many similar features and argues for the relevance of these ethical resources to the socialist market economy in China. It is an uncommon, yet interesting attempt to move toward a common ethical ground for business in this country.

Following are three chapters that struggle with a deeper understanding of the ethical foundations of the market economy. Xiuyi Zhao (chapter 4) investigates different economic motivations, that is, motivations for acquiring and creating wealth in a modern economy. While individual self-interest is an essential motivational force in a market economy—to be fully recognized also in a socialist economy—it is not and should not be the only one (otherwise it would degenerate into shameless greed and immorality). Concern for the welfare of one's nation, people, and fellow citizens provide other indispensable motivations. Given the relatively recent introduction of the market economy to China, the Chinese have difficulty coming to grips with contract ethics, a key ethical notion of a modern market economy. Huizhu Gao (chapter 5) first looks at the empirical evidence of contract ethics violations and then elucidates several moral principles of this core notion. The next chapter by Zhenping Hu and Kaifeng Huang (chapter 6) builds on the observation that the market economy has increased the spaces of freedom of the economic actors; however, unfortunately, these actors have often misused their autonomy in irresponsible ways. The authors call for moral education in which the Communist party and its members should play an exemplary role and fully implement democracy within the party and the Chinese nation.

In asking what kind of business ethics should be developed in China, two authors from the United Kingdom and Japan warn against embracing a widely held but narrow conception of Western business ethics and a misunderstanding of ethical theory as a powerless and unworldly type of thinking. Jane Collier (chapter 7) argues for a systematic approach that goes far beyond the study of individual and corporate business actions. She emphasizes the need for institutional reform in China in order to support "good business" effectively, reminding the reader of the need for institution building that is mentioned in other essays. Without such reform, institutional failure, moral failure, and market failure may threaten the success of China's socialist market economy. Yukimasa Nagayasu (chapter 8) proposes a new system of ethics composed of two dimensions: the living power or well functioning of actors like corporations, and the goodness or ethical level of their conduct. Similar to Zeying Wang's notion of "eco-economic ethics," these dimensions are to be integrated into ethical conduct in the real world. This approach that is explained in management science terms as the process of "Plan—Do—See," is well rooted in the East Asian region and can be applied to all actors in a global economy across diverse cultures.

PART II: MACRO-ISSUES

Part II of this volume deals with *more specific questions at the macro- or systemic level*: global competition, concepts of consumption, income distribution, corruption, finance, and demographic changes. As Xiaoxi Wang (chapter 10) points out, with its accession to the World Trade Organization (WTO) in 2000, China faces enormous challenges not only in economic and legal, but also in ethical terms, the latter being widely ignored. The country can survive in economic globalization only if it learns to compete in a fair and transparent manner and if it develops a sense of service that puts the interests of customers first. Moreover, government has to refrain from excessively interfering in economic activities, and companies should develop their intangible assets of corporate morality with determination. (These challenges are further pursued in part III of this volume.)

Inextricably linked to global economic integration is the consumption culture that displays sharply different features in China and in the West. Zhongzhi Zhou (chapter 11) compares these traditions and proposes a moderate approach to consumption, that is, to promoting "green consumption" and avoiding extreme consumerism. Another side of rapid economic growth in China is the emergence of wide discrepancies of economic benefits, leading to social instability, which are ethically evaluated by Jianwen Yang (chapter 12). He analyses five income types, from income based on labor to income drawn from illegal activities, noting that people's recognition declines from type one to type five. The main reason people perceive an unfair gap between the rich and the poor lies in a variety of wrongful acts to get quick money such as rent seeking of power including bribery, making and selling fake goods, corruption, tax dodging and evasion, prostitution, and drug smuggling.

The next two chapters describe, analyze, and evaluate the rampant problem of corruption. Dajian Xu (chapter 13) sees the main causes of business corruption in the imperfections of the current market system in China, in both formal and informal institutions. Critical about traditional Confucianism, he therefore proposes to build up Western formal institutions supported by moral values that are compatible with the market economy. George Brenkert (chapter 14) looks at corruption as a special case of "moral disparity," that is, the widespread noncompliance with widely accepted moral views, and criticizes as inadequate, three standard responses to this problem: legal and/or moral enforcement, appropriate incentives, and clear moral principles. He suggests examining how people see themselves vis-à-vis the roles (or offices) they inhabit and the rules and relations that define those rules. Several embracing, enabling, and ensuring conditions must also be in place in order to overcome corruption.

With the fast development of financial markets, the ethics of finance has become a hot topic nationally and internationally. The following two chapters (chapters 15 and 16) deal with crucial issues in Western countries, approached from an American and a European perspective. But it is not difficult to perceive their relevance for China as well. One might only recall the bankruptcy of the Guangdong Trust and Investment Company, the restructuring of Guangdong Enterprises, and the enormous challenges in the financial sector that became more visible in the early 2000s. Georges Enderle (chapter 15) analyzes the loss of confidence in the financial reporting system in the United States after the Enron and Andersen debacle. As discussed in the essays of Yiting Zhu, Richard De George, Xiaoxi Wang, and Lanfen Li, credibility, confidence, and trust are basic preconditions for a well-functioning market economy. And when the numbers in financial statements are not "honest," the users of these statements are misled, and, in the final analysis, business breaks down. The essay also attempts to show that business ethics should limit itself neither to the questions of institutions and rules nor to the questions of individual and organizational behavior, but rather embrace a three-level approach (indicated earlier) that pays due attention to the indispensable roles and responsibilities of persons, organizations, and systems. Peter Koslowski (chapter 16) examines the role of professional speculation at the stock exchange and elaborates its economic function of carrying the burden of uncertainty about the future marketability and tradability of shares and obligations. In contrast, insider trading is not speculation but pseudo-speculation that does not serve the absorption of uncertainty in the economy and is therefore ethically inadmissible.

In the concluding chapter of part II, Koichi Matsuoka (chapter 17) shares Japan's experiences in the late twentieth century, which might be of interest to neighboring China in the twenty-first century. He analyzes the demographic trends of declining birth rate and aging with their multiple economic, social, medical, and psychological consequences and makes a number of concrete proposals to use the information revolution to cope with these problems. As a consequence, several challenges for business and economic ethics are discussed.

PART III: PERSPECTIVES OF CORPORATE ETHICS

Part III of this volume is dedicated to corporate ethics or the ethics of business organizations. As stated earlier, with the economic reform and opening up to the outside world, business organizations in China have gained significant autonomy and freedom and, as a consequence, their roles and responsibilities have become increasingly important for the development of business ethics in China. This part includes four essays from Chinese authors and four from non-Chinese.

Lanfen Li (chapter 18) addresses the widespread tendency of Chinese management to avoid addressing ethical issues at all. She calls this phenomenon "moral reticence" (which, by the way, can be found in other cultures as well). She investigates major causes of this reticence and proposes strategies to overcome it. The next two essays present two highly successful SOEs, which not suffering from "moral reticence," have built up strong ethical cultures. These examples, though not representative of the majority of SOEs, are all the more impressive because China's cultural environment with the "ideology of the household" (familism) and the socialist society-wide tradition, is not particularly conducive to the creation of an organizational culture (as is the case, e.g., in Japan). Xiuhua Zhou, president of Dazhong Transportation Group, makes a strong plea for promoting an ethical culture in Chinese enterprises, provided they want to compete globally (see chapter 19). She then illustrates in concrete terms how her company in Shanghai has actually built up such a culture. Farong Qiao (chapter 20) reports on the experiences of the Xuchang Relay Group headquartered in the province of Henan. She also sees global competition within the WTO as a challenge for corporate ethics and describes the culture of "joint forces" that has shaped the Group's philosophy, environment, organization, technology, production, and management. The following chapter (chapter 21) by Hanlong Lu and Chi Kwan Warren Chiu offers the results of a research project among 500 major enterprises of various types in Shanghai. It focuses on donations to public welfare activities that companies intend to make, taken as an indicator of corporate citizenship behavior. The authors conclude by proposing various means to encourage this kind of social responsibility.

The contributions on corporate ethics by non-Chinese authors begin with Lynn Sharp Paine's reflections on the moral status of the corporation (see chapter 22). In a historical review she shows how the notion of the corporation has evolved from an amoral entity lacking any capacity for self-discipline or moral judgment to a "responsible agent" or "moral actor" in society. This major change is a reality today, forms the basis of any serious talk about corporate responsibility and accountability and should also be recognized by the theorists who, for too long, have built models of "fictional" companies operating in a presumably morally inert world. As the Chinese authors Xiuhua Zhou and Farong Qiao see global competition as a challenge for corporate ethics, so does Horst Steinmann from his German background (see chapter 23). He not only asks how to strengthen the international competitiveness of companies while maintaining (internal) peace in a less-regulated society but also examines what big corporations can and should contribute to a world economic order characterized by fair competition and social justice. Solutions to these problems are developed with the help of two practical cases (Volkswagen [VW] and Otto Versand). The next chapter focuses on corporate governance, an issue that has become a top priority both nationally and internationally. Deon Rossouw (chapter 24) discusses the relationship between corporate governance and business ethics from a developing country perspective and looks at an encouraging recent development in South Africa where the "Second King Report" (2002) gave particular prominence to business ethics. He explores its motivation and guidelines and closes with a critical review. Concluding part III of this book, Urs Baerlocher (chapter 25) explains how Novartis, a multinational pharmaceutical corporation headquartered in Switzerland, understands its mission of "global corporate citizenship," and strives for contributing to globalization with a human face. Being a "moral actor" with an evolving personality (Paine, chapter 22) in the global arena, the company needs "good governance" (see Rossouw, chapter 24) and has to be economically successful in a socially and environmentally compatible way in order to achieve sustainable success and social acceptance. As a consequence, Novartis has joined the UN Global Compact and also supports philanthropic activities, embracing a fairly comprehensive view of corporate citizenship that might inspire Chinese enterprises as well.

Good Beginnings: A Review of the International Conference on "Developing Business Ethics in China"

Xiaohe Lu

Following China's entrance into the World Trade Organization (WTO), how will business ethics in China develop? This is an issue of great concern for scholars of business ethics in China and around the world. From China's perspective, China's entrance into the WTO is accelerating the country's ongoing reform of the market system, promoting related changes in the superstructure, and increasing the scope and intensity of China's participation in globalization. As such, the role of business ethics in China is gaining greater importance. Many Western countries have learned hard lessons in this area. Less developed countries can and should learn from the experiences of the industrially more developed countries. The globalization of economic relations also requires an appropriate common ethical ground and calls for different countries to collaborate in the sharing of research and ideas. The world is more concerned with the question of the status of business ethics in China after the country became an important member in the world's economic system following its market reforms and entrance into the WTO. How can business ethics in China be developed? How do corporations in China view the issue of business ethics? Since China also needs to play its part in building a global business ethics, it is also necessary for international experts to exchange ideas with scholars of business ethics and entrepreneurs in this country.

Research on business ethics in China began in the first half of the 1990s and scholarship on business ethics in China has been growing for nearly ten years. Although a number of conferences on business ethics have been held in China, for the most part, the conferences have been confined to China's academia. Comparatively, the field of business ethics unfolded earlier in developed countries. Twenty-seven years have elapsed since the movement of business ethics first emerged in the United States in the 1970s. Since the mid-1990s, scholars from China and from around the world have shared their research and scholarship on business ethics. However, such sharing has been limited to a few academies and universities. Scholarship on international business ethics has largely been focused on the United States, Europe, and Japan. Since the end of the 1990s, however, the focus of research started to shift to other regions in the world, such as Latin America. Still, China was rarely considered. Although a small number of scholars from outside China have written papers on business ethics in China, research on business ethics in China, as a global enterprise, is still minimal.

The International Conference on "Developing Business Ethics in China," organized in Shanghai on May 29–31, 2002 played a significant role in changing this situation. The conference, held by the Center for Business Ethics at Shanghai Academy of Social Sciences also received support from Shanghai Municipal Government's Administration of Culture, Radio, Film and Television and the International Society of Business, Economics, and Ethics (ISBEE). Professor Jizuo Yin, president of Shanghai Academy of Social Sciences, hosted the opening ceremony; Mr. Tiechuan Hao, vice minister of the Shanghai Municipal Government's Administration of Culture, Radio, Film and Television; and Dr. Georges Enderle, president of ISBEE, provided opening remarks. Mr. Ying Chen, professor at Chinese Academy of Social Sciences, vice chairman of China Ethics Association and editor-in-chief of *Morality and Civilization*, came from Beijing, expressed his support and enthusiasm for the conference. Distinguished experts in business ethics from America, Europe, South America, Japan, and Hong Kong, in addition to well-known scholars in business ethics from Shanghai, Beijing, and the provinces of Jiangsu, Hunan, and Henan, joined more than 80 participants from affiliated areas in attending this international conference.

Centered on the theme of "developing business ethics in China," the conference addressed three main topics: important ethical issues of the modern economy and society, corporations and ethics, and how to develop business ethics in China. The conference featured twelve panels, including Fundamental Issues of Business Ethics; Motivation, Development, Environment; Consumption, Welfare State, Financial Markets; Honest Numbers and Corruption; Information Technology and Business Ethics; Corporate Ethics: Experiences in Different

Countries; Corporate Ethics: New Perspectives; Forum for Business Leaders: Need and Perspectives for Ethics in Doing Business in China; Developing Business Ethics in China: Foundations; Justice and Distribution; Integrity and Professional Ethics; and International Challenges and Perspectives for Business Ethics in China. Opening with a dialogue on how to view China's traditional business ethics, and closing with a discussion on the prospects of business ethics in China, the conference included not only many insightful discussions on broad and complex topics but also concentrated closely on the conference's main theme. Participants enjoyed many memorable moments, and the round table discussion with business leaders, in particular, was received with great enthusiasm. The proceedings of this conference are included in the Chinese book *Developing Business Ethics in China*, edited by Xiaohe Lu and Georges Enderle and published by the Academy of Social Sciences Press (Shanghai 2003). What follows is a review of the panels and discussions by panelists on the conference's three main topics.

THE DISCUSSION ON IMPORTANT ETHICAL ISSUES OF THE MODERN ECONOMY AND SOCIETY

China's entry into the WTO is not in itself responsible for introducing the challenging issue of business ethics in China. The field of business ethics in China does not merely address the question of how to deal with the challenge faced by the country after its entry into the WTO. Rather, the field grapples with the issue of the reformulation of ethics in China following the significant changes in the country's economic and social structures. After China's entrance into the WTO, reforms deepened and intensified across a broader scope of areas. As the pace of reforms sped up and propelled economic structural reforms at deeper levels, China urgently needed a set of ethical norms suitable for upholding the new economic relations.

The formation of business ethics for China's modern market, however, is not an issue to be viewed in isolation from the world. Due to the reality of economic globalization, all developing countries are embroiled, to varying degrees, in the modern market economic system and are grappling with the issue of their transformation from traditional ethics to modern ethics. East China Normal University's Professor Yiting Zhu commenced the discussion on the important ethical issues of the modern economy and society with his presentation entitled "On China's Traditional Business Ethics and its Modern Transformation." The issue of the remodeling of ethics he discussed—specific yet insightful—is significant for both China and the world. Following his presentation, panelists from China continued to address the issue from different angles. For example, Fudan University's Professor Weisen Li discussed the moral foundation of market economies. East China Normal University's Professor Xiuyi Zhao explored the degree to which and the ways in which business ethics is possible following the "legitimization" of economic motivation (or profit motivation). Hunan Academy of Social Sciences' Professor Zhiyou Zhu discussed the morality of economic development. Hunan Teachers University's Professor Zeying Wang argued that an ecological business ethics is necessary for adjusting to the development of the modern economy and society. Shanghai Normal University's Professor Zhongzhi Zhou investigated the transformation of the concept of consumer ethics. Starting with the ethical issues involved in the course of China's market economic reforms and the institutional causes of these issues, Shanghai University of Finance's Professor Dajian Xu remarked upon building an ethics based on and inspired by a market economy. The panelists' presentations all reflect the need to remodel and revise ethics. It is worth pointing out that scholars from China tended to focus on the experiences of Western countries in their transformation from tradition to modernity. For example, Professor Yiting Zhu noted that the transformation of China's traditional business ethics should be aware of the fact of "path reliance" (i.e., the reenforcement of traditional patterns in the process of transformation) while Professor Xiuyi Zhao's research focused on the experiences of Western economies where economic motivation has gained value in itself independent of political and ideological motivation. From another angle, Chinese scholars also looked toward the future, such as Professor Zeying Wang, who in his suggestion of ecological business ethics asserts that China must address both modern and postmodern issues. It is also worth noting the presentations by scholars from Western countries. The distinguished scholar Richard De George, professor of philosophy at the University of Kansas in the United States, summarized, in terms of both theory and practice, the experiences that Western countries learned in the course of developing an ethics of market economics. He also insightfully suggested that developing countries could use such experiences as a reference, but emphasized that in order to construct business ethics suitable for China, the country needs to combine the experience of the West with its specific practices, in accordance with its own conditions and the knowledge and values of its peoples.

The presentations regarding the transformation of traditional business ethics to those of the modern market economy sparked a lively discussion on how to deal with China's traditional business ethics. One view suggests that traditional Confucian ethics should be adopted to build a market business ethics, while another view holds that in introducing the market economic system, Confucian ethics as a whole cannot be integrated with it. Deepening the discussion on the remodeling of business ethics, the debate on Confucian ethics further prompted questions concerning the origin of market business ethics (e.g., transformation or transplantation) and whether a market economy itself can promote a market business ethics.

Many scholars also opened discussions on other important issues regarding the modern economy and society. Koichi Matsuoka, professor of economics at the University of Shimane in Japan, raised the issue of the social costs produced by economic development. Peter Koslowski, professor of philosophy and economic ethics from Germany, discussed the ethical problem of insider trading within capital markets. Professor Georges Enderle analyzed the issue of confidence in financial reporting. George Brenkert, professor of business ethics from the United States, discussed the issues of moral disparity and corruption. Yukimasa Nagayasu, professor of economics and social system theory at Reitaku University and the Institute of Moralogy in Japan, considered the issue of the process of adaptation to an ethical structure of global business players. Professor De George explored the ethical issues involved with the transformation from the industrial era to the information era in his presentation titled "Business Ethics, Globalization and the Information Age." Xincai Bai, general manager of Xinhai General Corporation, Shanghai Agriculture, Industry and Business Groups, reviewed the trend of technology displacing laborers from the perspectives of efficiency and fairness. East China University of Science and Technology's Professor Zonghao Bao discussed the issue of globalization and Internet. A number of these issues, such as the topic of ethics and capital markets, have already been encountered by developed nations, while China is just beginning to address them. Other issues, such as the ethical questions involved with globalization, the information era, and the Internet, are new issues faced concurrently by developed nations and developing nations, such as China. Panelists from outside China as well as from China summarized their most recent research findings and views related to these issues.

The Discussion on Corporate Ethics

Corporate ethics occupies an important position within business ethics. In fact, corporate ethics initially prompted the movement in global business ethics, and it remains a critical part within the research and scholarship of international business ethics. Corporations in China have already greatly developed since the country first began implementing its economic reforms. Following the further separation of government and enterprises and the opening of its domestic market to the world, the importance of corporate ethics has increased as companies play a greater role in China's contemporary economy. Professor Horst Steinmann, founder and former president of the German Business Ethics Network; Professor Deon Rossouw, chairman of the Business Ethics Network in Africa; Professor Lanfen Li of China's Suzhou University; and Professor Farong Qiao of Henan College of Finance and Economics exchanged their views on corporate ethics. Professor Lynn Sharp Paine of Harvard Business School; Dr. Urs Baerlocher, member of the Board of Directors of the Swiss multinational corporation (MNC) Novartis; and Hanlong Lu, professor at Shanghai Academy of Social Sciences, Chi Kwan Warren Chiu, professor at the Hong Kong Polytechnic University, provided their latest perspectives on corporate ethics.

Specially invited to attend the round table discussion for business leaders, five prominent speakers discussed (with the audience) the necessity and prospects for corporate ethics: Mr. Jianjun Yan (president and general manager of Shanghai's Zenitek Group), Mr. Jianning Zhang (vice president of BP China ranked second among the world's Fortune 500 companies), Ms. Xiuhua Zhou (president of Shanghai's Dazhong Transportation Group), Mr. Paul Lau (CEO of Novartis China), and Mr. Tianle Gao (president and general manager of Tengen Group). They all agreed that business leaders concerned with the long-term development of their enterprises must value the establishment of corporate ethics. Business leaders from China also indicated that they wanted to learn from the successful experiences of others in developing the economy, raising the level of ethics, and strengthening competitiveness. China's business leaders also stated: "China's listed and outstanding private enterprises should take the lead in transforming themselves into respectable ethical organizations" (see Xiuhua Zhou's essay in this book, chapter 19, pp. 209–210).

The discussion on corporate ethics not only served as a platform for exchanging views between both scholars and business leaders on the practice of ethics, but also provided a clear message that Chinese enterprises and multinationals in China urgently need to develop business ethics. Business leaders and scholars together need to accelerate the development of business ethics in China.

How to Develop Business Ethics in China?

After exploring both broad and specific questions of business ethics mentioned earlier, the conference returned to the subject of how China's business ethics can be developed with a particular focus on theoretical foundations, ethical norms regarding economic systems, professional integrity, international competition, and the direction of development. Joanna Lam, Professor at the Hong Kong Baptist University, Fudan University's Professor Tao Ma, and Shanghai Normal University's Professor Huizhu Gao, respectively discussed different foundational theoretical issues of China's socialist market economy, including Confucianism and Christianity, contract ethics, and China's traditional notion of "governing the country through morality." Shanghai University of Finance's Professor Xiong Zhang, Jianwen Yang, professor of economics, and Dr. Xiaopeng Hu from Shanghai Academy of Social Sciences as well as Zhongdao Ren of Shanghai Academy of Social Science's Institute of Philosophy, respectively discussed the ethical issues of systems, including economic fairness, distribution ethics, and equity and rights. Shanghai University of Finance's Professor Xinhan Chen, Yejing Wu and Anmin Chen of Shanghai's Chengkai Group discussed their views on the issues of *homo oeconomicus* and professional integrity. Professor Byron Kaldis of Athens University of Economics and Business suggested a transformation of the prevailing model of business ethics. In the very end, on the issue of the development of business ethics in China, Nanjing Normal University's Professor Xiaoxi Wang and Zhenping Hu, Kaifeng Huang, and Zehuan Chen, professors at Shanghai Academy of Social Sciences, respectively spoke on enhancing moral competitiveness, strengthening official governance, and promoting the development of the discipline of business ethics.

Throughout the conference, many differences emerged between the views and approaches of scholars from China and those from other countries around the world. For example, most scholars from China were concerned with comparatively macro-theoretical issues, while scholars from other countries focused more on ethical issues raised by specific research cases. Or, scholars from China investigated the problems of corruption and counterfeiting by pursuing their systematic cause and the transformation of the system of morality. Scholars from Western countries, however, specifically examined how people see themselves vis-à-vis the roles they inhabit and the rules and relations that define those roles. Of course, these differences in approach are largely due to the responsibility that scholars in China are taking on within this transformation of ethics, but they also represent differences in ways of thinking and research methods.

This international conference achieved its objective of "encouraging the exchange and dialogue between Chinese and international scholars and between scholars and business leaders, promoting the development of the study of business ethics, and sharing and learning from the achievments and experiences of Western countries in business ethics," as stated in the invitation to the conference. During the meeting, participants exchanged their ideas on how to develop business ethics in China and their views on the important ethical issues of the modern economy and society. In addition, participants also arrived at a common understanding regarding developing corporate ethics in China as shown by the round table discussion. For both scholars and business leaders in China, the conference introduced new ideas to them, expanding their research field and facilitating their understanding of views from outside their country. By deepening their understanding of many issues of business ethics, the gathering facilitated learning from the research accomplishments and experiences of other countries and further promoting the development of the formation and practice of the discipline of business ethics in China. For scholars researching international business ethics and multinational corporations, the conference fostered and deepened a dialogue between them and their respective colleagues in China, providing an opportunity to understand perspectives from scholars and business leaders in the country. International scholars also realized that developed countries can also learn from a developing China. The meeting helped them to understand the economic reforms of China and understand the research on business ethics in that country. The conference also offered the opportunity for scholars from China and from around the world to exchange ideas on issues of international business ethics related to China's entrance into the WTO. Such an opportunity will assist in having China play a role in the building of a global business ethics, thereby contributing toward the goal of "bringing all peoples of the world closer to a just and peaceful world in which we will all prosper."

PART I

Foundational Questions

CHAPTER 1

On China's Traditional Business Ethics and Its Modern Transformation

Yiting Zhu

The topic of this essay is a complicated and difficult one that cannot be treated comprehensively by a single author. What is intended in the following is to raise initial comments based on our current understanding of the topic for further discussion.

INTRODUCTION: ON CHINA'S TRADITIONAL BUSINESS ETHICS

China's traditional business ethics was based on three fundamental characteristics of China's premodern "traditional economy." They are as follows:

1. The economic structure of the valued agricultural activities above commercial enterprise that is based on the small agrarian economy (natural economy).
2. A social structure built on a hierarchy of an ancient clan system centered on patrilineal authority.
3. The authoritarianism of the "traditional model" of monarchic governance unified politics and economics into a single structure.

"The nation was established as holding the highest right to property ownership,"[1] while individual property rights for commoners lacked systematic legal protection. Such an economy, political system, and cultural environment formed the business ethics of China's "traditional agrarian society." It valued "public [*gong*] over private [*si*]" and "righteousness [*yi*] over profit [*li*]." Management was rooted in the family clan system. Wealth was to be distributed according to the "status based on propriety" and "evenly distributed among the poor and the rich." Extravagant consumption was rejected and frugality upheld. The virtues of labor were diligence and dedication to work. As for market behavior, "trustworthiness" was taught and "competition" opposed.

INITIAL REFORMS OF TRADITIONAL BUSINESS ETHICS SINCE THE LATE 1890S

Business ethics in premodern China that belongs to the "natural economy" essentially stands in direct opposition to the business ethics of a market economy and is neither appropriate for a free market economy nor a socialist market economy. It therefore needed thorough transformation in order to become suitable for the socialist market economy (Chen Jun and Ren Fang 1996).

In fact, the reform of these traditional business ethics began as early as the end of the nineteenth century and the beginning of the twentieth century. At that time, along with the Westernization movement and the rise of modern commerce, a large debate emerged concerning the fate of China's modern industrialization. This debate centered on the rationale and the means for which a commercial industry could be established. Business ethics was concerned with the types of business ethics to be adopted in the process of industrialization. The crux of this problem involved the ethics of property rights. The ultraconservative party ("*wan gu pai*"), the Westernization party ("*yang wu pai*"), and different reformist groups all proposed their own solutions to these issues.

The ultraconservative party of the Late Qing government maintained the traditional ethics of "valuing agriculture and despising commerce" and "valuing righteousness and despising profit" under the guise of "people being the foundation of the country." They vilified the establishment of modern industry and commercial industry as the corruption of the agricultural economy, alleging it to "deprive people of their livelihood." The party held that "virtue rather than equipment was the measure of the country's strength." They aimed to abort the modern commercial economy while it was still in its infancy. The Westernization party raised the notion of "combining Chinese systems with Western techniques." Although its political purpose really entailed "defending the nation" and "preserving China's moral teachings," it discarded in the least the rather bizarre theory of the ultraconservative party that machines were "perverse shenanigans." A basis for legitimizing the establishment of industry was found in terms of utilitarianism and of dealing with foreign affairs. The assertion that using machines and building railways achieved, not frittered away, benefits for the people and was necessary to create a prosperous society and strong country, refuted the fallacy held by the ultraconservative faction that machines robbed people of their livelihood. This broke through the traditional idea of valuing agriculture and suppressing commerce. Citing the conviction that "prosperity is necessary for a strong country and commerce is necessary for prosperity," the suppression of commerce was changed to "valuing commerce."[2] Concerning this economic structure, Zhang Zhidong clearly raised the ethical principle of "the equal importance of agriculture and commerce."

However, since China's modern industrialization was impacted from the outside, it naturally developed from the top down with commerce taking orders from the government and government officials maintaining authority over commerce. Therefore, the phenomena of "officials overseeing commercial activity," "joint management between officials and commercial enterprises," and the government's monopoly powers naturally and inevitably emerged and essentially meant that government officials maintained control over property rights. This resulted in an enterprise management system in which the government protected commerce and commerce aided the government; or, in other words, a family-like mode of business ethics in which government and commerce are unified, work together and share a common fate. The relationship between the government and commerce has even been compared to that of the relationship between father and son. In accordance with this understanding of the ethics of property rights, the Westernization party objected to free competition asserting that competition would only lead to illicit activities and fraud in the pursuit of self-interest. It was stated: "As the masses begin to pursue profit, they begin to behave in a selfish and illicit manner, not heeding the complete picture, thereby causing the decline of various industries."[3] Clearly, they had not yet broken from the hold of tradition.

The ideas of the reformist and revolutionary factions clearly adopted the features of modern capitalism. They combined the premodern notion of "people first" with modern Western ethics to promote enlightenment, new virtues and rights for people, and enriching people's livelihood. Enriching people's livelihood was adopted as the ethical motivation and target for developing China's modern industry. Sun Yat-Sen's (1866–1925) *The Three Principles of the People* (1975) asserted that developing capital and stimulating industries could "resolve the problems with people's livelihood." To criticize the notion of valuing agriculture and despising business, Qian Zhang argued that industry and agriculture together were the basis for building up the country. Kang Youwei raised the notion of "building up the country through commerce" and Liang Qichao (1873–1929) proclaimed the idea of "building up the country through industry." Furthermore, revolutionary factions thought "those who advocated the notion of 'valuing agriculture and despising business' maintained fallacious views." For example, it was stated: "Now in order to remedy the country's faults, it is necessary to commence with a focus on commerce." They opposed the notion of "agriculture as the country's foundation" and supported the idea that "the foundation of the country is commerce, industry, agriculture, and mining." They objected to the government's control over business enterprises and claimed independence for property rights and autonomous economic liberalism.

While Liang Qichao called for "free competition," in accordance with Bernhard Mandeville's mantra of "the private vices as public virtues," Yan Fu (1853–1921) raised the concepts of "uniting righteousness and benefit" and "the self and group as one." He thereby countered the Confucian outmoded maxim of "dividing righteousness and benefits." He opposed the government's rights to intervene in the market and promoted a set of capitalist principles of business ethics, including free trade, liberal self-marketing, fair competition, and so on. Sun Yat-Sen of the revolutionary faction clearly pointed out the principles of "liberalism and equality for all" in his *The Three Principles of the People* (1975). He asserted that "all obstacles posed by the officials must be eliminated." Zhu Zhixin emphasized the "spirit of independent self-management" and the principle of economic liberalism to theorize the ethical principles of autonomous and independent business property rights.

The reforms in modern ethics broke away from the system of traditional business ethics and established principles of business ethics imbued with the features of modern capitalism, such as industry and commerce building up the country, industry saving the country, the independence of business property rights, free competition, and so on. These provided the ethical vindication and vigorous support necessary for the development of China's modern industry and promotion of its industrialization. Accomplishments should have been clearly secured. However, because of the semicolonial and semifeudal nature of society in modern China, under the encroachment and oppression of the economic might of the imperial powers and bureaucrat-capitalist ensembles, the development of capitalism on a national basis was rather delicate and difficult. Facing this kind of political and economic environment, it was impossible to complete any transformation of China's traditional business ethics.

After the founding of the People's Republic of China, since a market economy did not exist nor could it be established under the planned economy, it was impossible to return to the historical problem of continuing to reform traditional business ethics. However, a new starting point for the "modern transformation" of traditional business ethics was formed during this era. The planned economy required traditional business ethics to adopt a new form. Tradition, just as long as it's not entirely disconnected, can always perpetuate through different historical forms. Therefore, just as Shils says: "It is currency past, but it is similar to any newborn things, and is a part of current" (Shils 1982, 16). What we confront today and aim to change is primarily not the original form of traditional business ethics. The reason for researching China's premodern business ethics is because we want to better grasp the traditional business ethics that has become a part of today.

MODERN TRANSFORMATION OF TRADITIONAL BUSINESS ETHICS SINCE THE END OF 1970S

Reform of the Ethics of Property Rights

Directed by the Chinese Communist Party, economic reform, namely the transformation of the planned economy into the market economy, began at the end of 1970s. The basic characteristic of the market economy is that the market, for the most part, allocates resources throughout society. This requires the reform of the system and structure of property rights, the establishment of diverse independent markets with autonomous property rights, and the establishment and refinement of the basic economic system of the "central public-owned system developing together with the economies of diversely owned systems." This involves the deep reform of the ethics of property rights. In the early stages of socialism, concerning the system and structure of property rights, it was neither "the more public, the better" nor the "purer the 'public,' the better." The public-owned system not only can and should be diversified, but also the state-owned enterprises must establish a modern enterprise system. Such an endeavor involves "clear property rights, clear and definite rights and responsibilities, separation between government and business, and scientific management" to distinguish ownership from management rights, while enabling business enterprises to become market-based corporate and competitive entities. Nonpublic economic systems need to be encouraged, guided, and developed, a legal system for ownership needs to be constructed with individuals given legal protection, and privately owned property rights need to be legitimized. This would establish equal treatment of citizens, while also affirming that those who are engaged in nonpublic economic activities are also "builders of a socialism with Chinese characteristics." Such initiatives have essentially negated the former traditional concept of valuing public and despising private (even to the extreme of completely wiping out the private), and established the ethics and values of property rights informed by the coexistence and equality of the "public" and the "private" in accordance with the socialist market economy.

In the modern reform of the ethics of property rights, the substantial ethical breakthrough occurred by departing from the traditional concept in which property ownership rights were founded on social ranking. Now, under the planned economy, property rights were classified into different grades and allocated in accordance with the contributions that the resources made to total production.[4] This is an enormous accomplishment for the modern reform of traditional business ethics. It intensifies the reform effort and the development of the socialist market economy. However, toward the task of truly establishing widespread recognition by society, the implementation of the liberalization of property rights and the social obligations intended by such property rights must be unified in order to further establish a moral foundation for the legitimization of property rights.

Reform of the Ethical Principles on Wealth Distribution

In terms of the distribution of wealth, China had long ago negated the premodern clan-style system of allocating status in accordance with propriety. However, the traditional ethics of "fear of not having the same rather than of having little" still maintains a critical influence within China's modern society. Although this traditional concept connotes the prevention of and opposition to wide gaps between the poor and the rich, this was by all means an ethics developed within and for a low level of economic efficiency if not total inefficiency. The result would inevitably be widespread poverty within society, obviously violating the essence of socialism.

The socialist market economy fundamentally changed the traditional ethics of wealth distribution by establishing the strategic principle of the "mutual coordination of efficiency and social equality." Social equality of the socialist market economy implies not only equal opportunity, but also the enabling of large numbers of people to share in the fruits of economic development. The goal is to head toward an equality in which the result is commonwealth. This involves a kind of evening out of the poor and the rich—not egalitarianism or the doctrine of "even distribution" within the historical context of low efficiency—but an increasing efficiency that continues to promote economic development. An equality based on the continuous increase in the total social wealth is to be achieved, thereby preventing and overcoming the bipolarization of the poor and the rich. In the end, a shared social wealth is to be realized. Efficiency and equality, as mutually enforcing and complementary, form a constructive cycle that propels the ongoing social development. Here lies the true meaning of modern reform in the traditional ethics of wealth distribution.

The Traditional Notion of Business Trustworthiness versus Modern Market Credibility

The teaching of "trustworthiness" was a positive tradition within China's premodern ethics. However, this premodern notion of business trustworthiness referred almost entirely to the moral character of businessmen, in which social trustworthiness was represented by the moral standards of the individuals. Therefore, the notion could more precisely be called the "trustworthiness of businessmen." At the same time, business trustworthiness in premodern China was established via personal connections—a kind of limited, parochial "acquaintance society" composed of connections based on family and hometown relationships. Businessmen on both sides engaged in a kind of "exchange based on moral character." Trustworthiness was embodied by a kind of personal guarantee. Therefore, the premodern notion of businessmen trustworthiness is not the same as the modern concept of "market credibility."

Market credibility moved beyond personal relationships to apply to a system in which market transactions occur between "strangers." Commercial contracts precisely establish a kind of ethical relationship based on impersonal exchange. It is a two-way mutual relationship between both contract parties requesting the rights and obligations of credibility. Credibility here is the reliability of honoring and implementing the commitments promised within the contract. Such credibility includes the moral credibility of the market in general. However, due to the primary role of *homo oeconomicus* within the market, market credibility must necessarily appear within the restrictions of the system, namely the "credit system." Following the financial market's development, market credibility has become a designated type of transaction behavior or targeted transaction. These are termed "credit-worthy transactions."

Therefore, market credibility is a system of credibility composed of moral credibility, market credibility, and the credit system. Therefore, as a kind of economic morality, credibility is very similar to trustworthiness. However, as a kind of system, credibility is very different from the notion of trustworthiness. The fact that we usually say "credit system" rather than "trustworthiness system" precisely reflects the divergent connotations of these two phrases. Obviously, the traditional notion of business trustworthiness, as molded by the society of relationships, can to some degree serve as a cultural reserve for establishing a modern market credibility. However, it is impossible to convert it directly into market credibility. It is worth noting that once commercial behavior adapted from a system of personal relationships faces the impersonal exchange of strangers, the quality of "person-person trustworthiness" will be cast off. Moreover, even as propelled by self-interest the leveraging of its credibility will intend the death of the utilization of personal relationships. Therefore, as a type of cultural reserve (Fukuyama 1998), the virtue of traditional trustworthiness can only play a positive role in the formation of market credibility under the condition that it submits to the system of credibility. In terms of the market credibility of the system, the traditional notion must be reformulated and redeveloped. China still has a long way to go in realizing such a reform.

The Tradition and Reform of Household Enterprises and the Ideology of the Household

Following the development of private enterprise, the increasing tension between a changing organizational pattern of business and the traditional ideology of the household has gradually become more prominent and has become a hot issue for both business and scholarship. "Household enterprises," as a form of business organization, are so called because the property rights of the business belong to or are controlled by the same household, and at least two generations within the same household manage the company or enterprise. "Ideology of the household," or the "ideology of household enterprises," is a kind of "corporate culture" manifested within the management of the business. There is an inherent relationship between the household enterprise and the ideology of the household, but they are not the same concept and should not be lumped together. The importance here doesn't lie in the organizational form of the household, but rather involves the cultural implications of the ideology of the household. The original ecosystem of the clan-style ideology of the household no longer existed after China's successful institution of modern social reforms and the national policy of family planning within the last 20 years. However, as a kind of cultural tradition emerging in a new guise, it still plays a definitive role.

The influence of the ideology of the household can be seen, for example, within private enterprise. As a type of centripetal mode of management (or "personal administration"), the head (i.e., family elder) of the enterprise commands the business. The ideology of the household also appears in the notion of family inheritance (the business is passed down from father to son), the strong awareness of kinship (only those within the family are trusted), and the human resources practice of only employing relatives, and so on. Admittedly, these traditional cultural values played an active influence during the early stages of the business. However, as they necessarily conflicted with modern business culture, and following the enterprise's development, the negative impact of the ideology of the household arises when it becomes a pitfall in the enterprise's development. In fact, many famous household businesses, apart from "son inherited business," have more or less changed their mode of management after reflecting upon the household business management style. They implement the businesses' share-ownership system, employ professional managers, strengthen a democratic management style and competition for talent, and upgrade the company's social capital. This trend indicates that within the context of an ongoing developing modern market economy and scientific management, concrete changes are taking place in terms of the cultural implications of household businesses.

This is the secret as to why some well-known household business enterprises are filled with vitality and may be an important reason why household businesses are still "one of the most widespread and critical forms of business organizations in the world today." In a nutshell, within our scrutiny of household businesses, we should differentiate the form of organization of household businesses from the business culture of the ideology of the household. Only in this way can we interpret the modern household business phenomenon with the household business continuing to survive. That is to say, as compelled by the outside, the household business should continue to reform its cultural tradition of the ideology of the household and realize the fusion between modern business culture and the household enterprise form of organization. The household business can thereby inherit a new vitality amidst fierce market competition.

The four problems listed are only examples, however they can assist in illustrating the issues. In order to establish a system of business ethics in the socialist market economy, the modernizing reform of traditional business ethics must continue to proceed.

CONCLUDING REMARKS ON THE DIFFICULTIES OF THE TRANSFORMATION PROCESS

As a conclusion, I want to point out that the modern transformation of "traditional business ethics" is a very difficult process. An important reason for this is due to the issue of "path dependence," a concept developed by the American economist of institutional economics Douglass C. North (North 1994). This notion of path dependence says that a system, which had been selected in the past, through its transformation produces a kind of mechanism. Due to this type of mechanism, as soon as a certain path is selected within the transformation, its direction will be self-strengthening in the future. Thereby, it makes the system continue along the same path. If the original path is incorrect, then the system will be "pinned down" to an inefficient position, and once it is pinned down then leaving it will become very difficult. The key point here is that once the system is established, a type of "pressure cluster" that profits from the current system is formed. They will seek to reinforce this type of system and obstruct further changes to it, even if a new system is relatively more efficient. These circumstances not only exist within the transformation of formal systems but also exist within informal systems (such as customs and habits, ethics and morality, and religion and faith).

Certainly this principle also exists within the course of the transformation of traditional business ethics. For example, why is it so difficult to change certain phenomena, such as the "interpersonal ethics" of "making connections," within the reform of the economic system? The reason lies in the path dependance to the ethics of personal exchange within the traditional acquaintance society. The transaction style of the personal guarantee, as produced through its long evolution by trustworthiness amongst acquaintances, formed a type of habitual thought or collective unconsciousness—namely, acquaintances are dependable, can be trusted, and get things done well. Precisely under the domination of this kind of consciousness, an ethics of personal relationships formed. Such an ethics became divorced from a system and was steadily enhanced as it gained currency. Eventually, it turned into an incurable "ethical syndrome."

This is often seen within the processes of system transformation. An exceptional illustration of this is the leveraging of the "indivisibility between state and business" and "government approval system" (these systems have already been informed by a type of "path dependance"). These "platforms" provide the conduit for different types of irregular and illegal methods of "making connections." As soon as the connection has been forged, both parties become the benefactors of a "win–win" situation, even to the degree of facilitating high, if not exorbitant, returns with little capital outlay. It is precisely under the motivation of profits that the deluge of connection ethics will become disastrous because it develops into a significant obstacle to establishing market credibility and economic fairness. Other practices such as traditional property rights ethics, ethics of wealth distribution, ideology of the household, and so on are also informed by this tendency toward path dependence. We should offer a high degree of thought to such issues. In his lecture entitled "Outline of the Theory of Institutional Change" at Peking University on May 4, 1995, North stated:

> Path dependence still plays an important role. That is to say, within the evolution of our society until today, our entire cultural tradition and our system of faith are fundamentally restricting factors, and we must still consider these restricting factors. That is to say, we must be very sensitive in noticing: how did you get here from the past? How did the transition proceed? We must really understand all of this. Then, we can clearly confront the restricting factors that we must face in the future and choose which opportunities we have.[5]

This is exactly why we need to research the role of traditional business ethics during the course of the formation of business ethics in the socialist market economy.

NOTES

1. This is Professor Jiafan Wang's expression about Marx's treatise on Asia's premodern form of land ownership. He uses this expression to summarize the historical characteristic of China's premodern agricultural ownership. See Wang Jiafan. *The General Theory of Chinese History*. Shanghai: East China Normal University Press, 2000, 96.

2. Institute for Early Modern History of China. Yangwu yundong (Westernization movement). In: *Data of Chinese Early Modern History* (series). Edited by China's Association for Historiography. Shanghai: Shanghai People's Publishing House/Shanghai Book Company, 2000, 6.
3. Zhang Zhidong. Zhang Wenxiang gongquan ji, Zouyi. Vol. 37. In: *Zhang Zhidong Complete Works*. Edited by Yuan Shuyi et al. Shijiazhuang: Hebei People's Publishing House, 1998.
4. See Liang Huixing. *Zhongguo wuquanfa jianyi ago* (Suggestions concerning China's property rights). Beijing: Social Science Data Publishing House, 2000, 97. [No English publication.]
5. North, Douglas, C. Theoretical Outline of Institutional Change. (A Lecture at Beijing University.) In: *Economics and Economic Reforms in China*. Edited by Yi Gang et al. Shanghai: Shanghai People's Publishing House, 1995, 8–9.

REFERENCES

Chen Jun and Ren Fang. 1996. *Business Ethics and Social Transformation*. Wuhan: Wuhan Publishing House.

Fukuyama, F. 1998. *Trust: The Social Virtues and the Creation of Prosperity*. London: Hamish Hamilton (1995). Chinese version translated by Wanrong Li. Hohhot: Yuanfang Publishing House.

North, D. C. 1994. *Institutions, Institutional Change and Economic Performance*. New York: Cambridge University Press (1990). Chinese version translated by Shouying Liou. Shanghai: Sanlian Publishing Company.

Shils, E. 1982. *Tradition*. Chicago: University of Chicago Press (1981). Chinese version translated by Fu Keng and Lu Le. Shanghai: Shanghai People's Publishing House.

Sun Yat-Sen. 1975. *The Three Principles of the People (San min zhu yi)*. Translated into English by F. W. Price; edited by L. T. Chen. New York: Da Capo Press.

CHAPTER 2

The Ethics of an Ecological Economy

Zeying Wang

Contemporary economics is developing in a direction that combines ecology and ethics, while ethics is exhibiting the tendency to unify ecology and economics (Daly and Townsend 1996, chap. 19). If ecological economy becomes the most important economic model in the twenty-first century, then there will surely appear a kind of new ethics that unifies the integrity of ecological ethics and economic ethics. We call this new kind of ethics eco-economic ethics, which, in our view, will become a powerful moral force to push forward the sustainable development of the ecological state, economy, and society.

WHY ECO-ECONOMIC ETHICS ARISES

Eco-economic ethics develops when people have a deep understanding of the advantages and disadvantages of modern industrial civilization and of the market economy, when the theory of sustainable development has been put forward, and when people have come to consider and study the ethical issues arising in the developing course of the ecological economy. Thus, it comes in essence from contemporary people's criticism of the developing course of modern economy and the study of the sustainable development of human economy and society.

In specific, there are at least three reasons for the birth of eco-economic ethics. First, eco-economic ethics is the inevitable product of the selection of the ecological economic model and the strategy of sustainable development. The chief capitalist countries of the West entered the industrial revolution in consecutive order at the turn of the eighteenth century, changing from agricultural societies to modern industrial societies marked by a tremendous accumulation of riches and great productive forces. However, the process of industrialization is a contradictory one with a lot of side effects. Motivated by anthropocentrism, extreme egoism, and narrow utilitarianism, the Western nations chose to pursue nothing but efficiency without giving attention to the evolution of the environment. The path that the Western countries pursued turned out to be one based on surprisingly high consumption of natural resources and extremely serious pollution. This concentration on the economic development of one area will do great harm to humans fundamentally and in the long term, so it is marked by obvious immorality and amorality. With the shortage of natural resources and the serious environmental pollution causing an imbalance in the ecological system, there appear to be numerous difficult problems. It is under such circumstances that in the second half of the twentieth century some economists and ecologists of great insight began to question the modern economic model of Western countries. In theses or published books they disclosed the defects of the economic model formed after the industrial revolution, and they criticized the economic theory of seeking only speed and amount without recognition of the environment, holding that contemporary peoples should develop an ecological economy based on the unity of natural law and economic law (Daly 1996, chap. 15). The rise of and support for ecological economy indicates that humans are separating themselves from the fetters of an economy of pure utility, and that a systematic analysis has been made of the possibility of balancing ecological concerns and economic development, pointing to the developing and future direction of economics.

The rise of eco-economic ethics is also closely related to the economic ethical movement and the ecological movement, which took place in the second half of the twentieth century. As mentioned earlier, in Western society before the middle of the twentieth century, economists and moral philosophers had discussed economic ethical issues in their books and theses, but their discussion showed that the general tenor of academic thought was marked by the logic of economics without ethics. People believed in Darwinism whose basic principle was the law of the jungle. According to this basic principle, the economic market was characterized by a jungle-like competition among people, which favored elimination of all competitors. This kind of belief continued until the 1960s and 1970s when a large-scale crisis broke out with a number of economic scandals, leading to the development of the economic ethical movement, which advocated abandoning the ethics of the jungle. In this context economic ethics began to draw attention from the circles of economic theorists. At the same time as the explosion of the economic ethical movement, there appeared a global ecological movement. The ecological movement, characterized by an emphasis on ecological ethics, first appeared in America with the publication of Rachel Carson's *Silent Spring* (1962/2002). With the co-development of the economic ethical movement and the ecological ethical movement, the attention of the economic ethical movement was gradually drawn from a fixed focus on society to an awareness of the need for unity between society and nature. From this awareness arose the ecological theory of economic ethics. Meanwhile, the ecological movement also began to replace its "light green" attitude with a "dark green" approach, signifying its increased attention to the unification of the idea of environmental protection with the idea of economic development so as to push forward the sustainable development of economy, society, and environment. Therefore, eco-economic ethics results from the development of the economic ethical movement and the ecological movement.

Finally, the birth of eco-economic ethics is the outcome of unifying ethical promotion, economic development, and environmental protection. The ecological crisis caused by the limitless exploitation of nature by humans in the development of our modern industrial civilization with its market economy warned people to pay special attention to environmental protection for the well-being of human development. The rise of eco-economic ethics has much to do with the choice of an ecological economy and of the ethical character of that ecological economy. The ecological economy requires that the economy should be developed without harm to the environment. The sustainable development of the economy should be keyed to concern for the environment. According to the ecological economic model, economies should emphasize the interdependence of efficiency, social effects, and environmental effects. Therefore, the efficiency model that the ecological economy requires is eco-economic efficiency. The ecological economy not only posits beneficial relations between humankind and nature and between the individual and society, but also suggests the unity between the present benefit and the long-term benefit as well as the benefit of the present generation and that of the future generations. Thus, the ecological economy has an ethical implication. It is the only economic model that contains both ethical and nonethical elements. If it is right to say that economic development cannot go without environmental protection and without moral regulation and direction, then it is also proper to say that environmental protection in the present age cannot do without consideration of economic development and without moral justification and support. Environmental protection without consideration of economic development cannot last long. Accordingly, the ethical promotion of the present day cannot make progress without keeping pace with economic development and environmental protection.

As the developing history of human moral life shows, morality has experienced three developing stages, that is, the stage of interpersonal morality, the stage of social morality, and the stage of universal morality. At present, we are in a transitional period of time between the second and third stages. The developing course of morality is a reflection of the expansion of human moral life space, the deepening of human understanding of morality and social practice. In the past, people usually restricted their understanding of morality to interpersonal relations. Not until the appearance of environmental issues did people come to realize the moral implication of the relations between humans and nature (Worster 1994, chap. 15). The tendency to give equal consideration to environmental issues, economic development, and moral construction has paved the way for the birth and development of eco-economic ethics.

The Features of Eco-Economic Ethics

Eco-economic ethics, formed in the process of developing an ecological economy, is a kind of ethics that sums up the moral consciousness, the moral concepts, the moral principles, and the moral activities that are reflected in the form of good-and-evil valuation and value pursuit based on the principle of inseparability between nature, society, and humans. This kind of ethics presupposes an ecological economy. It supports and justifies the development of the ecological economy with the purpose of solving the ethical problems that appear in the developing course of the ecological economy, holding that ecological ethics, economic ethics, and human ethics should be unified organically, that economy and humans should develop on the prerequisite that ecological ethics is emphasized and valued, and that the environment should be protected on condition that economy and humans get developed.

The development of an ecological economy created the possibility of a new kind of ethics: eco-economic ethics. Different from either ecological ethics or economic ethics, it is an assimilation of ecological ethics with economic ethics. First, eco-ecological ethics is an expression of economic ethics but in a nontraditional way. It is the rational option based on the experience and lessons derived from the developing economy. Eco-economic ethics holds that people's spiritual happiness—the glorification of the spiritual and cultural life of humankind—must be based on a decreased expenditure of substance and resources. Further, equal consideration should be given to both natural riches and national riches, reflecting the ideal unification of heaven and humans. If we say that economic ethics in its early period was an ethics confined to economic life alone and largely an ethics of utility, then eco-economic ethics has surpassed that level. It extends the research scope of economic ethics to the environment, holding that the sustainable development of an economy cannot be realized without consideration of environmental issues; therefore, economic development should be achieved under the regulation of ecological ethics and should be carried out with a combination of utility and morality. In eco-economic ethics there is an unprecedented moral completeness and unity of values. In this sense, eco-economic ethics is an ideal economic ethics, without question.

Just as eco-economic ethics is a nontraditional form of economic ethics, so too, second, is eco-economics a nontraditional form of ecological ethics, for it is a form of ecological ethics that gives special attention to economic development and economic progress. This kind of ethics has exceeded the "light green" level of environmental concern, progressing to the "dark green" level. If we say that the former level of concept has been characterized by description of environmental issues and emphasis on the importance of solving environmental issues, then the latter level of concept has been marked by the analysis of the economic and social causes of environmental issues and corresponding approaches to solve these issues. Eco-economic ethics advocates the idea that positive economic and social measures should be taken to realize the value of unifying environment with development. Thus it attaches great importance to the renovation of human civilization, human productive patterns and human living patterns. Eco-economic ethics has lifted ecological ethics to a higher level, representing the developing prospect of ecological ethics.

The third feature of eco-economic ethics is the blending of ecological ethics with economic ethics. We can call it ecologized economic ethics or economized ecological ethics. In fact, the solution to environmental issues must occur within the context of economic development, while the solution to economic ethical issues must take into consideration the relations between humans and nature. In addition, ecological ethics will inevitably be adapted to the economic activities of the enterprise and commercial activities; will be closely connected with the economic decisions, economic arrangement, and economic administration of the government; and will be linked to the economic consciousness and economic activities of the individual. Similarly, contemporary economic ethics will have to pay attention to concerns addressed by ecological ethics. To achieve the sustainable development of economy, economic ethics has to rely on the aim set by ecological ethics to develop the economy. In forming a bridge between economic ethics and ecological ethics, eco-economics has surpassed the limitations of economism and ecologism. It not only has the ecological-ethical implication of respecting nature, protecting environment, and maintaining the ecological balance, but it also has the economic-ethical implication of developing economy, exploiting natural resources properly to meet the rising physical and cultural needs of humans, and leading people to a happy and harmonious life.

Eco-economic ethics has risen in support of the development of an ecological economy. It is the outcome of the interaction between ecological ethics and economic ethics in the particular situation of our contemporary society. Eco-economic ethics reflects the double requirements and properties of both ecological ethics and economic ethics, so it is in essence a new ethics growing from modern morality and standing for the latest developing tendency and the latest study achievements of modern morality.

The Structure of Eco-Economic Ethics

As a brand new kind of ethics, eco-economic ethics has its own internal structure and content. The internal structure of this kind of ethics is composed of three levels, that is, the macro-level, the meso-level, and the micro-level, and three parts, namely, eco-economic ethical consciousness, eco-economic ethical relations, and the application of the eco-economic ethics.

Eco-economic ethics at the macro-level is concerned with the internal unity between the universe and the earth. This is expressed in the moral responsibility of humans to other living beings, the connection of human economic development with the macro- or super macro-environment, and the picture of globalization or the eco-economic ethical concepts, the eco-economic ethical principles, and the eco-economic ethical conduct of human beings. All people must respond to the ecological crisis, at this macro-level of concern, for the occurrence of, effects of, and solutions to the ecological crisis have global implications. Furthermore, eco-economic ethics at the macro-level may find its expressions in the eco-economic decisions, the eco-economic system, the eco-economic operation, the eco-economic distribution, and the eco-economic activities of every country or nation.

Eco-economic ethics at the meso-level is chiefly reflected in eco-economic planning, eco-economic management, eco-economic valuation, eco-economic education of regions and departments of various kinds. Thus it is closely related to such issues as regional and departmental environmental protection, regional and departmental economic development, regional and departmental construction of spiritual civilization, and so on. Eco-economic ethics at the micro-level is largely found in eco-economic ethical concepts, eco-economic ethical consciousness, eco-economic ethical selection of conduct, and the formation of the eco-economic ethical quality of the enterprise and the individual. After all, the eco-economic decisions and strategies at the macro-level and the eco-economic planning and management at the meso-level must be carried out by the eco-economic consciousness and conduct at the micro-level. Every enterprise and every individual has the responsibility to protect the environment and to push forward the sustainable development of the world.

Eco-economic ethical consciousness consists of two parts, that is, the consciousness of the eco-economic ethical principles and that of the eco-economic ethical thoughts. The consciousness of the eco-economic ethical principles is an organic system that reflects people's conceptual grasp of the eco-economic ethical principles, regulations, categories, and so on. The basic principle of eco-economic ethics is that of sustainable development, which finds its concrete expressions in the principle of fairness, the principle of common responsibility and duty, and the principle of improving life quality. The principle of fairness includes fairness in the same generation, fairness between different generations, and fairness in the distribution of limited resources. The principle of common responsibility and duty requires that people should regard humans and the earth as belonging to all and should fairly undertake the responsibility and duty to realize sustainable development. The principle of improving life quality respects the basic needs of human beings, maintains the health of human beings, and aims at creating a society that can guarantee equality, freedom, education, and human rights among its members, and that can keep its members immune from violence, persecution, and threat. Eco-economic ethical regulations include that of developing and protecting natural resources, developing industries and consumption, which are harmless to the environment, satisfying the diversified needs of humans by cultivating human intelligence, and pushing forward the all-around development of humans. Eco-economic ethical categories include eco-economic ethical obligations, eco-economic ethical conscience, eco-economic fairness, and eco-economic ethical happiness. The eco-economic ethical theory consists of production, productive value, riches, development, and so on. In general, eco-economic ethical relations are a kind of relations between people and nature. However, this kind of relation shows itself in the relations between the individual and society, between organizations and organizations, and between the individual and himself.

Eco-economic ethical activities refer to people's activities based on their understanding of eco-economic ethical concepts, eco-economic ethical principles, and eco-economic ethical regulations. It includes the selection of eco-economic ethical conduct, eco-economic ethical valuation, eco-economic ethical education, eco-economic ethical accomplishments of social members. What can be used as the good-and-evil criterion to judge the eco-economic ethical conduct is the eco-economic ethical principles and rules. Eco-economic ethical principles and regulations have reflected the integral benefit and the long-term benefit of the whole of humankind, and the fundamental benefit of a country or a nation. In the contemporary world, the conduct and phenomena that are instrumental to the realization of sustainable development are morally good, while the conduct and phenomena that are harmful to the cause of sustainable development are morally evil. The key point of eco-economic ethical education and accomplishments is to cultivate people's eco-economic ethical consciousness in order for them to overcome a pragmatic eagerness for instant success, quick profits, and narrow utilitarianism, and to understand the ecological crisis accurately so as to develop an appropriate plan for conquering the crisis. Eco-economic ethical education and accomplishments are also marked by an emphasis on the propagation and advocacy of the concept of sustainable development, and on the fact that we only have one earth. Such education emphasizes the necessity of protecting the earth and its resources by focusing on the individual's connection to a hometown, a particular corner of the earth, and the fundamental benefit to the individual of the earth's resources. In this way the sustainable development of the economy and the environment is inextricably tied to the existence and happiness of every individual who can embrace the cause of environmental protection, the cultivation of green products, and green consumption as a compulsory responsibility.

Studying and advocating eco-economic ethics is of great significance and value for both economic construction and ethical construction in the new century. The formation of this kind of ethics has opened a new area in the field of ethical study and has cultivated new room for the development of ethics. In the new century, ecological issues are economic issues, and vice versa. Accordingly, ecological ethics and economic ethics will demonstrate a tendency to assimilate. Eco-economic ethics is the lucky child of the new century, whose growth will be sure to add tremendous vitality to the ethical construction of the new era.

References

Carson, R. 2002. *Silent Spring.* 40th anniversary edition. Introduction by L. Lear; afterword by E. O. Wilson. Boston: Houghton Mifflin.

Daly, H. E. 1996. *Beyond Growth: The Economics of Sustainable Development.* Boston: Beacon Press.

Daly, H. E. and K. N. Townsend (eds.) 1996. *Valuing the Earth: Economics, Ecology, Ethics.* Sixth printing. Cambridge, MA: MIT Press.

Worster, D. 1994. *Nature's Economy: A History of Ecological Ideas.* New York: Cambridge University Press.

CHAPTER 3

Confucian and Christian Ethics about the Market Economy

Kit-Chun Joanna Lam

INTRODUCTION

This essay studies the historical development of Confucian and Christian ethics about the market economy. As both traditions contain some socialist elements, a study of how each has responded to the historical changes in market institutions in order to maintain the dynamism and vitality of their traditions may give us insights into the development of business ethics for contemporary Chinese economy as it develops into a socialist market economy with Chinese characteristics.

The major source of authority of the Confucian tradition can be traced back to Confucius (551–479 B.C.) and Mencius (forth century B.C.), while the final source of authority of Christian teachings is the Bible, which Christians believe has been inspired by God over an extended period of time. The Classical Confucians, in general, have acknowledged the beneficial existence of market exchanges and the influence of supply and demand conditions on the price of a good. Rather than accepting market forces unconditionally and without limit, they inherited a tradition for government to regulate market exchanges. The Christian biblical writings also accept the pursuit of personal gain, including that attained through market activities, perhaps even more positively than the Confucians, although it also emphasizes that exchanges have to be carried out in a correct way, and that there should be honesty rather than cheating or stealing. In both traditions, the right to private property is not absolute. Confucius thought that responsibility for the poor should fall equally on wealthy people as well as on the government. Excessive inequalities could destroy social harmony and cause social disorder. Similarly, the Bible teaches that the ultimate ownership of wealth belongs to God and thus wealth has to be managed according to the will of the loving God, which may mean sharing with the poor.

With this background of the two classical traditions, we study the later development of their ethical thinking about market exchanges and distribution of wealth. We then discuss the relevance of Confucian ethics and Christian ethics about the market economy as applied to the socialist market economy of China.

DEVELOPMENTS OF CONFUCIAN AND CHRISTIAN ETHICS ON MARKET ECONOMY

Confucian Ethics

From the time of Han Kao Ti (202–195 B.C.), there were policies and laws applied to the whole empire for the suppression of merchants in China. Public sentiments were against merchants because people thought that the merchants did not make anything themselves, and they stored up commodities in order to raise their prices and then sell at a profit.

The Neo-Confucians of the Sung dynasty (960–1279) were more negative about the profit motive than the Classical Confucians. For example, the Sung Neo-Confucian Zhu Xi regarded calculating profit and advantage as being inconsistent with rectification of moral principles. He thought that if people "understood moral principle, [then] poverty and baseness would be incapable of doing them harm, and wealth and honor would add nothing to them." He did not assert that it was impossible for a merchant to live according to the "Principle of Heaven," but he regarded such an achievement as unusual, for the world was deeply confused morally. The problem actually did not lie in the occupation of the merchant, any more than it did in the occupation of farmer or artisan. Rather, the problem was common to all occupations. The problem resulted from turning one's mind "to wealth and extravagance every day," instead of pursuing one's work diligently and living simply (Chu Hsi and Lu Tsu-Chien 1967, chap. 8, 5).

The attitude toward profit and market exchanges became more positive with the advent of the Ming dynasty (1368–1644). An influential Neo-Confucian of this period, Wang Yang Ming, even acknowledged the possibility of merchants becoming sages if they could harmonize their bodies and minds (Wang Yang-Ming 1963, 56). The principle that each of the four groups of people—officer, farmer, merchant, and craftsman—is equally useful to society was noted by a Confucian scholar, Yeh Shih, who said, "It is because the four groups of people all together contribute their usefulness to society, that civilization can be advanced. To depress the secondary occupations and to promote the primary one is not a correct theory" (Chen 1974, 412).

After China suffered humiliating defeats by Western political and economic powers in the nineteenth century, there was a dramatic shift in attitude toward the morality of market activities. Many Confucian scholars became convinced that commerce and industries were necessary to save the nation from her weakness, so government should take a strong supportive role in this respect. There was a clear shift from the metaphysical orientation of the Neo-Confucians to the consequential approach taken by the political Confucians of the nineteenth and twentieth centuries, including Kang Youwei and Suen Yixian (Sun Yat-Sen).[1]

The belief in industrial development and the strength of active government leadership in the economy was inherited by the modern Confucians, and Tu Weiming in particular, tried to relate the miraculous growth of some East Asian economies to Confucian values.

Concerning distributional issues, the Neo-Confucians followed the Classical Confucians' tradition of ascribing to the government and the wealthy people social responsibilities to help in poverty relief. For example, a system of village granary was established by Zhu Xi in 1168 when the people of his district were hard pressed for food. As a form of relief, the people received rice from the government, and, in the winter, they returned it together with interest. Zhu also called for the wealthy merchants to participate in this poverty relief program.

This Confucian belief in the priority of people's welfare and poverty relief was shared by the political Confucians in the late Qing dynasty. Kang even formulated an ideal form of utopia in his later stage of thought, which was built on social ownership of factors of production. He was concerned about the moral problem of inequalities resulting from the buying and selling of private property, so he envisioned an ideal society with no social stratification and with the disappearance of family and private property (Hsiao 1975).

On the other hand, his contemporary, Suen Yixian, a Christian convert brought up in Confucius tradition, expressed his socialist ideal in the "Principle of People's Livelihood," which shows the influence of both Confucian humanism and Christian compassion for the poor. The goal of People's Livelihood was to build a "wealthy and equitable" state by implementing "equalization of land-ownership and regulation of capital."[2] He was concerned that in the natural evolution of market capitalism, workers were given unfair treatment. Thus he proposed the nationalization of natural monopolies like railroads and public utilities so as to use the monopoly profit to finance social welfare programs; only small businesses should remain in the private sector (Hsiao 1975, 367–369). He also proposed a land tax to prevent the idle landlords from reaping excessive monopoly rent.

In response to the globalization of competitive markets, the modern Confucian Tu acknowledged that the competitive market has been a major engine for economic growth. But at the same time, he was concerned about the widening of the gap between the haves and have-nots as unintended negative consequences of globalization. He regarded it as "just" that the beneficiaries of globalization share their resources more equitably with the world, implying that the beneficiaries in the competitive market do not have absolute right over the gains they make in the market, but indeed have a responsibility to share them with the marginalized, underprivileged, disadvantaged, and silenced (Tu 2001).

Christian Ethics

The biblical morals on market exchanges are followed very closely by theologians of all ages, although they may extend their interpretations and applications of biblical writings to their life situations in accordance with their understanding of the market institution in their times. The thought of Thomas Aquinas (1225–1274) dominated the church life in the medieval period. He referred to Jesus' Sermon "Do to others what you would have them do to you" [Matt 7:12] as the basis of commutative justice. While Aquinas condemned unrestricted profit seeking, he thought trade, "considered in itself . . . does not imply a virtuous or necessary end" (Aquinas 1981, II–III, Q.77, A.4). He saw no injustice in selling something for a higher price than the purchase price, provided that the value of the thing sold has been increased in some way, and if profit realized is "lawfully intended, not as a last end, but for the sake of some other end which is necessary and virtuous," such as supporting one's family or enriching one's sovereign. Compared to the Confucians, Aquinas seemed less willing to accept a price determined by supply and demand as just.

In the sixteenth century, the influential Protestant reformist Martin Luther (1483–1546) warned in "On Trade and Usury," that "The love of money is the root of all evil." He also thought that a just price should be cost-determined, and that it was against Christian love and natural law that sellers sell their goods as dear as they can. Luther saw very clearly the sinful nature of man. Therefore, he thought that the government should come onto the scene "to appoint wise and honest men to compute the costs of all sorts of wares and accordingly set prices which would enable the merchants to get along and provide for them an adequate living" (Stackhouse et al. 1995, 174). What he objected to most were trading companies, which at his time made a lot of monopoly profit and got richer than kings and emperors within a very short time.

Another Protestant reformist of the sixteenth century, John Calvin (1509–1564), had an important influence on the development of the later economic order when he expanded the biblical principle of stewardship. Endowments were regarded as blessings, but in living the present life, Christians should "observe a mean," lead an ascetic life and "indulge as little as possible" (Calvin 1989, Book III, Chap. VII, Sec. 10). The conception of a sacred "calling" encourages workers to work hard even under difficult working conditions and also justifies the position of the middle-class business people.

As the productive nature of market activities became more apparent, the Christians increasingly saw that making gain in the market could be a good thing and money could be put to use for "glorious ends." The famous rule of John Wesley (1703–1791) to "gain all you can, save all you can and give all you can" has remained an important dictum for Christians till the present time.

In modern times, the efficiency of the market has gained pervasive recognition among Christians, especially after the fall of the Soviet Union. However, many Christians think that efficiency is not enough since we have to be concerned about morality and justice (Griffiths 1982). There is a general awareness that the market economy fails when there are externality problems (Wogaman 1986) and that government regulations would be necessary in case of market failures, to control, for example, environmental pollution. There are also concerns that free international trade results in terms of trade that are favorable to the rich industrial nations but unfavorable to the poor agricultural economies. In other words, these Christian concerns extend from equalities within a nation to that equality across nations and to the issue of international justice.

Concerning distributional issues, there is not much question among Christians in modern times about the charging of interest on loans, although Christians regularly make appeals for the rich countries to relieve the heavy interest burden of the very poor nations as an expression of Christian compassion. The major Christian concern is the widening income gap between the rich and the poor or, more importantly, the existence of poverty even in affluent societies. As a result of supply and demand conditions in the free market, the market wages for low-skilled workers are very low, and this has forced a lot of minorities into poverty and distress. There is thus a demand on the government to take up responsibility to care for the weak by creating various welfare programs. Internationally there are also concerns to find ways to share more equitably the resources of the world as the income gap among nations widens with globalization (National Conference of Catholic Bishops 1997, 101–102; United Methodist Church, Chap. IV). The basis for appropriate redistribution is the biblical principle that private ownership of property is a trusteeship under God; no person or any group of persons has exclusive and arbitrary control of any part of the created universe. Therefore those entrusted with wealth have a responsibility to share their resources with the poor in accordance with the will of the compassionate God (Griffith 1984, 63–80).

Relevance to the Socialist Market Economy of China

Since the three traditions of Socialism, Confucianism, and Christianity share a deep concern for the welfare of the common people, it would be helpful for Socialist China to study the Confucian and Christian market morality under different market conditions in its attempt to develop business ethics.

One important observation from our study is that both Confucian and Christian traditions consistently take a holistic approach to moral issues. There is never a complete separation between morality of persons and that of the market institution. The emphasis is on the moral character of persons, regardless of socioeconomic institutions. Although there is an increasing awareness of the moral nature of the market institution, whether individuals or groups of individuals are doing justice and practicing mercy to other people remains a major concern.

The emphasis of the Confucian and Christian traditions on personal ethics has a favorable effect on the growth of the market economy since honesty and trust can reduce transaction costs in voluntary market exchanges. The recognition of the importance of building up spiritual development alongside with material development in China in the 15th Congress of the Chinese Communist Party is thus commendable (Li 1999, 581). On the other hand, the negligence of moral aspects by modern economic analysis of the market economy is deficient.

Another important observation is that, although both the Confucians and the Christians accept the market as morally good to the extent that the market is efficient in production and creation of wealth, they have found it undesirable to let the interplay of supply and demand conditions in the free market to completely determine the allocation and distribution of resources in the economy. For Confucians, transfer of wealth to the poor can be justified because the government and wealthy people have social responsibilities toward the poor in a society where different people are interconnected and mutually dependent. Even though Christians put more emphasis on individual freedom and private property than the Confucians, the concept of stewardship and accountability to God again imposes a moral constraint on the use of resources, and a responsibility on the part of the government and the wealthy people to take care of the poor in a society. Both Confucian and Christian ethics have provided the moral constraint to prevent the absolutization of wealth and enabled the provision of a safety net to the poor. Adequate welfare support and poverty relief from government and nongovernment charitable organizations have been important in maintaining social stability in market economies of many Western countries, and many of these are of Christian origin.

Since the introduction of market mechanism in socialist China, the socialist market economy has experienced much productivity gain within a short time, largely attributed to the efficiency and incentive inherent in the market structure. At the same time, troubling signs have emerged which indicate that without the appropriate development of market morality that goes with the development of the market, unconstrained selfish profit-maximizing activities in the market can easily lead to frauds and dishonesty that raise transaction costs and inhibit the healthy growth of the market economy. Besides, undesirable market outcomes like widening income disparities, unemployment, and insecurity as a result of the privatization and marketization of public enterprises may also threaten social stability; the Classical Confucians warned of this long ago. The Confucian and Christian ethics on market economy illustrate the need to strike a balance between efficiency and equity, incentive and security, as well as between private property and social responsibility. How to strike a balance amidst contradictions of these kinds in the specific context of China will demand much wisdom and moral strength.

Notes

1. Kang Youwei (1858–1927) is best known as the leader of the "Hundred-Day Reform" in the late Imperial Qing Dynasty while Suen Yixian (1866–1925) is known as the "Father of the Republic."
2. Conference on Dr. Sun Yat-Sen and Modern China. *Proceedings of the Conference on Dr. Sun Yat-Sen and Modern China*. Taipei, Taiwan: National Sun Yat-Sen University, 1985, Vol. IV, 444.

References

Aquinas, Thomas. 1981. *Summa Theologica St. Thomas Aquinas*. Translated by Fathers of the English Dominican Province. Westminster, MD: Christian Classics.

Calvin, John. 1989. *The Institutes of the Christian Religion*. Translated by Henry Beveridge. Grand Rapids: Eerdmans.

Chen Huan-Chang. 1974. *The Economic Principles of Confucius and His School*. New York: Gordon Press.

Chu Hsi (Zhu Xi) and Lu Tsu-Chien. 1967. *Reflections on Things at Hand (Jin Si Lu)*. Translated with notes by Wing-Tsit Chan. New York: Columbia University Press.

Griffiths, B. 1982. *Morality and the Market Place*. London: Hodder and Stoughton.

———. 1984. *The Creation of Wealth: A Christian's Case for Capitalism*. Downers Grove, IL: Intervarsity Press.

Hsiao Kung-Chuan. 1975. *A Modern China and a New World: Kang Yu-Wei, Reformer and Utopian 1858–1927*. Seattle and London: University of Washington Press.

Li Zhan-Cai. 1999. *Modern Chinese Economic Thought (Dang dai zhong guo jing ji si xiang she)*. Kaifeng: Henan University Press.

National Conference of Catholic Bishops. 1997. *Tenth Anniversary Edition of Economic Justice for All*. Washington, D.C.: National Conference of Catholic Bishops.

Stackhouse, M. L., D. P. McCann, S.J. Roels, and P. N. Williams (eds.) 1995. *On Moral Business*. Grand Rapids: Eerdmans.

Tu Wei-Ming. 2001. The Context of Dialogue: Globalization and Diversity. In: UN Eminent Person Group. *Crossing the Divide*. New Jersey: Seton Hall University, 51–96.

United Methodist Church, U.S.A. *The United Methodist Social Principles*. At http://www.umc-gbcs.org/sp.html.

Wang Yang-Ming. 1963. *Instructions for Practical Living, and Other Neo-Confucian Writings*. Translated by Wing-Tsit Chan. New York: Columbia University Press.

Wogaman, J. P. 1986. *Economics and Ethics: A Christian Enquiry*. London: SCM Press.

CHAPTER 4

Economic Motivation and Its Relevance for Business Ethics

Xiuyi Zhao

EMANCIPATING ECONOMIC MOTIVATION AND ESTABLISHING A ROLE FOR BUSINESS ETHICS

The assessment of economic motivation, that is, the will to acquire and/or create wealth, has varied in accordance with the status of economic life within different social environments and during different historical periods. It was not until the rise of the market economy that economic motivation received significant recognition. In his analysis of the development of economic motivation in the history of Western civilization Max Scheler (1874–1928) points out that during ancient times and the Middle Ages, social class by birth and heredity determined the "privileges of political status, and only with such political status could one acquire wealth." What could be acquired through different pursuits was determined by a standard in which "livelihood corresponded to status." Political power and status absolutely determined and delimited the opportunities and pure activity space created by wealth (Scheler 1997, 10). In other words, political status with its corresponding morality was the highest standard for measuring all economic activities. The critical issue was social hierarchy, since only 'livelihood that corresponded to status was lawful, moral, and normal. Economic motivation not subject to the limitations of status, however, was abnormal, immoral, and illegal. For this reason, the only way to rise above economic activities restricted by status was through the quest for treasure, turning worthless metals into gold, controlled pillages, and unlawful activities such as cheating people out of money. A pivotal factor in the transition from a traditional society to a modern society is that the economic motivation that had been viewed as abnormal or improper gradually became normal and proper. Scheler's historically situated analysis, which reveals the problems of economic motivation in social transformation in the course of modernization, contains a certain widespread application.

A similar development also occurred in the process of transformation of Chinese society. Traditional Chinese society acknowledged economic motivation to a certain degree. The Chinese traditional aspiration for *fu* (happiness), *lu* (salary), and *shou* (longevity) in everyday life implies an acknowledgment of economic motivation. However, status also limited economic motivation in premodern China, most apparently in the value of *lu*—the salary received from the emperor on account of social status. The main feature of *lu* is its correspondence between a certain economic benefit and a political rank. For the vast majority of people, who were not officials, economic motivation was limited to "matching one's social status" and "making a livelihood." However, Confucianism, as the official ideology of the ruling class, taught that "Confucius rarely talks about profit" (Confucius 1992, *Analect* 9:1) and that "one should pursue righteousness rather than financial gain"(Confucius 1992, *Analect* 4:16).

During the last century in China, economic motivation achieved a certain degree of autonomy. The Chinese Communist Party persistently pursued the political objective of bringing economic benefits to the Chinese people. But under the planned economy, economic motivation in reality was substantially restricted to a level of subsistence only. Although the party pursued a line of egalitarianism, social class distinctions were actually preserved, especially for the peasants, for whom economic mobility was greatly limited. Despite this, political status and its related morality were the highest standards for measuring all economic activities. A situation related to this stands out in particular. At times, due to politics, even the economic motivation to make a livelihood was restricted and assailed. Such limitations had been abolished gradually during the course of China's economic reforms and opening up, especially in the transition to a socialist market economy since the 1990s. Political status and corresponding morality no longer served as the top criteria in measuring all economic activities. An important part of this undergoing process is the legitimization, or emancipation, of economic motivation. Today, society affirms the legitimization of individual economic motivation. The ability of people to pursue personal economic gain through honest labor and legal business endeavors has already been encouraged. People's notion of this is also changing. In the more developed areas of China, not only do most people realize that legally pursuing economic motivation is a citizen's legitimate right, but they have also adopted the principle of "money making more money." Personal wealth management has gained great attention, as we can see, for example, by the best-selling book *Rich Dad, Poor Dad* (Kiyosaki and Lechter 1997).

However, development in China has not been even, and the divide between urban and rural economies created under the planned economy still exists. As such, the limitations on the status of economic motivation have not been entirely eliminated, especially the restrictions on economic motivation for rural residents. Following increased reforms in the country's social transformation, especially following the next phase of integration with the global market introduced by the country's entrance into the WTO, we can predict that economic motivation will gain even greater autonomy and influence in the near future.

After economic motivation gains legitimacy, identifying the limits of such legitimacy becomes a pressing question. The emergence of a large number of immoral activities within the present economic life indicates that following the affirmation of economic motivation, an issue that must be resolved is how to regulate economic activities in terms of morality. This is the reason why so many different fields are interested in business ethics and the field has gained recognition. To regulate economic activities, we should first theoretically clarify whether or not, given the confirmed legitimacy of economic motivation, morality in the field of economic activities is possible.

The Implications and Theoretical Justification of Economic Motivation

In the history of Western thought, neoclassical economists provided the most influential analysis of the implications of economic motivation and its rational justification. The crucial point of their theory is based on the hypothesis of *homo oeconomicus*. The main idea is that economic motivation is an individual's pursuit to maximize benefits. According to the neoclassical economists, economic motivation is the incentive for fulfilling individual preferences and personal gain. In more concrete terms, it is the motivation to maximize the fulfillment of material desires, as represented by the incentive for profit. Participants in economic life are rational economic individuals; namely, "individuals rationally pursuing greatest efficient use." Rationality here refers to instrumental rationality. It is said that

> The title of *homo economicus* is usually reserved for those who are rational in an instrumental sense. Neoclassical economics provides a ready example. In its ideal-type case the agent has complete, fully ordered preferences (. . .), perfect information and immaculate computing power. After deliberation he chooses the action which satisfies his preferences better (or at least no worse) than any other one (Eatwell et al. 1987, 54).

The theoretical justification for the hypothesis of *homo oeconomicus* can be summarized as follows.

The first one is an empirical justification asserting that all economic activities are in fact motivated by self-interest. As Adam Smith said, "It is not from the benevolence of the butcher, the brewer, or the baker, that we expect our dinner, but from their regard to their own interest. We address ourselves not to their humanity but to their self-love, and never talk to them of our necessities but of their advantages" (Smith 1976, 26–27). Economic research must be founded on such a premise. Therefore, it is stated that the first principle of economics is that all behavior must filter through personal profit in order to be realized.

The second one is a justification based on a theory of human nature. It assumes that people by nature are selfish. This premise has been widely adopted by economists. It has received theoretical support from philosophy and ethics during the last several centuries. From Thomas Hobbes, the philosophy of Britain's empiricists accepted the theory of the sensualists, taking happiness, namely the satisfaction of desires, as goodness, and viewing the "desire to power, desire to wealth, desire to knowledge and desire to honors" (Hobbes 1985, 54) as the basic desires of human beings. In the eighteenth century, with France's Bernard Mandeville, such a theory of human nature took a more radical form in being used to justify selfish economic motivation. According to Mandeville, pride, self-interest, and the desire for material goods, which were the vices in the view of traditional morality, became the basis for the economic well-being of the entire society (Philosophy 1963, 457).

The third one is a moral justification, claiming that parochial private benefit of individuals is a virtue in its own right. Thinkers in the tradition of British utilitarianism provided the philosophical and ethical grounds for this position. In Benthamian utilitarianism, the essence of human nature was regarded as attaining pleasure or averting pain, while the maximum possible amount of happiness resulting from individual behavior was regarded as good. J. S. Mill revised Bentham's theory, yet his proof, "that which is desired is desirable" (Robson 1996, 235) objectively provided a methodology for the conclusion of "the pursuit of one's own interest is itself good" deduced from the "fact that people are pursuing their own interests."

In summary, neoclassical economists base their interpretation of economic motivation on three propositions. The first proposition is that economic motivation can be completely reduced to the maximization of individual benefits. The second is that the pursuit of an individual's parochial selfish benefits is a kind of virtue and goodness in its own right. The third is that the pursuit of parochial private benefits is not only the single motive for all economic behavior, but also the single motive for all kinds of human behavior. Thus the hypothesis of *homo oeconomicus* can be used to interpret various types of human behavior, including political, altruistic, and even biological behavior. This third view, also referred to as the "declaration of economic imperialism" is represented by Gary S. Becker's book *The Economic Approach to Human Behavior* (Chicago 1976).

Although widely influential, this idea has been subjected to several kinds of criticism. Without denying the fact that people's economic motivation stems from their pursuit of material benefits, these criticisms argue that it is too simple just to equate economic motivation with the maximization of an individual's benefits. Friedrich List, a German economist in the nineteenth century (1789–1846), believed that people's motives for economic behavior must also be linked to cultural customs and patriotic ethos, and thus cannot be accepted unconditionally. He proposed the concept of the "moral person," which was positioned in direct opposition to the concept of the "economic person" (or *homo oeconomicus*). He asserted that any given person is subordinate to a specific country: "One's happiness is linked to the independence and progress of one's country" (List 1997, 31). Therefore, we cannot view an individual as a self-sufficient entity. He relies upon Hegel's view that a country is comprised of common ethics, in which morality functions as the linchpin for the country and the individual is viewed as a moral person. Here moral person does not denote a person who possesses typical moral behavior or moral character, but rather refers to the individuals who have been linked together by the linchpin of patriotism to form the object of nationhood. Therefore, he emphasizes that as for the individuals' pursuit of economic benefits, it can be unconditionally affirmed in terms of morality. He believes that specific analyses and evaluations are necessary for different types of economic motivation. First, he emphasizes that in order for wealth to be acknowledged it must be acquired through legal means. In addition, as for the pursuit of wealth, it can only be affirmed if it is combined together with the efforts to develop the economy and culture for future generations. The pursuit of wealth for wealth's own sake and/or as motivated by hedonism is not worth affirming from a moral perspective.

Francis Fukuyama, a contemporary American scholar, asserts that the neoclassical conception of economic motivation can interpret 80 percent of all economic phenomena but is ineffective with regard to the remaining 20 percent. He states: "The fact that our values are able to be influenced by the praise or recognition of those people we admire and of whose judgment we trust is more important than anything else" (Fukuyama 1998, 224). Relying upon Alexandre Kojeve's explanation of Hegel, Fukuyama states that struggle for recognition is the fundamental motive of human being's behavior, and the pursuit of property is just one of its aspects. Material gain is not the only motivation for human behavior, even within economic activities. The relentless pursuit of personal benefits is not necessarily all that is to economic motivation. Likewise, the motivation for the desire for wealth and pleasure cannot be entirely affirmed.

Thinkers belonging to the tradition of romanticism had revealed long ago the negative side of economic motivation. Thomas Carlyle in nineteenth-century Britain (1795–1881) is a typical example. He asserted that the rise of the notion of economic motivation caused a moral crisis and spiritual paralysis. He believed the rise of economic motivation led to greed becoming fashionable and the widespread suspicion of morality. The world had become filled with charlatans promoting false teachings, while the educated preached the bold words of morality while sinking into a life of money, luxury, and dissipation. He criticized Bentham's utilitarianism: "It turns humankind's limitless sacred spirituality into a type of hay or thistles and fuses together happiness and suffering . . . These people are victims of paralysis in terms of spirituality" (Carlyle 1988, 122). He mocked the "principle of maximizing happiness" as "Mormon gospel," accusing Bentham of viewing making money and enjoying pleasures as Heaven and neglecting the obligations required by morality, thereby negating spiritual values.

The debates and divergent views on economic motivation not only existed among scholars, but also existed in everyday life in general. This discussion on Western social values and morality took shape ever since the rise of the market economy.

A similar controversy regarding the meaning of economic motivation and the justification of its legitimacy has emerged in contemporary China as well. Years have passed since the adoption of a market economy in China, and few today are still denying the legitimacy of economic motivation and the pursuit of material benefits. Economic motivation is no longer viewed as a negative value, but rather has essentially become a right for citizens, thereby legitimizing the pursuit of economic benefits attained through earnest labor and legal business activity. However, people still disagree over whether or not economic motivation can be simply reduced to individual private benefit. In other words, can economic motivation also involve spiritual and cultural aspects such as patriotism and faith? Many have also pointed out the negative moral and spiritual impact exerted by the rise in the legitimization of economic motivation. The resonant call for trust throughout society provides evidence of this concern. Indeed, whether self-centered economic motivation is right or not, and to what extent it is right, remains a controversial issue in China.

POSSIBILITY AND LIMITATIONS OF ECONOMIC MOTIVATION

Divergent views over the implications and legitimacy of economic motivation is related to the basic questions of whether or not and how business ethics is possible. Addressing these questions requires an understanding of business ethics, including the ethical norms in economic life, the relationship between business ethics and social ethics, and the relationship between the ethics of the modern market economy and China's traditional ethics. In reference to these questions, I will compare three alternative understandings of economic motivation.

The first one is to understand economic motivation simply as the maximization of one's private benefits. Then, a possible response is that morality and ethics cannot be articulated within the field of economics. This is the conclusion reached by Bernard Mandeville. According to Mandeville, since economics are motivated by personal gain, what had been earlier viewed as negative aspects, such as greed, extravagance, and arrogance, have all become the enabling force behind economic prosperity and artistic and technological advancement. In his *The Fable of the Bees*, Mandeville notes that lawyers, motivated by self-benefit, intentionally take advantage of legal loopholes to gain reputation and wealth. Different fields are filled with deception with vice pervasive: doctors treat life lightly and businessmen knowingly sell fake goods. A return to honesty would only lead economic prosperity and technological advancement to disappear into thin air. Mandeville's view that the market is a place of mutual deception is evident in everyday life and refutes the possibility of a business ethics based on the notion of the motivation of self-gain.

The second position holds that people pursue their private interests in all economic activities. This is a type of game based on individual benefits. As the game is repeated time and time again, as a result, a relationship of reciprocal cooperation is gradually established. Since the possibility of future cooperation requires both parties to meet, the future is very important to both. However, if it were necessary to hold a meeting in the future, then the optimal choice for both parties would be cooperation. Therefore, mutually beneficial cooperation, based on reciprocity within this game, will be generated over and over, playing out endlessly. Through its evolution, the market economy will be shaped into a system composed of reciprocal cooperation. In this scenario, private interests generate a relationship based on the expectation of reciprocal cooperation and corresponding market ethics. Since the system requires a morality consisting of mutual benefits and mutual trust, it raises the possibility of business ethics. At the same time, here we can see that an important function of business ethics is that it establishes and maintains a type of ethical relationship based on private benefit and whose main aim is mutually beneficial cooperation within the market. Various moral requirements emerge that are based on ethical principles, such as contractual relationships. Although this viewpoint affirms the possibility of business ethics, the moral requirement mentioned here, stemming from Bentham's utilitarianism principle of maximizing happiness, is based on individual utility. Its main sanctioning force comes from external means such as legal or economic ones. Therefore, what is emphasized is the use of legal administration and economic means to form society's business ethics.

There are many advocates of this conception of business ethics today, especially in reference to the current discussion in China on the virtue of integrity. Many advocates of this view actively support the use of legal administration to construct reciprocal cooperative relationships within the marketplace, while at the same time encourage integrity for the sake of the individual's long-term interests (i.e., benefits gained through repeated games). There are also some objections to this idea. The first objection is that a conception of ethics based on self-interest, or more exactly, based on long-term self-interest, can only rely upon amoral sanctions, such as law and economics. If the temptation for profit is greater than the calculated profit, then how can we guarantee that a legal loophole would not be sought? The second objection is that the acting out of the process of weighing benefits is more of a tactic than a morality. From the perspective that morality entails self-sacrifice or some degree of altruism, it is difficult to construct business ethics on the basis of self-interest. The third objection claims that traditional morality has no role to play in the construction of business ethics if we just base it on self-interest. How can we build a modern business ethics if we depart from the reliable resources of traditional morality?

These objections urge us to consider whether economic motivation can be entirely tied to individual self-interest. Therefore, a third possible position should be considered. We should recognize that economic motivation cannot be detached from individual self-interest, and in addition, an ethical relationship built on the basis of reciprocity is a requisite component of business ethics. At the same time, economic motivation is multifaceted and cannot be simply reduced to the motivation for self-benefit. Economic life, interconnected with spiritual and cultural life, is only part of all social life. Agents of economic actions are both economic beings and moral beings. As citizens of a specific nationality, individuals possess an intrinsic relationship with their nation's history, language, and culture. Concern for the welfare of one's nation and people, and to pursue the appreciation and recognition of one's fellow citizens, would provide motives, in addition to private benefits, for economic activities.

This is an acceptable hypothesis because only with such a hypothesis can business ethics achieve a degree of autonomy within the field of economics. We may hold that the ethics of market economics stems from a motivation out of self-interest. However, the research of market ethics not only needs to assume that people's economic motivation arises out of self-interest, but also needs to consider that people's economic activities have additional motives. It is precisely due to the presence of other motives, which also to a certain degree restrict the motive for personal gain that self-interest does not necessarily have to degrade into shameless greed and immorality. It is only with this kind of assumption that we can find a basis for people to uphold moral norms within economic activities. Business ethics that are based on this presupposition can also better receive the support of the resources of traditional morality. Due to the fact that morality within premodern society was formed under the historical conditions in which self-interest within economic activities was not recognized, such traditions can only be carried on given the recognition of the existence of other motives (Fukuyama 1995; Sen 1987, 1999).

REFERENCES

Becker, G. S. 1976. *The Economic Approach to Human Behavior*. Chicago: University of Chicago Press.

Carlyle, T. 1988. *On Heroes, Heroworship, and the Heroic in History*. Boston: Houghton (1907). Chinese version. Shanghai: Joint Publishing Company Ltd.

Confucius. 1992. *The Analects (Lun yu)*. Translated by D. C. Lau; second edition. Hong Kong: Chinese University Press.

Eatwell, J., M. Milgate, and P. Newman (eds.) 1987. *The New Palgrave: A Dictionary of Economics*. Vol.2. London: Macmillan.

Fukuyama, F. 1995. *Trust. The Social Virtues and the Creation of Prosperity*. New York: Free Press.

———. 1998. *The End of History and the Last Man*. New York: Free Press (1992). Chinese version. Hohhot: Yuanfang Publishing House.

Hobbes, T. 1985. *Leviathan*. New York: Cambridge University Press (1991). Chinese version. Beijing: Commercial Publishing House.

Kiyosaki, R. T. and S. L. Lechter. 1997. *Rich Dad, Poor Dad—What the Rich Teach Their Kids About Money—That the Poor and Middle Class Do Not!* TechPress Inc.

List, F. 1997. *National System of Political Economy*. New York: Garland (1974). Chinese version. Beijing: Commercial Publishing House.

Philosophy in 18th Century France. 1963. Edited by the Teaching and Research Section of Foreign Philosophy History, Department of Philosophy, Beijing University. Beijing: Commercial Publishing House.

Robson, J. M. 1996. *Collected Works: John Stuart Mill—V. Essays on Economics and Society*. New York: Routledge.

Scheler, M. 1997. *Die Zukunft des Kapitalismus und andere Aufsätze* (1979). Chinese version. Beijing: Joint Publishing Company.

Sen, A. 1987. *On Ethics and Economics*. Oxford: Blackwell.

———. 1999. *Development as Freedom*. New York: Knopf.

Smith, Adam. 1976. *An Inquiry Into the Nature and Causes of the Wealth of Nations*. New York: Oxford University Press.

CHAPTER 5

On the Moral Principles of Contract Ethics

Huizhu Gao

In China contract ethics has gained paramount importance with the development of the socialist market economy. Before, in the planned economy, the enterprises didn't have to be concerned with contract ethics because they only had to execute the instructions of the central government. Contracting policy has now been gradually introduced and is becoming popular. However, simultaneously, the phenomena of not honoring one's promises and of breaking one's contracts have spread widely. According to the (incomplete) statistics of the Chinese Ministry of Industry and Commerce, in 1998 the courts tackled 2,890,000 cases nationwide involving creditors' rights and repayments of debts, estimated at 51 percent of all cases in China. The overdue funds between enterprises in China have reached more than 5 percent of the whole trade volume, compared to only 0.25–0.59 percent in fully developed market economies. While domestic enterprises have annually drawn 4 billion contracts, the ratio of fulfillment has been far below the average level in developed countries. Unsurprisingly, this has aroused substantial concern of high-ranking officials in China's provincial and municipal governments. And the report of the country's Tenth Five-Year Plan explicitly stated that "we will make tremendous efforts to tidy up and regulate the market order, reinforce the market system, consolidate trustworthiness and establish a system of confidence."

Since 2002, measures have been taken to penalize those who break their contracts. Several provincial governments presented "warnings" to the enterprises that were short of credits. For example, the

Zhejiang provincial government excluded some enterprises from the list of "the top cultivated enterprises," while in Shanghai the licences of ten corporations were suspended because of cheating activities. In Qingdao, a director, blacklisted as the leader of a bad enterprise, is prohibited from taking any business leadership position in the coming years. In Beijing, a documentation center has been established that gathers the credibility records of enterprises. On February 7, 2002 the Price Bureau of the Beijing government exposed cheating activities of nine commercial enterprises and took due measures to tackle the case (*Xinhua Digest* 2002, vol. 3).

People have come to realize that contracts, as an indispensable component of modern economic activities, constitute, to a certain degree, the modern market economy. It is generally agreed that confidence in the effective fulfillment of contracts is key to whether the market economy runs smoothly. Ethics, with the exception of law, makes up one of most important means in guaranteeing the effective fulfillment of contracts. Contract ethics is the moral standards that both sides should adhere to during the course of signing the contract and during its execution and afterward as well. Contract ethics, as adapted to the socialist market economy, adopts trustworthiness as its core principle and consists of the principles of voluntarily entering into contracts, fairness and justness, and compensation for damages.

The Principle of Voluntarily Entering into Contracts

As pointed out long ago, as early as Roman law, the fundamental meaning of the contract is its formation through mutual intent. In the second chapter of his *Institutes of Gaius* (1988), the Roman legal scholar Gaius (115–180) states: "A contract could be established either through material means, oral means, or through mutual intent." Elaborating upon the concept of mutual intent, Gaius continues: "We say that the establishment of a contract's obligation through the afore-mentioned forms is based on mutual intent because they do not require any special form of expression or writing other than that both parties share the identical agreement." As evident here, mutual intent refers to mutual agreement. This notion that mutual intent is the basis of contracts was also pointed out in the *Civil Code of France*: "A contract is a kind of expression of mutual intent, in accordance with which one individual or several individuals owe a certain liability or debt to one or more individuals." The *Civil Code of Germany* (viewed as representative of strongly positive law) also clearly accepts mutual intent as the fundamental basis of contracts. However, it developed the notion by dividing it into two parts: the intention of the contract parties and the expression of this intention. It maintained that intention could only become fact through its expression by explicit action.

It is precisely because a contract is a type of expression of mutual intent that the voluntary signing of contracts becomes the fundamental ethical principle of contract ethics. Contracts are formed only through the free and mutual agreement of the parties involved and are not a result of external coercion or the wishes of just one party. Rather, contracts involve two parties voluntarily and self-consciously willing to join hands in a shared endeavor. Therefore, contracts established through any external pressure or from one party's coercive threats or deceit could be totally rescinded. Such actions are not ethical contract behavior. Likewise, an established contract can also be cancelled due to lack of mutual intent or other defects such as in the case where the contract parties fail to be equipped with normal decision-making faculty (e.g., suffer from psychiatric disorders or under the legal age). Entering into contract with such parties is considered unethical contract behavior. Thus, as stipulated in the *Contract Law of the People's Republic of China* (issued March 3, 1999), the signatories of contracts must adhere to the principles of equity, voluntarism, fairness, and trustworthiness. The law also states: "The contract parties are equal under the law and neither side has the right to force its will upon the other side . . . The contract parties in accordance with the law possess the right to sign contracts on a voluntary basis without the illegal interference of any other individual or entity."

THE PRINCIPLE OF FAIRNESS AND JUSTNESS

Under the market economy, contracts are the means for essentially ensuring fair distribution. Therefore, the principle of fairness and justness, as an essential part of business ethics, naturally also comprises an important principle of contract ethics. Within contract ethics, the principle of fairness and justness is expressed in the following ways.

First, involving the justness of contract motives, the motive for establishing the contract cannot run counter to the principles of social justness. In establishing a contract, the autonomy of the individuals and their mutual "intent" must be based on the principles of fairness and reason. The requirement for fair and just motives for establishing contracts was created to suppress unlawful contracts. The signing of contracts through coercive or deceptive means, or by unauthorized representatives, stems from unjust contract motives.

The second issue concerns the fairness and justness of the contract's contents. This means that the contract's contents in terms of its stated business or trade must not break the law, violate "public order and customs," or violate society's welfare. Public order and social customs refer to positive social order and exceptional social mores and customs. Society's welfare refers to different types of social benefits, including the benefits derived from natural resources and human resources and benefits associated with economic, political, and cultural development.

The third issue concerns fairness in the execution of the contract. This is the guarantee for conducting safe business or trade, and includes the fairness of the means involved in executing the contract, honesty of the contract parties in executing the contract, and the principle of not withdrawing a promise. Since a promise is a type of pact, and because the party making the promise willingly enters into the pact, the other party has the right to expect the fulfillment of the promise, and the party making the promise should comply with the pact. On a fundamental level, the existence of contracts is precisely due to the fact that the contract parties willingly establish the contract in accordance with their promises. Promises can therefore be considered the fundamental concept and function of contracts. "The principle of not withdrawing promises" is also a fundamental principle in terms of sustaining the fairness and justness of contracts. Of course, the "promise" that we speak of must be a promise willingly made by a rational and normal person while not under any form of external coercion. In the process of executing the contract, another expression of the principle of not withdrawing promises is in terms of the principle of assuming responsibility for defaulting on a contract. Since this principle concerns the "penalty" for the unethical behavior of transgressing the contract's principles of trustworthiness and fairness and justness, it holds an important position within contract ethics.

The Principle of Responsibility for Defaulting

Generally speaking, there are two types of defaults: rational and irrational. Irrational default refers to instances in which the contract parties break the contract when obligations are to be met due to objective inabilities (such as uncontrollable or accidental events), economic inabilities (such as failure to execute the contract due to poor business), and unreasonable economic factors (punishment for the contract parties' unreasonable economic management). Rational default means that when the obligations are to be met or about to be met, a contract party, although possessing the ability to fulfill the contract, rationally and deliberately breaks the contract after financial analysis and evaluation reveal that such an action results in greater maximization of profits. Rational default includes two types: default based on opportunism and default based on efficiency. Opportunistic default refers to instances in which after receiving goods from the other party (mainly borrowing money), the party fails to execute the contract and rather uses the capital or materials received from the other party to pursue other business opportunities. Efficiency default means that the contract parties choose to break the contract after carefully calculating that the profits derived from breaking the contract would considerably exceed the anticipated profits gained by the contract's fulfillment. It is evident that of these two types of contracts, rational default clearly involves subjective malice. The rational contract violator not only disregards the other party's interests and social welfare, but also intentionally manipulates the law, thereby resulting in dire social consequences.

In regards to assuming responsibility for defaulting, regardless of whether the default is rational or irrational, the defaulting party commits substantial damage to the other party of the contract. Therefore, the concrete manifestation of the default principle is compensation for damages incurred. In his book *Contract as Promise: A Theory of Contractual Obligation* (1981), American legal scholar Charles Fried points out:

> With any commitment made to you, I should try what I can to fulfill; if failing, I should present the equivalent amount of compensation . . . in the case of contract theory, with the expected measurement . . . and the aggrieved party should receive what he deserves when, otherwise, the breaking didn't occur.

Here, Fried points out both the necessity and the "degree" of compensation.

However, in terms of ethics, there exists indeed a tremendous difference between rational and irrational default. Thus, scholars of law and ethics in China, from a standpoint of both civic liability and public law, assert that rational default should be accompanied by severe compensation and punishment. The rational defaulting of economic contracts, due to their civic and economic features, affects both the contract parties as well as the entire society. This kind of breech causes significant damage to both individuals and society. In addition, due to the damage caused to social interests, law should exact punishment. In terms of the form of assuming responsibility, the defaulter should be responsible for paying a penalty for defaulting, such as compensating the loss incurred by the other party as a result. Additional penalties including confiscation of possessions, fines, and so on should also be exacted by the defaulter. This is in accordance with moral justness. Assuming responsibility for defaulting will be trivial if punishment is overlooked at the expense of compensation, especially in the case when financial gains resulting from defaulting exceed that of compensation, which then creates a motive for defaulting.

A large number of default cases can be observed in economic activities in China. This is in part related to neglecting, for a long period of time, to establish punishment for defaulting. Nowadays, following the development of China's socialist market economy, the country faces a large number of rational defaults. Many kinds of rules have been revised on defaulting to emphasize greater punishment, as stipulated in *The Regulations on the Buying and Selling of Agricultural By-products* (Article 17):

> When failing to fulfill the contract on account of selling goods through one's own channels or illegally selling at increased prices, the defaulting party must pay the aggrieved contract party from 5 percent to 25 percent of the total value of the goods for the unexecuted portion of the contract as a fine for defaulting and return the amount gained from increasing the price and all commodities to the aggrieved party; the excess income earned through selling through one's own channels shall be confiscated by the Department of Industry and Commerce Administration and remitted to China's central financial administration.

Such a law positively influences and raises the moral standards of the execution of economic contracts in China. In reality, whether a given act of defaulting should be punished depends on the degree to which the defaulter's motives are malicious and the precise damage caused by the act of defaulting (including whether compensation was proactively offered). Penalties requiring compensation for rational default is precisely the means for preserving and maintaining the principles of trustworthiness, fairness, and justness in contract ethics.

BIBLIOGRAPHY

Fried, C. 1981. *Contract as Promise: A Theory of Contractual Obligation.* Cambridge, MA: Harvard University Press.

Gaius. 1988. *The Institutes of Gaius.* Translated by W. M. Gordon and O. F. Robinson; with the Latin text of Seckel and Kuebler. Ithaca, NY: Cornell University Press.

Koslowski, P. 1996. *The Ethics of Capitalism*. Chinese edition. Beijing: China Social Science Press.

———. 1997. *Principles of Ethical Economy*. Chinese edition. Beijing: China Social Science Press.

Li Yining. 1995. *Ethical Issues in Economics*. Beijing: Sanlian Publishing House.

Lu Xiaohe. 1999. *Out of Jungle*. Wuhan: Hubei Education Publishing House.

Wan Junren. 2000. *The Sole Guidance On Ethics*. Guangzhou: Guangdong Education Publishing House.

Wong Guomin. 2001. *The Legal Protection of the WTO Entry and Globalized Management*. Beijing: World Books Publishing House.

Xinhua Digest 2002, vol. 3. Beijing.

Ye Dunping, Gao Huizhu, Zhou Zhongzhi, and Yao Jianjian. 1998. *The Evolution and Adjustment of Business Ethics*. Shanghai: Shanghai Education Publishing House.

CHAPTER 6

Fundamental Business Ethics Issues in Contemporary China

Zhenping Hu and Kaifeng Huang

MARKETS INVOLVE SPACES OF FREEDOM AND ETHICAL OBLIGATIONS

Following the rise of business ethics in the West since the 1970s, during the last few decades in China a greater number of scholars have focused their attention on business ethics in this country. If the rise of business ethics in Western countries had been linked to crises in corporate ethics, public trust, and corporate well-being instigated by the exposure of a series of scandals in the corporate world, the rise in business ethics in contemporary China was rooted in the emergence of critical ethical issues during the transformation of the country's economic system (Lu 1999). Although China's sociopolitical, economic, and cultural background is radically different from those of Western countries, many of the issues regarding business ethics that emerge are related to the market economy. Therefore, in analyzing the emergence of such issues in contemporary China, it is important to first understand the relationship between the market and ethics.

The market and market economy are two different concepts. The market economy is essentially an economic system in which market mechanisms serve as the fundamental method for allocating resources. In *Capital*, Marx pointed out:

> We saw . . . that the exchange of commodities implies contradictory and mutually exclusive conditions. The differentiation of commodities into commodities and money does not sweep away these inconsistencies, but

develops a form in which they can exist side by side. This is generally the way in which real contradictions are reconciled. (Marx 1975, 122)

During the phase of the natural economy in which productive forces stand at a relatively low level and national output matches national demand, the market has already reached the stage of accommodating surplus agricultural and small handicraft production. Toward the end of the medieval period in the West, following the increased scope and efficiency of production, especially in relation to the appearance of mechanized industry, the level of the socialization of production rapidly increased. The contradiction of privatization became more and more pronounced and pointed to a solution based on the continued development of a market-based economic system.

Due to various kinds of economic motivation and complex social consequences within the market economy, business ethics involves difficult problems that should be faced and solved by scholars in the field of ethics. In the history of business ethics in the West, the relationship between economics and ethics has been discussed from three different points of view. First, economics and ethics are understood as closely related and compatible; thus what fits the market also fits ethics (natural coincidence). Second, the market is conceived as morally neutral; thus whatever relates to the market is neither good nor bad (value neutrality). Third, regulations embody ethical demands of the market economy; thus ethical behavior in the economy is equivalent to compliance with the regulations (game theory; cf. Gan 2000, 20–21). These viewpoints indicate some fundamental questions of economic ethics and point, in particular, to the need of investigating the origin of ethics and morality in the market economy. The emphasis should be placed on the study of the degrees of freedom pertaining to the conditions and the functioning of the market economy and the concomitant spaces of freedom of its actors. There is no ethics and morality without freedom. The need for business ethics and morality depends on how much freedom exists in relation to different types of constraints within the economy.

It is well-known that the individual markets and the market economy as a system are the results of the productive forces of society. As the market institutions have grown over time, human beings have developed abilities to overcome natural obstacles, their spaces of freedom have increased, and economic independence has become the basis of personal independence. Accordingly, the way of restricting personal action has greatly changed as well. Under the conditions of the market economy, personal dependence on people and organizations have been diminished or even eliminated. Now market rules can be used to restrict or to enlarge the degrees of personal freedom. The actors in the market can acquire more and more opportunities. They can freely enter the market or withdraw from it and choose their own way to participate in the market.

To act freely presupposes that the actors act in accordance with their own self-consciously determined will. There is no freedom without self-consciousness and voluntariness. The development of the market economy plays a critical role in promoting a widespread self-awareness of freedom. In the latter part of the medieval period, people were moving to free themselves from the constraints of theology and feudalistic authoritarianism and calling for freedom. These were at the time the prerequisite conditions for the development of the market and market economy.

The enlargement of the spaces of freedom does not necessarily mean that the freedom of human beings are actually realized. Freedom not only involves self-consciousness and free will, but also implies "the principle of self-awareness," that is the conscientious recognition and utilization of regular behavioral patterns, including the relationships between the individual and the group and between the individual and the society. In this regard, Confucius had remarked: "I may follow what my heart desires without transgressing the limits" (Brooks and Brooks 2001, 2: 4). Marxism more thoroughly treated the issue: "Freedom is the necessary transformation of our recognition and our world" (Mao Zedong 1999, 198). In order to realize freedom, one has to have a true recognition of objective regularity and correctly deal with the relationships between the individual and other people and organizations. This is a matter of morality. Marx and Engels precisely pointed this out:

> Only within the common group can individuals obtain a method for the complete development of their abilities, and that is to say that freedom is only possible within the common group . . . Within the conditions of a true common group, individuals within and through their unity to the group obtain their individual freedom. (Marx and Engels 1975, 119)

In order to realize individual freedom, it is necessary not only to truly recognize objective human behavior, but also to correctly deal with the individual's relationship to others and society, and this is an issue of morality. However, because economic interests are strongly emphasized in the market economy, the ethical issues in dealing with relationships tend to be neglected. The development of a more perfect market economic system is directly connected to the process of optimizing such recognition and behavioral standards. The rise of the study of business ethics is directly related to the criticism by academics and others of the notion of the profiteering business people. If a public discussion of the issue of corporate ethics creates a crisis in public trust for corporations, then the management of corporations will have little choice but to begin to pay attention to the problems of its corporate image and business ethics (cf. Feng 1996, Chap. 10).

As the discussion earlier indicates, the development of the market and market economy greatly increases the scope of freedom, and while questioning interpersonal relationships, consequently highlights the problems of business ethics. At the same time, under the market mechanism, due to the limitations of economic interests necessary to ensure the normal operation of the market economy, people must pay greater attention to market regulations and business ethics. Not only is it critical to improve market laws and regulations, but also to deepen people's recognition of social relations and relations to the environment.

THE PROSPECTS FOR BUSINESS ETHICS IN CHINA

Historically, China has pursued a kind of ethical idealism. China's self-sufficient economy and patriarchal clan system have led to ignoring the role of public ethics. Confucianism has played an important role in ethical life while pure religious ideals have been far less influential than in other countries. After the proclamation of the People's Republic of China in 1949, the communist ideal and belief became the spiritual pillar of the nation. However, with the transformation from the planned economy to the market economy, the conflict between ethical idealism and the present economic system has become considerably aggravated. Due to the acceleration of economic change, people have been painfully realizing the loss of their ethical ideals, and as the spaces of freedom and monetary benefits have increased, some people have even been advocating moral nihilism.

China is currently implementing reform of its economic system. It will take a long time to improve the market laws and regulations and make them reasonably perfect. Although people are receiving many types of ethical education, the educational impact is quite limited compared to that of the past. Moreover, due to a very different moral environment, the divide between moral education and the experiences of reality has become more aggravated.

All this exacerbates the urgent problem of business ethics in China. Thus, there are objective reasons for China's ethical problems, namely as related to the transformation of the country's economic system and the long process required for the market mechanism to reach a relatively mature stage. Internal reasons, such as the instability of the value system and vacillation and loss of ideals, have led to a frailty of morality and even moral nihilism. In addition, the large divide between moral education and reality indicates the difficulties and failure of moral education. These conditions have created a sharp contradiction between the moral goals of socialism and society's real moral condition, attracting attention to these ethical problems for ethicists and different segments of society.

China is currently facing a serious situation with regard to economic ethics. This is not just apparent in the relatively widespread proliferation of different types of deceptive behavior and scams, drawing attention to the problem of integrity with a great drop in credibility throughout society. In addition, due to the corruption of legal and administrative institutions, these problems cannot achieve prompt and thorough exposure and commensurate restrictions and punishment. Therefore, various strange phenomena have become prevalent and normalized, such as handing out presents to the extent that bribery is commonplace, the use of power by cadres within the government and state-owned corporations to seek personal gain even involving openly soliciting bribes. Within this type of immoral atmosphere, public pressure faces great difficulty in increasing the exposure and rectifying these problems.

However, it should also be noted that the ethical problems of China's market economy are closely related to the fact that in the Party's conscious effort to follow a path of reform and implement the transition from a planned economy to a socialist market economy system, the market system has not yet reached a mature stage and laws and regulations are far from being infallibly enforced. These have been exacerbated by the instability and vacillations in ideology and values. These problems can be resolved as the system matures, laws become better established, and moral beliefs are reformulated.

In the last few years, the construction of China's market economic system, legal system, and legal enforcement has certainly made strides forward. China's 15-year plan clearly points out the importance of building a socialist country that is ruled by law. This indicates the correct direction for China's market economy and development of society in general. China's government and Communist Party were aware of the difficulty involved with the transition of the country's economic system, and therefore China's entry into the World Trade Organization (WTO) has breaking through various obstacles associated with the nation's traditional system, standardized the market economic system, and enhanced external pressure upon it. This illustrates China's resolute determination to establish a standard modern market economic system.

The Chinese Communist Party has always focused on morality, and with China's reforms, the Party is still very concerned with issues of spiritual morality. In the past 20 years, in terms of ideological theory, we have seen the formation of Marxist thought in contemporary China, such as Deng Xiaoping's Theory. This banner has been raised to unite Party ideology and encourage the establishment of the ideals and belief system for socialism with Chinese characteristics. In terms of morality, after endorsing the policy of "governing the country through law," the Party promoted its link to "governing the country through morality," adopting a series of concrete measures such as the "Outline of Implementing the Construction of Citizen Morality." The persistent implementation of these legal regulations and moral education efforts will result in helping to resolve China's problems with business ethics through the formation of a more mature market economic system and value system.

In addition, there exists an intrinsic relationship between economic development and business ethics because problems of business ethics are always related to insufficient economic development and insufficient satisfaction of the desires stimulated by the market economy. More than two thousand years ago in China, the philosopher Guanzi stated: "With the granaries full, there can be propriety. With sufficient clothing and food, there can be honor." China's Communist Party was aware of such an idea, as Deng Xiaoping emphasized that "principles are strengthened through development," and Jiang Zemin had emphasized that the problems emerging with reform can only be resolved through the deepening of the reform effort to encourage continued economic development. In the last 20 years, the world has recognized China's rapid economic growth and many agree that such a trend will continue. When economic development moves to a new phase and scientific technology, especially development of the Internet industry, provides strong support to enforce legal contracts, many types of problems that have emerged within business ethics will gradually be solved.

It is critical to point out that business ethics is an issue for all people within China and solutions to such problems must rely upon all people. The socialist market economic system is developing the independence of individual citizens and has forged a systematic foundation for the protection of legal self-interest. An important problem for business ethics is to adopt various means to confront the infringement of the benefits of others or the public benefit. In order to effectively halt this infringement, it is important for every individual to objectively understand and self-consciously preserve his or her own personal interests and related public interests, thereby creating public pressure to monitor their interests. This is precisely a problem for democracy. This is the only way a relatively fair and just legal system can be formed and implemented. This is the only way the widespread abuse of freedom can be checked. Throughout China's history, the lengthy period of feudal authoritarianism has led to the weak sense of autonomy for its people, and a certain psychology of obedient dependence still maintains a strong hold. This type of psychology is an obstacle to the development of China's social market economic system and the establishment of healthy principles of business ethics. In general, the establishment of China's socialist system, especially the socialist market system, is beneficial for reforming this psychological weakness of the Chinese people, overcoming the flaws of the planned economy's limitations, to providing a concrete systematic plan for developing healthy individuals. Although this requires time and great effort, dedication will ensure that China rapidly gets out of its current predicament.

REBUILDING THE COMMUNIST PARTY OF CHINA

The transformation of the economic system is an important decision based on historical experiences and lessons learned by the Chinese Communist Party. The problems that exist in the field of economic ethics are intimately related to the Communist Party. First, the leaders of all ranks in the Party, holding different types of authority and control over resources, not only form the backbone of economic development, but are also the main targets of corruption within the market system. Second, the Party's objective will have a large impact on the formation of the market system considering its position of authority and self-conscious transformation of the system.

The Communist Party, without a doubt, has selected the path of economic reform for the prosperity of the country. This is reflected in Jiang Zemin's written statement: "The Party has no other special interests other than the interests of the broad masses" (Jiang 2001). However, at present, in the course of economic transformation, some Party cadres utilize their power for their own interests. This is the main reason for the considerable lack of social decency, the growth of Party corruption, and for the urgent problems in the field of business ethics. If these corrupt practices become so pervasive as to affect the Party in power and generate vested interests, the nature of the social-ist market economy will totally change. Therefore, if the urgent problems of economic ethics cannot be addressed and solved, a well-functioning socialist market economy cannot be built either. On the one hand, the Communist Party of China must use its authority to carry forward modern market economic development; on the other hand, it should overcome and prevent the misuse of its power and authority, especially as such abuse corrodes the market mechanism. In order to establish a fair and just economic environment, one has to overcome the problem of "rent seeking" and corruption that exists in the Party by cutting off the influence of money on public authorities. The formation of a positive environment for business ethics first requires a standard of morality within the Party. Rebuilding the Party in power becomes an increasingly important task. In order to be a healthy and dynamic organization, the Party should implement Jiang Zemin's "Three Representations"—represent the advanced produc-tive forces, China's advanced culture, and the basic interests of the people. While maintaining the Party's leadership, democratic processes within the Party must be developed to promote democratic structure for all people in China. Lenin has pointed this out: "If victorious socialism does not fully implement democracy, then the victory achieved cannot be sustained and will even lead to the extinction of the nation" (Lenin 1975, 168).

In a nutshell, to develop good and reasonable business ethics, the leadership at all ranks should set positive examples for the common people, while everybody has to shoulder his or her own responsibility. Such individual and concerted efforts will create a more ethical environment.

REFERENCES

Brooks, E. Bruce and A. Taeko Brooks. 2001. *The Original Analects*. English translation. New York: Columbia University Press.

Deng Xiaoping. 1993. *Deng Xiaoping Anthology*. Vol. 3. Beijing: People's Publishing House.

Feng Qi. 1996. *Human Freedom and Truth-Goodness-Beauty*. Shanghai: East China Normal University Press.

Gan Shaoping. 2000. *Ethical Wisdom*. Beijing: China Development Publishing House.

Jiang Zemin. 2001. *Remarks Congratulating the Eightieth Anniversary of China's Communist Party.* Beijing: People's Publishing House.

Lenin, W. 1975. *Complete Works of Lenin.* Vol. 28. Beijing: People's Publishing House.

Lu Xiaohe. 1999. *Out of Jungle.* Hubei: Hubei Education Publishing House.

————. 2001. On a Characteristically Chinese Study of Business Ethics. *Philosophy Studies*, No. 8, 54–59.

Mao Zedong. 1999. *Mao Zedong Anthology.* Vol. 8. Beijing: People's Publishing House.

Marx, K. 1975. *Capital: A Critique of Political Economy.* Introduced by Ernest Mandel; translated by Ben Fowkes. New York: Vintage Books (1977). Chinese version. Vol. 1. Beijing: People's Publishing House.

Marx, K. and Engels, F. 1995. *Selected Works.* Chinese version. Second edition. Vol. 1. Beijing: People's Publishing House.

CHAPTER 7

Business Ethics in China: A Systemic Perspective

Jane Collier

INTRODUCTION: TEXT AND CONTEXT

In *The Blackwell Encyclopedic Dictionary of Business Ethics* we read that "business ethics is the study of business action—individual or corporate—with special attention to its moral adequacy" (Werhane and Freeman 1997, 51). In that same publication we read that "business ethics in China rest upon a . . . heritage that emphasises personal virtue and . . . right ordering of personal relationships in social organization" (ibid., 72). In their focus on persons and organizations as units of analysis, these approaches regard the context of business activity as "given." For instance, market universalism, methodological individualism, and the primacy of technology are simply taken for granted. A further set of presuppositions relate to the wider institutional context of business defined by such attributes as private property and ownership rights, open and competitive market structures and stability of contractual arrangements, as well as supportive regulatory and financial frameworks.

This acontextual approach, which treats the organization as atomistic, is arguably not always appropriate even in American or European contexts where organizations are increasingly subject to transformative shifts due to mergers and acquisitions, global market forces, and technological upheavals. In the case of China, however, a country that has undergone and is undergoing profound institutional, social, and cultural change, neglecting the context of business activity and focusing on organizations as discrete entities yields neither sufficient information nor adequate understanding of the normative issues specific to the Chinese business situation, nor does it provide any guidance as to how one might approach the task of "developing business ethics" in the Chinese context. This paper begins from the premise that the task of theorizing business ethics in China must start with a focus on context.

CONTEXT AS SYSTEMIC

There are two ways that this can be done. One is to regard social, cultural, political, and institutional contexts as analytically separable from, but "impacting" on organizations. The other is to opt for a systemic perspective that will create understandings of the social world by using the analogy of systems in the natural world seen as webs of interconnected elements (Simon 1996). A systemic perspective regards organizations not as separate entities, but as "nested" within the context in which they exist (Scott 1998), open to and responsive to that context (Collier and Esteban 1999). Taking the analogy further, we note that whereas subsystems in the natural world survive by exchanging energy with their systemic environment, in the social world organizational subsystems survive by the exchange of information between agents at every level. Information provides feedback from the environment and helps agents to adapt to fast-changing external demands and to change behavior in appropriate ways. Feedback can be negative or regulatory, reinforcing the stability of the system, but it can also be positive, thus generating fluctuations that render systemic processes nonlinear and hence unpredictable (Cilliers 2000). Small changes in initial conditions can produce great effects: the production of hurricanes in the South China Sea by the beating of butterfly wings in the Amazonian basin is frequently cited as an example of how systemic processes work in this manner.

MARKET SOCIALISM AS SYSTEMIC COMPLEXITY

The emergence of market socialism in China is understandable only in systemic terms. Webs of multiple and interconnecting systemic relationships provide the variety and differentiation required for successful adaptivity to a fast-changing global economic situation. But adaptivity can only happen at the price of increasing complexity. We can distinguish two aspects of complexity. The first of these has to do with the nature, scope, and variety of the information flowing through the system: we might term this "cognitive complexity." The second has to do with the structure and density of the relational webs within the system along which the information flows: we might term this "relational complexity" (Boisot and Child 1999, 241).

Social systems handle complexity in different ways. They can aim to reduce complexity by getting to understand the information and/or controlling its flow, or they can try to absorb it by aiming to keep options open, to hold multiple representations of the systemic environment, thereby creating a range of responses, including collaborative relationships with other subsystems so that risk can be shared. Cognitive complexity can be reduced by codifying and abstracting information so it becomes manageable, relational complexity can be decreased by reducing the number of agents (bureaucracies) or simplifying and ordering the nature of their relationships (markets). Complexity absorption, on the other hand, needs trust and shared values in collaborative relationships where the risks associated with uncertainty and ambiguity can be pooled (Boisot and Child 1999, 244). Complexity reduction is the usual Western response, but complexity absorption is more consistent with Chinese culture and the realities of the Chinese situation (ibid., 237, 238). China as a socioeconomic system is immensely differentiated and "cellular," with high levels of cognitive complexity and ambiguities of governance, power and responsibility at the institutional level, and complexity absorption does not handle these. However, the additional tensions introduced by the wide range of unethical behavior leads to an increasing emphasis on relational networks as a risk management strategy, and it is here that complexity absorption manifests itself.

The Significance of Institutions

A systemic approach allows us to picture the context of business in China, and thus the locus of the business ethics discourse, as dynamic flows of interactions and information within or between organizations, moving along networks that are stronger or weaker depending on the intensity of the relationships, which generate those interactions. These interactions are framed by their context: they are governed and shaped by the structures of organizational, systemic, and institutional arrangements and procedures within which they are embedded (Emanuel 2000). Sometimes "institutional structures" are explicit—formally or informally constituted bodies that articulate and maintain widely observed norms and rules (Child and Tse 2001, 6). Sometimes they are tacit—culturally embedded "ways of doing things." Institutions constitute the social framework in three different ways. They have a cognitive function in the sense that they provide shared meanings, ways of thinking, and repositories of learning and experience. They are regulative in that they embody implicit or explicit rules for the governance of procedures, practices, and behavior, both collective and individual. They are normative in the sense that they introduce prescriptive, evaluative, and obligatory dimensions into social life (Scott 2000). Institutions are also the repositories of the values and norms that underpin social stability.

A systemic approach allows us to realize that any discussion of business ethics in China or elsewhere needs to take into account the enabling and constraining effects of institutional, social, and organizational structures on decision taking. The ethical consequences of these effects are rooted in, and can be traced back to, the normative nature of these structures. We know from practical experience that structures can promote or block "good" or "right" decisions and outcomes. Structures can be inherently ethical or unethical, so that the notion of "structural ethics" relates to the attributes of structures that determine, influence, or pertain to ethical or unethical performance of individuals, organizations, or institutions (Emanuel 2000, 152). The idea of structural ethics may be novel in the business ethics literature, but it is implicitly and explicitly dealt with in the literature on institutions (Scott 2000).

We can distinguish the pathways through which these attributes are realized in their effects on outcomes.

1. Structures govern and shape relationships, and once structures become implemented they become "animated" by the interactions of people who carry out their functions and purposes. The structures that underpin systemic organizational interactions can be said to be causally implicated in outcomes of those processes that have adverse normative consequences.

2. Structures embody values and norms, and these in turn empower and enable actions and interactions, conferring rights as well as responsibilities, privileges as well as duties, licenses as well as mandates (Scott 2000, 55).

3. Relationships within and between organizations are guided by purpose and intent. Purpose and intent imply a capacity for moral responsibility not merely at the level of the individual or indeed the organization, but at the structural institutional level that governs their systemic interactions. Structures are ethical in the measure that they are designed to be consistent with, and to facilitate good purpose and intent.

Western business ethics regards the organization as a moral agent, with collective moral responsibility for its decisions and actions (Werhane 1985). The attribution of responsibility always carries with it the requirement of accountability, whether at the structural, the organizational, or the individual level. But who is to be accountable, to whom and for what? Individual accountability is an easy idea to understand; most of us know for what and to whom we are accountable. But in Western economies there is now a sustained effort to establish accountability at the corporate level by identifying corporate responsibilities to stakeholders and measuring the extent to which they are fulfilled (Jones et al. 2002). In these economies it is also realized that accountability at the institutional level is essential if corporate responsibility is to work. Institutions—economic, legal, political, and social—are accountable to the wider public for the normative consequences of their functioning. This accountability is at the core of democratic governance.

CHINA AND INSTITUTIONS

The significance of institutions is particularly relevant in the Chinese context. Not only is China undergoing the swift and wide-ranging institutional changes common to other transition economics, such as marketization and privatization, but it has a tradition of strong institutional influence, with government at every level playing a major part in economic and social affairs. Furthermore, changes in the ownership and structure of firms and industries, together with the growth of business support systems, are fostering the emergence of a complex, multifaceted Chinese business system. As China embraces market socialism, her institutional structures will need to adapt to support efficient market functioning.

The institutional context of Chinese business is likely to be profoundly affected by the opening up of Chinese markets to the wider systemic context of global capitalism. The primary structural feature of the global business revolution is that business organizations are no longer "stand-alone" entities, but are linked together in an integrative web of systemic transactions driven by the conscious coordination and planning activities of the core "system integrator" companies who in their drive to control costs establish long-term "partner" relationships not only with suppliers upstream, but also with distribution, servicing, and logistics companies downstream (Nolan 2001a, 39). This process has a "cascade" effect throughout the system. Core businesses put intense pressure on first-tier suppliers to meet their global needs: these in turn put pressure on second-tier suppliers, and so on all the way down the value chain. Resource allocation, location, and product development are driven by this process. Chinese businesses are likely to be sucked into this allocative system as their firms and industries are identified as low-cost/high-value providers of supplies for global companies. The primary role of Chinese firms is likely to become that of outsourced suppliers to the world's leading systems integrators (Nolan 2001b).

China must now face the reality of systemic integration within a global capitalism that increasingly demands transparency, accountability, and stakeholder satisfaction. The country has a strong tradition of moral thinking based on an ancient and rich culture. In order for China to realize the transition to market socialism and global capitalism she must not only build on this tradition, but she must aspire to the achievement of excellence in all three pillars—of personal integrity, corporate responsibility, and institutional structures that are both ethical and effective. China has opted for market socialism, and notions of "market" carry with them institutionally supported ways of behaving as well as ways of avoiding the worst adverse social consequences of market functioning. Good training practices make the newly unemployed more employable, quality control maintains product standards, environmental protection helps future generations, and so on. China has different aspirations, different expectations, different values, and different ways of living out these values in a market context. But if China is to realize her potential as a great global economic power she must develop the institutions to support free and fair markets as well as create the business practices that enable business to satisfy human needs, and the personal commitment, which rejects the temptations of greed and corruption.

INSTITUTIONAL REFORM

It is at the level of institutions that the task of creating the context where ethical business can flourish must start. The most basic of all reforms relates to the allocation of resources. The transition from a situation where resources are allocated by administrative "fiat" to a situation where resources are allocated by market forces has not yet been achieved (Wu 2000), and yet it is fundamental to the creation of a market economy.

The first and most significant need is for a bureaucratic reform that will enshrine the principles of transparency and open and consistent dealings. The political system must serve the good purposes of market socialism (Maosen 2000). Chinese conceptions of state and society, interpersonal relations (*guanxi*), together with a strong bureaucratic control of economic activities, encourage an allocation of resources based on privilege and familiarity rather than on viability and productivity (Dahlman and Aubert 2001). The present system breeds a corruption that is corrosive and enormously damaging to the building of competitive market functioning because it increases costs (Norton 2001). Bribery increases the costs of contracts; control of financial resources through state banks leads to corrupt and inefficient allocation of loans; payment for the right to set up a new company or a joint venture weakens the competitive potential of these businesses. Systemic change is the only way in which China will beat the problem of corruption and thus enhance productivity, efficiency, and innovation.

Associated with this is the need to strengthen the legal basis of business. The new global context of business means that China's economic objectives can be achieved only in the context of a transparent legal framework operated evenhandedly. The legal system in China is complex, but the several key legal pillars required to operate a market economy are lacking. Clear property and ownership rights and well-defined rules governing ownership of state enterprises are essential for efficient restructuring, not least because there is a close link between property rights, incentives, and efficiency (Cauley and Cornes 1999). So also is the establishment of effective corporate governance in the private sector (Coudert 2002). The regulatory environment is deficient: two examples here are the regulations of financial institutions and the establishment of intellectual property rights. Collaboration with other countries, together with proper enforcement measures, are essential prerequisites for progress in this regard.

A third need is for measures that will strengthen internal competition in order to allow the market to achieve allocative efficiency. China's progress in the global free trade economy will be hampered if internal and interprovincial barriers to trade prevent the achievement of economies of scale and if monopoly power is not checked. The establishment of free and fair trade must be supported by measures to deal with safety standards and environmental regulation, with the development of efficient tax levying and collection mechanisms, and with improvements in government collection and dissemination of economic statistical and other imformation.

The fourth need, that is, a climate of free and fair trade is particularly important if small and medium-sized enterprises, the most promising type of corporate vehicle for growth and for the introduction of new technologies, are to flourish. SMEs provide the setting for entrepreneurial creativity and ingenuity, they can react swiftly and responsibly to new market opportunities, and because they tend to be labor-intensive they can provide much-needed employment, particularly within the service sector. But the establishment of a strong SME sector requires, as a first step, a favorable and proactive policy stance and a clarifying of the law on private property. There is plenty to learn from ways in which other countries have tackled this particular aspect of economic change (Dahlman and Aubert 2001), yet each economy must find its own way of realizing the potential contribution of entrepreneurship.

A fifth arena of needed institutional change relates to the freeing up of the labor market. The problem of creating greater labor market flexibility without destabilizing migration requires a stepwise adjustment process that will have elements of retraining, of labor-using development policies such as the provision of infrastructure, urban construction and development of service sectors, and of the strengthening of social safety nets. The transition to a fully funded social welfare system will combine the protection given to workers in the previous system with a level of incentives for the unemployed, which will encourage retraining and hence greater flexibility.

Yet another structural adjustment relates to the financial sector. An emerging economy will move from a bank-dominated financial system to one that provides specialized financial intermediation, equity financing, and secondary paper asset markets. China needs a larger and more efficient financial sector, and the role of the government in the financial sector will need to be rethought (Baldinger 2000). Hitherto the government has acted as provider of finance as well as facilitator and guarantor of loans, using the banking system to support ailing SOEs and to pursue special policies without clear accountability mechanisms. The government now needs to act as architect of China's developing financial sector by establishing the regulatory and supervisory frameworks necessary to generate a wider and deeper provision of financial services.

SOCIAL ETHICS

The argument of this paper has been that institutional reform is the central plank in the development of "good" business in China—good in the sense of achieving the good purposes of allowing China to become a significant actor on the global economic stage. This is not to say that corporate social responsibility and personal ethical behaviour are not important. But without institutional reform at every level China will neither achieve market socialism nor become part of global capitalism because market failure becomes likely, perhaps even inevitable. Here we are talking both of market failure in the structural sense and of endemic factors, which bring about the same effect. Structural market failure has to do with manipulation of market processes either by monopolization, for example, of natural resources or by government interference in market functioning. Endemic market failure comes about because of uncertainties and externalities that impact on market processes—unpredictability and volatility in financial markets such as we witnessed in the East Asian financial crisis, information asymmetries, moral hazard of investors, or the costs of alignment to technological change. Market failure is to a large extent (although not entirely) rooted in the failure of institutional "networks." However, institutional and market efficiency are not the only requirements for market socialism to succeed. The moral dimension in society shapes the working of market capitalism and generates the commitment of institutions and individuals to improving its functioning (Dunning 2001, 34). If personal morality falters and social responsibility fails, market socialism will founder.

Throughout history successful economies have had a strong moral ethic, and China is surely one of the societies with the most articulated moral perspective (Dragga 1999, Koehn 1999, 2001). China has an ancient and respected moral tradition that is role-centerd and duty-based. That tradition demands unconditional loyalty to superiors, and first to the state or ruler. But China is in transition, and loyalty to superiors can weaken when expediency demands that personal need or greed should come first, when consumerism or hedonism seems more attractive, or when it is clear that state or ruler has not the interests of the people at heart. In addition, if business is politicized and responsibility is collective it is hard to introduce notions of individual moral autonomy. The future of China's economic prosperity hinges on the development of a coherent corpus of values and norms of behaviour that can support the efficient functioning of markets, and this in turn requires the development of new kinds of moral perception on the part of economic agents (Sherwin 2001).

Global capitalism is characterised by three dominant features. It is driven by knowledge and intellectual capital, shaped by alliance-driven global networks, and perceived as the shrinking of "world" to a global village (Dunning 2001). The virtuous qualities that therefore need to be nurtured, at a personal and at a social level, if socially responsible and sustainable global capitalism is to be achieved are as follows:

- *Creativity*—imagination, initiative, entrepreneurship, a willingness to learn, self-discipline, self-confidence, and self-respect.

Creativity realizes the potential of the person, increases intellectual capital, and leads to the embodiment of new knowledge.

- *Cooperation*—trust, forbearance, reciprocity, adaptability, a willingness to listen, an appreciation of the common good, and a respect for the opinions and viewpoints of others. Cooperation builds relationships, increases social capital, and the alignment of different approaches to the common purpose.
- *Compassion*—a sense of fairness and justice, an awareness of the needs of others, an acceptance of difference, and a profound respect for the "otherness" of the other. Compassion opens eyes and ears to the needs of others, develops critical faculties and the need to question the status quo, generates commitment to work for social justice not simply for those who are close, but for everyone.

We can see that different varieties of capitalism possess these virtues in different measure. U.S. capitalism, for example, is strong on creativity but not on compassion. European capitalism manifests cooperation and compassion; Asian capitalism is strong on cooperation but not on creativity; and Chinese capitalism has much to teach us about the virtue of cooperation, but is weak on compassion and on creativity.

What have creativity, cooperation, and compassion got in common? Each of these virtues is founded on a conception of the intrinsic worth and dignity of the human person. The "modern" way of saying this is that these virtues embody a conception of human rights. Following Chen (2000), I see human rights not as a Western idea, but as an idea, which as concept and discourse, is a phenomenon of modernity, reinvented in the twentieth century from its roots in Christian thought and its rediscovery in the intellectual and political revolutions of the seventeenth and eighteenth century. In the Chinese tradition there are elements that support a conception of human rights, just as there are elements that are inconsistent with that thinking. The Confucian principle of benevolence, the affirmation of moral autonomy and capacity for growth and perfection, and the duty of care for others all affirm the worth and dignity of the human person. Confucianism also supports specific rights, such as the right to education and the rights of the less fortunate. It would appear that China is similar to the West in that it is now rediscovering the basis of human rights in its own cultural tradition, and is thus on the way to making the same kind of qualitative transition into modernity and ethical maturity. Chen points out that Mou Zhongsan, the greatest Confucian philosopher of the twentieth century, believed that notions of human rights, democracy, and the rule of law are essential if Confucian values are to be fully realized and a "new mode of outward kingliness" is to be attained by the Chinese people (Chen 2000). China's moral tradition is strong and profound. All that is necessary is that China rehabilitate the virtues and insights of the Confucian tradition so that she may be able to achieve the institutional reforms, the democratization, and the protection of human rights on which she can found the success of market socialism and her full participation in the benefits of global capitalism.

REFERENCES

Baldinger, P. 2000. China's Green Markets. *China Review*, 27(2), 44–49.
Boisot, M. and J. Child. 1999. Organizations as Adaptive Systems in Complex Environments: The Case of China. *Organization Science*, 103, 237–253.
Cauley, J. and R. Cornes. 1999. Stakeholder Incentives and Reform in China's State-Owned Enterprises: A Common-Property Theory. *China Economic Review*, 10(2), 191–207.
Chen, A. H. Y. 2000. Chinese Cultural Tradition and Modern Human Rights. At www.oycf.org/Perspectives/5_043000/chinese_cultural_tradition_and_m.htm
Child, J. and D. Tse. 2001. China's Transition and Its Implications for International Business. *Journal of International Business Studies*, 32(1), 5–21.
Cilliers, P. 2000. What Can We Learn from the Theory of Complexity? *Emergence*, 2(1), 23–33.
Collier, J. and R. Esteban. 1999. Governance in the Participative Organization: Freedom, Creativity and Ethics. *Journal of Business Ethics*, 21, 173–188.
Coudert Brothers Worldwide. 2002. Corporate Governance in China: Obstacles and New Development. At www.coudert.com/articles/corporate_governance_china.htm
Dahlman, C. R. and J.-E. Aubert. 2001. *China and the Knowledge Economy: Seizing the 21st Century*. WBI Development Studies, Washington D.C.: World Bank Institute.
Dragga, S. 1999. Ethics of Intercultural Technical Communication: Looking Through the Lens of Confucian Ethics. *Technical Communication Quarterly*, 8(4), 365–383.
Dunning, J. H. 2001. *Global Capitalism at Bay*. London: Routledge.
Emanuel, L. 2000. Ethics and the Structures of Healthcare. *Cambridge Quarterly of Healthcare Ethics*, 9, 151–168.
Jones, T. M., A. C. Wicks, and R. E. Freeman. 2002. Stakeholder Theory: The State of the Art. In: N. Bowie (ed.), *The Blackwell Guide to Business Ethics*. Oxford: Blackwell, 19–37.

Koehn, D. 1999. What Can Eastern Philosophy Teach Us about Business Ethics? *Journal of Business Ethics*, 19(1), 71–79.

———. 2001. Confucian Trustworthiness and the Practice of Business in China. *Business Ethics Quarterly*, 11(3), 415–430.

Maosen, L. 2000. Chinese Officials: Faithful to the State or Faithful to the Self. Paper given at the IIPE Conference, Ottawa, September. At http://strategis.ic.gc.ca

Nolan, P. 2001(a). *China and the Global Business Revolution*. Basingstoke: Palgrave.

———. 2001(b). *China and the Global Economy: National Champions, Industrial Policy and the Big Business Revolution*. Basingstoke: Palgrave.

Norton, P. 2001. Management Fraud in China. *China Business Review*, 28(2), 26–31.

Scott, W. R. 1998. *Organizations: Natural, Rational and Open Systems*. London: Prentice-Hall International.

———. 2000. *Institutions and Organizations*. Second edition. London: Sage.

Sherwin, S. 2001. Moral Perceptions and Global Visions. *Bioethics*, 15(3), 175–188.

Simon, H. A. 1996. *The Science of the Artificial*. Third edition. Cambridge, MA: MIT Press.

Werhane, P. 1985. *Persons, Rights and Corporations*. Englewood Cliffs, NJ: Prentice Hall.

Werhane, P. and R. E. Freeman (eds.) 1997. *The Blackwell Encyclopaedic Dictionary of Business Ethics*. Oxford: Blackwell.

Wu, J. 2000. China's Economic Reform: Past, Present and Future. At www.oycf.org/perspectives/5 043000/china.htm

Toward an Integrative Theory of Business Ethics: With Special Reference to the East Asian Region

Yukimasa Nagayasu

THREE DIMENSIONS OF COMMON ETHICS TO OVERCOME THE MYTH OF AMORAL BUSINESS

A prejudice exists, "the myth of amoral business," which claims that ethics is useless in the business world. Professor De George notes this fact in *Business Ethics* (1990). The roots of this myth lie in a prevailing wrong view of the content of ethics. When people think about ethics, they only take notice of improving the dimension of human values and relations. In other words, people do not pay enough attention to the necessary and hidden dimension of ethics that makes the living power of a system stronger.

Two Dimensions of Power and Goodness in Ethics

Generally speaking, each human conduct aims at creating stronger living power and a higher level of goodness. Thus a company always tries to increase its competitiveness in the market; at the same time, the company should take a course of just conduct of business. In our lives we should not violate justice or fairness to increase human goodness.

Functional Principles to Increase the Power of System

Ethics is, therefore, expected to be both a theory and a guideline, as well as a practice itself in order to increase the living power of a total system. From the viewpoint of system theory, human beings build various systems such as an individual's life, organizations as business corporation, nation–states, and the information system of a society. By disregarding the dimension of power inherent in ethics, the "anti-ethics" dogma insists that ethics is useless. People, however, need to realize that ethics should be and is closely related to the power of system.

Axioms of Human Relations to Guide the Dimension of Good and Bad

In human society, basic human values, integral to human society, are truth, goodness and beauty, and, additionally, sacredness and profit. Ethics is essential to the value of goodness in order to develop human lives in their coexistence. In order to increase goodness not only for itself but also for its stakeholders, a system like a business corporation wants automatically, and is expected by society, to behave in an ethically sound way.

Third Dimension That Integrates Power and Goodness

In order to increase sustainability and creativity, ethical conduct in the real world should be a practice to combine the two dimensions of power and goodness. Such ethical behavior can also be understood as a process of PLAN—DO—SEE according to management science.

Let me mention an example here. In 1912 Titanic, the luxurious ship collided with an iceberg and instantly sank in the North Atlantic Sea. The Titanic, as a whole, is a total system, composed of a human system of crews and guests, a physical system, and an information system of sailing. The environment for it was the iceberg-filled sea, the telecommunication network, and the emergency system. The dimension of human relation is a subsystem composed of crew and guests. This total system failed, however, while sailing on the sea, because the Titanic failed to sustain itself and get to its goal, North America, because of its weak design, which had not paid enough attention to safety or crisis management for sailing on the dangerous sea. The Titanic's system lacked the ability to respond to the dangerous environment, and nobody realized its fragility because of ignorance. This accident shows that a system such as a ship should operate by integrating strong functions as well as good human relations.

FUNCTIONAL PRINCIPLES

Let me describe functional principles in detail. If the physical dimension of the system of a ship is weak, the guests and crews are in a dangerous situation. Functional principles should, therefore, first be taken into consideration. No matter how sound and happy the human relations are, human lives cannot be safe without proper consideration of functional principles. Every kind of system, as an "autopoietic" and self-generating system, has four functional principles to develop itself. They are as follows:

Stability or Safety

Each system has a border that separates its internal situation from its external conditions as a means of protection. The human body, for example, is a system that has a "homeostasis" or balancing function. This means that it can sustain itself within a limited realm in which the internal situation remains the same and stable to some extent. Stability is needed for coping with the internal disorders generated from inner factors such as occurs when metallic deterioration happens to the body of a car. Sound functioning is necessary in order to be able to absorb external shocks. A yacht can restore its stance, or achieve sound functioning, even when it meets a sudden attack by big waves. A classic Chinese saying points to the applicability of homeostasis in the human realm: "Know the enemy, realize the self, and respond to change."

Efficiency

Efficiency is the relationship between cost and aim, so saving costs is a major target of efficiency. While efficiency is quite often criticized being antihuman, it is wrong to regard all kinds of efficiency as always wrong. Efficiency in a comprehensive form is necessary to save resources and restrict pollution on our planet Earth.

Reliability

The probability of attaining the expected aims can be called reliability. In other words, reliability is the extent of certainty to actualize aims. A person is regarded to be credible or reliable if he keeps his promise and attains his aims with a high degree of certainty. Reliability is indispensable for the development of all systems.

Creativity

All kinds of creatures and their systems continually live in an ever-changing environment. For instance, our planet Earth is a system often bumped by small meteorites. Evolution is the result of creative adaptation to such an ever-changing environment. The economy of human kind faces innovation in the field of such an environment, information, and life. Creative innovation in these fields produces a suitable environment for the actor itself. Companies always interact with each other by remodeling their own transaction strategies. Thus, the interaction is not simply a passive adaptation, but a positive one as well.

AXIOMS OF HUMAN RELATIONS

Every system has a dimension that aims at improving goodness for human beings. The dimension is composed of four concepts related to individuals and their mutual relationships (see Beauchamp and Childress 2001).

Autonomy

The individual human being seeks to be free by keeping its decision making autonomous. And the autonomous person naturally takes responsibility. According to the autonomy principle, people should harvest products that their plants produce. Autonomy should be the first condition for business conduct in the market; otherwise free transaction can not occur.

Justice

Human beings from birth have a natural drive to reach the highest possible level of self-actualization. Happiness, then, is generally regarded as the cultivation of an individual's possibility. Equal opportunity for happiness is granted by nature to every individual person. This basic content of justice is applicable to all creatures. Every individual has equal value when he or she is born. Thus, justice is composed of fair opportunity as well as the concept of fair causality. Causality is the fair relationship between human effort and its result.

Non-Malfeasance

Because there can exist no community where citizens are taught, "you may or should violate others' rights," children are taught, "You should not harm others." This guideline is called the axiom of non-malfeasance.

Malfeasance includes the harm or violation of common social goods such as the natural environment, just social rules, and cultural goods.

Beneficence

Mozi, ancient philosopher in China, teaches us that all human beings have in their given nature an inclination to feel sympathy, a reasonable feeling of joy, or sadness about their neighbors. Making efforts to increase goodness for others is critically important for human beings.

INTEGRATIVE PRINCIPLES OF ETHICAL CONDUCT

Ethics is, on the one hand, a system of principles of conduct or guidelines to vitalize the life power of a system. On the other hand, ethics is a body of methods to improve human relations systematically. In order to construct a comprehensive body of ethics, ethical principles should derive from an integration of these two vectors, the human and the functional (see Hiroike Chikuro 2002; Institute of Moralogy 2001; figure 8.1).

Integration of Functional Principles and Human Axioms

Ethics has the following three dimensions: (1) functional principles to make a powerful system, (2) human axioms to improve goodness, and (3) behavioral principles of the system to integrate these principles and axioms. Ethical theories ought to show effective clues to real problems in business activities. However, many ethical theories fail to give useful guidelines for real business activities, guidelines that would lead behaviors with both standards of goodness and power in a competitive market.

PLAN—DO—SEE as a Process of Ethical Conduct

According to the PLAN—DO—SEE model, the process of ethical conduct is composed of the three stages. The first stage is PLAN that includes (1) motivation as implicit energy—human motivation can be said to be the energy generated by biological genes and cultural genes. However, because motivation has no clear direction, aims should be

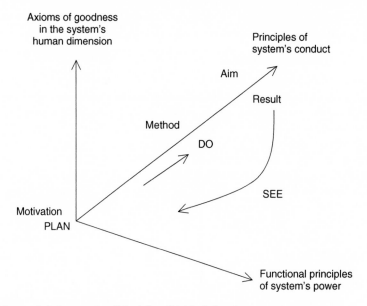

Figure 8.1 Integrative Principle of Ethical Conduct

given by intentional decision making; (2) aim as an explicit ideal—
motivational energy seeks for an aim. In the market system, each actor
pursues separate aims. Every company aims at maximizing its profit
while competing with each other. In setting aims, functional principles and human axioms should correctly be taken into consideration.
Aims should be organized toward "triad" goodness, which is a balance of merits among all stakeholders. For example, a corporation
should fairly distribute opportunities and benefits to its workers,
shareholders, managers, consumers, and traders.

The second stage is DO or the method, that is, means or
procedures, to attain aims. In order to construct rational methods, it
is necessary for a business corporation to consider the following
factors: (1) functional principles; (2) human axioms; and (3) effects
on the global environment. Human axioms are related to improving
human relations in a system. An organization with good human relations can develop both its autonomy and justice within the organization and the creativity of its members, and can also develop the
functional power of the system. A company should make a system
according to which a worker's creative contribution is sufficiently
rewarded. In this way, human axioms and functional principles are
integrated in the management of human resources.

The third stage is SEE or a comparison between aims and results. Every system wants to sustain and to develop. For this purpose, it is necessary for it to make a comparison between aims and results as a process of SEE. The steps of SEE are the following: (1) to accept the results with a sense of thanks by interpreting all results as meaningful; (2) to check errors by understanding that efforts provide a precious textbook for learning and development; and (3) to devise the next step.

In such ways of valuing the results, the psychological viewpoint is important. Ethical thinking should consider the following points of goodness: (1) effects on actor; and (2) effects on others.

The first is composed of effects on internal goodness, that is, on the actor's mind and body, and on external goods. When we consider effects on internal goodness, ethical conduct can be understood to produce mental results instantly and constantly. Positive thinking is useful to increase the sense of joy in action. Ethical conduct creates peace and positive joy as the "positive thinking" theory teaches us. The second point of goodness is composed of direct effects on other persons. We need to know how much our conduct gives positive feelings to persons with whom we interact. Effects on social common goods and on the global environment should simultaneously be noticed carefully because they are necessary conditions, which have a deep influence on all human beings.

A CASE OF NINOMIYA SONTOKU

Just before the Meiji restoration in Japan, Ninomiya Kinjiro Sontoku (Ninomiya Sontoku 1970) was born in a rural village not far from Mount Fuji. He played a great role in the economic and social development of Japan. His life and efforts illustrate the idea of integrative ethics (mentioned earlier). While he lost his parents when he was about ten years of age, he successfully transformed bad fortune toward happiness in a broad sense, and the fundamental principle in his effort was in accordance with wisdom.

As was typical of students in the Far East, Kinjiro studied the classics such as the ancient Chinese writing *The Great Learning* in the *Book of Rites* (1965), which tells us, "Educate yourself, govern in order and harmony your family, your country, and the world." Kinjiro's wisdom is based on his study of ancient Asian classic texts. It is from such teachings that Kinjiro derived his understanding of the East Asian philosophy of common ethics, one which is indicated by the subtitle of this paper "with special reference to the East Asian Region." Globalization is now making a system of common morality mainly based upon market ethics developed in advanced countries like North America and the European Union. But, as Kinjiro showed, the principles and content of common ethics can also be found in the classics of non-advanced economies in the East. Kinjiro's conduct is analyzed according to the integrative PLAN—DO—SEE process as follows:

Motivation

At the level of Kinjiro's unconscious mind existed the stock of potential energy with the desire to escape from poverty and the uncertainty of life.

Aim and the Transformation of its Meaning

His first aim was to restore his family life in a normal sense. His first small but important task was to cultivate his own paddy field. However, he did not have his own hoe. He was determined to ask a neighboring family to lend him a hoe. Then he realized that would be a sorrow of heaven if he kept his body and mind idle without working until the hoe becomes free when the neighboring family finished cultivating. Because he thought heaven had granted him a mind and body through his parents and ancestors, he proposed to the neighboring family to allow him to help cultivate their field. This would be a real way of devotion to a public purpose, beyond the private one to cultivate his own field. In Kinjiro's thinking, human beings are granted their lives by heaven. Heaven intends to help human life develop. In order to respond to this gift and intention, Kinjiro first devoted his mind and body to cultivating the land of the neighboring family. The land of the neighboring family is thus regarded as being owned by heaven in a transcendental sense. Such a way of thinking is the first step of transforming the mind. That is the improvement of ethical character.

Method

While working in such a way with improved consciousness, cultivation by a borrowed hoe was an instrument, but it was also the aim of life in response to heaven's grace and gift. This results in a unification of instrument and aim in a higher sense. Stability and safety are here indispensable points because human beings are weak and tend to generate errors. Kinjiro devised a method of very stable planning and cultivation as a way of farm management according to nature's potentiality of production. He took this idea from China's classic *The Book of Rites* (1965). Behavior to devote oneself to universal creation, with a pure and egoless mind, promises sustainable development. Kinjiro's life and experience provide a clue to achieving it.

In the current economic system, we tend to forget a natural course of sustainable development because we are dazzled by the capitalist and market economy based upon pecunialism as well as speculation. We should pay more attention to this fact of a natural course. Classics in the East can suggest guidelines for us to develop a natural course in this age of the crisis of global environment.

REFERENCES

Beauchamp, Tom L. and James F. Childress. 2001. *Principles of Biomedical Ethics*. New York: Oxford University Press.

The Book of Rites (Liji). In: Chai Chu. *The Sacred Books of Confucius, and Other Confucian Classics*. Edited and translated by Chu Chai and Winberg Chai. Introduced by Chu Chai. New Hyde Park, NY: University Books, 1965.

De George, Richard T. 1990. *Business Ethics*. New York: Macmillan.

Hiroike Chikuro. 2002. *Towards Supreme Morality*. Kashiwa-shi, Chiba-ken: Institute of Moralogy.

Institute of Moralogy. 2001. *Management Theory Towards Triad Goodness*. Kashiwa-shi, Chiba-ken: Hiroike Gakuen Publishing Section.

Ninomiya Sontoku. 1970. *Sage Ninomiya's Evening Talks*. Translated by Isoh Yamagata from *Ninomiya-ô yawa*. Westport, CT: Greenwood Press.

CHAPTER 9

Business Ethics, Globalization, and the Information Age

Richard T. De George

Business today has clearly moved into the era of globalization and the Information Age. If it is to remain relevant, business ethics must also do so. This chapter looks to the future by first looking back on the past. In the first part of this chapter I ask: what has been learned about business ethics from dealing with business in the developed industrial countries that others interested in pursuing ethics in business can adopt? In the second part I extend the consideration to ethical issues in business connected to globalization. In the third part I ask what are the new ethical issues of business in the Information Age with which all countries are struggling and from which we can all learn from one another.

LESSONS ABOUT BUSINESS ETHICS

Marx noted that countries can and should learn from one another. With respect to the development of industrialization he noted that although no country could skip over stages, it can lessen the birth pangs of moving into a new era.[1] Marx saw many of the ills of the way capitalism was developing in the nineteenth century. His approach to solving them was the complete overthrow of the existing system. But history has shown that there are other, more fruitful and less extreme approaches to curbing some of the ills of a market economy that he described. Central to these are considerations of benefiting people, which is at the heart of business ethics. I suggest five lessons that advanced industrial countries have learned through hard experience from which others may profit.

Good Ethics is Essential for Good Business

Consumers, workers, and most of those engaged in business have come to see that in the long run good ethics is essential for good business. This insight explains the popular reaction to scandals in business, the acceptance of legislation benefiting workers and protecting the environment, and the popular demand for more and more transparency in business activities. Any company or multinational interested in its own long range reputation, future development, and profit will come to see the need for adopting and adhering to ethical standards. The general population, workers groups, environmental activists, and human rights watchers are all putting pressure on companies to act as ethics demands. This applies both to what the companies do in their own countries and to what they do in other countries in which they operate.

Each company must adhere to ethical norms, but this does not mean that each company must come up with a new set of rules or Commandments, or enter the ethical seas without a chart or compass. The basic moral rules, such as don't kill and don't steal, apply everywhere, despite differences in local customs. As company after company has struggled with developing a set of guidelines for its employees, a certain consensus has emerged on the need for adopting a code and on the ethical issues it should address. These include respect for human rights and guidelines on the ethical treatment of workers and customers, protection of health and safety, the avoidance of conflict of interest, and concern for the environment.

Ethical Business Requires Ethical Leaders

Experience shows that ethical businesses require ethical people. However, this does not simply mean that ethical business requires ethical workers, who, for instance, do not steal from the company. More importantly, the people at the top—the chairman of the board, the CEO, and in some contexts the chief government officials—who set the tone for the company, must be ethical. They have to act as ethically as they demand that their workers act, or their workers will do as their leaders do and not as they say. Unethical leaders will result in unethical employees who follow unethical practices.

Ethical Structures are Indispensable

We have learned that although ethical people are necessary, they are not enough. Ethical structures are also required. Corporations can be structured so as to reward, directly or indirectly, unethical behavior or amoral behavior. They can also be structured to reward ethical behavior. The better companies have built into their organizations structures that reinforce ethical behavior. As examples, many companies have implemented hot lines (also called help lines) or telephone lines that allow employees to raise ethical concerns or report unethical behavior; they have developed codes of conduct that are implemented; and they have included among considerations for salary increases and promotion whether the employee has maintained high ethical standards. The more transparent the actions of a corporation are, the better from an ethical point of view.

Enforced Legislation is Necessary

We have learned that some ethical problems cannot be solved simply by ethical people or ethically structured companies because the problems are industry-wide or reflect inadequate laws or are caused by corrupt governments. Enforced legislation is necessary not only to enable business to develop, but to protect workers, consumers, and the environment.

Often legislation is required to correct unethical business practices. As we look back over a century-and-a-half we see that moralizing by itself can do only so much. It is only when moral concerns are translated into legal demands that changes are widespread, reliable, and enduring. It took legislation in England to eliminate the abuses of child labor so poignantly described in the Sadler Report. It took legislation to outlaw sweat shops, to guarantee workers their rights in the workplace, to provide a basic minimum wage, to promote safe working conditions, to protect consumers from false advertising and misleading interest rates, to prevent gross environmental damage, and so on. Not everything that is unethical can or should be made illegal. But legislation is important.

Legislation Needs to be Demanded by the Population

We have found that legislation of the type needed tends to get passed only when demanded by the general population, including demands by workers groups, consumer groups, environmental groups, and human rights groups. Usually the political sensibilities of people have to be raised before legislation is passed on issues that previously only raised moral concern. Hence, there is a correlation between a truly responsive type of government and the level of ethical business behavior.

The developing countries can and should learn from the developed countries the need for adequate, enforced legislation, which often goes against the entrenched interests of the rulers, of the ruling class, of the nascent capitalists, and of unscrupulous millionaires. The transition of Russia from a socialist country in 1991 to its present condition shows the importance of having national laws that enable and enforce contracts, that keep the market fair for all, and that curb corruption. Failure to do these leads to the economic chaos characteristic of Russia today. The past years of the stumbling development of a market economy in Russia provide a clear argument for the passage and enforcement of laws that are adequate to control the abuses, which an unrestrained market system brings with it.

ETHICAL ISSUES IN BUSINESS CONNECTED TO GLOBALIZATION

Globalization in its current predominant meaning is a fairly recent phenomenon with a variety of different aspects. One is the development of multinational corporations (MNCs) that not only operate in many countries, but also functionally divide their activities in different countries, producing one part of a product here, another part there, assembling them elsewhere, and marketing them throughout the world, while coordinating all the operations from a home base. This is made possible by the globalization of communications, which makes it as easy to communicate with a fellow employee on another continent as with one a room away in one's own building. A second focus of what goes under the name of globalization is global institutions, such as the World Bank, the International Monetary Fund, and the World Trade Organization. A third aspect has to do with the disparities between the rich and the poor countries of the world, and the national policies that lead to or foster these disparities. This in turn leads to issues of cultural domination, as well as to environmental preservation, global warming, and other issues that can be adequately addressed only at a global level. They are all interrelated.

At the turn of the new millennium we see that many of the ethical issues that multinationals are facing in less developed countries are issues that are familiar ones, practices whose immorality is already widely recognized, and problems for which the developed countries, as I noted earlier, have already found solutions. Many of the ethical problems of the Industrial Age have been transferred together with industry to the less developed countries. Bribery, child labor,[2] human rights abuses, pollution, unhealthy working conditions, below living wages, and so on, are serious ethical issues. The major drawbacks to ethical global business in less developed countries are the absence of adequate background institutions and conditions—such as uniform enforced laws, enforced standards, consumer and worker organizations, and pressure—and the presence of institutionalized corruption, which leave less developed countries vulnerable to abuses that the more developed countries have more or less eliminated. Having been through the problems, they are neither new nor should each country have to discover how to deal with them. Although solutions to these problems are complex and difficult, there is a certain growing consensus about how to deal with them on a national and international level.

Global Codes of Conduct

The UN Universal Declaration of Human Rights has been ratified by almost every country on earth, and is used as a standard both by companies and by their critics. On January 31, 1999, Kofi Annan, the Secretary-General of the United Nations, addressing the World Economic Forum in Davos, Switzerland, called on firms collectively and through their business associations "to embrace, support and enact a set of core values in the areas of human rights, labor standards, and environmental practices . . . areas in which universal values have already been defined by international agreements . . . and areas . . . where . . . if we do not act, there may be a threat to the open global market" (see www.unglobalcompact.org).

A group of U.S., European, and Japanese companies have drawn up a code of conduct known as the Caux Principles, named after the Swiss town in which they met and continue to meet. The Caux Principles are based on two principles: the Western notion of respect for human dignity and the Japanese principle of *kyosei* or working together for the common good. Companies from many nations have adopted these principles (see www.cauxroundtable.org).

Following the Bhopal disaster, chemical manufacturers worldwide adopted a "Responsible Care" initiative, which commits them to a set of Guiding Principles they both pledge to abide by and to pressure all other chemical companies to abide by. They clearly preferred self-policing to legislation (see www.responsiblecare.org).

International Background Institutions

At the international level, just as at the national level, self-regulation by companies and industries is important, but background institutions are also necessary. International agreement that bribery is unethical and should be made illegal was necessary before bribery could be adequately attacked. Although the United States took the lead in this regard in 1977 by making it illegal for American companies to bribe non-American high level government officials, and although the OECD countries a few years ago passed similar legislation, the other developed and, even more essentially, the less developed nations must all join in the effort.

Legislation and international agreements are crucial for those truly global problems that are not strictly business ethics problems, such as the gross discrepancies between rich and poor countries, the depletion of the ozone level, and similar global problems, which require the correlated action of nations.

Moreover, multinationals can play a positive role in transferring knowledge and technology and in helping developing countries improve the condition of the ordinary people. Although multinationals from developed countries are responsible for some harm to developing nations, many of the problems found there are not caused by the multinationals. For those who are interested in trying to improve the situation in such countries, it is essential to get the causes right. Unless they do so, they cannot get the solutions right. Outside agencies—whether they be multinationals, global institutions, non-governmental organizations (NGOs), or foreign governments—can only do so much, and lasting solutions require significant changes in the countries themselves, which must be made by those within the country. The changes require, as I have already suggested, adequate and appropriate legislation to tame market forces.

If an industrial society develops anywhere, it changes the agricultural culture from which it springs. It does not matter whether the system is capitalist or socialist, whether there is government control or free enterprise. An industrialized country is different from its agricultural antecedent. And the change produces a change in culture, broadly conceived.

The introduction of TV, cell phones, and the Internet into rural communities in countries will change them. This is all part of globalization. Although multinational corporations are guilty of abuses, they are transferring knowledge and know-how as well as international standards—technical and ethical. The stories of abuse by them should be weighed against such stories as those of the multinational companies that fought apartheid in South Africa by following the Sullivan Principles; of McDonald's in Guatemala raising standards for bread as well as for cleanliness and working conditions; of Unilever's policy in India of protecting the environment and developing products for the poor; of companies that adopt and follow the Caux and other international principles.[3]

Central Role of the Countries and Their Peoples

Governments of developed countries, international organizations, multinationals, NGOs, and others all have a positive role to play in fostering development worldwide. That is all part of the globalization phenomenon. But the central actors in development remain the country itself and its people.

As business becomes more and more complex, it is more and more difficult for governments to try to exercise centralized planning and control. Such planning and control can take a country only so far in its development. For full development the creativity of individuals must be unleashed, which is the heart of the argument for a market system and for free enterprise. Free markets, among other things, establish many sources of economic power, which seek a voice in the government and a hand in running the country.[4] If the market is truly free and not kept under the control of a small number of families or oligarchs, it allows entry and new entrepreneurs, who ultimately wish a voice in government. Hence, free markets tend to lead to the democratization of governments. Whether the full development of free markets requires political freedom in the form of democracy is a pressing question for many countries. History tends to indicate the two fit well together, although, whether democratic or not, usually a strong government can foster business better than a weak one, such as those in many of the African nations.

In any event, the people must change their country. Responsive governments cannot be imposed on countries from the outside. They must be formed from within. Changing conditions of labor will not result from outsiders recommending changes. The conditions must be changed internally—usually by their being demanded by the people and brought about by a responsive government. Globalization will not change this. But as countries become more closely tied through trade and communication, there will be growing pressure—external and internal—for authoritarian governments to respond to the needs of their people.

New Ethical Issues of Business in the Information Age

To unleash the potential of the Information Age requires the freedom to experiment, to take risks, and to try new approaches that are not

allowed under the strict control of any person or group or government. India in recent years provides an example of the rise of computer-
based software and programming industries that presage a wave of the
future. Modern technology, the Internet, cell phones have all made it
possible for people anywhere not only to become informed about
what is happening elsewhere, but also to compete in areas that do not
require large plants and capital investments for entry. The new areas of
business are where we find the new ethical issues raised by the transition from the Industrial Age to the Information Age.

The Transformational Power of Computers and Information Technology

Computers and information technology are transforming the way we
work, the way we live, the way we learn, the way society functions.
Even though the developed world is entering into the Information
Age ahead of the less developed world—where, for instance, in some
countries more than half of the population has never spoken on a
telephone—the Information Age is global in reach and is having an
impact on the less developed countries as well, albeit in ways that are
different from the ways it is impacting the more developed countries.
The differences give rise to different ethical issues in the two cases, as
well as to questions of inequality and domination of new types. In
such a situation, all countries should both have a voice and be heard
by the others.

In the Information Age companies are learning to do business in
new ways. The computer has entered and is entering more and more
into all the realms of business so that it leaves none of them
unchanged. This means that marketing is done differently, that manufacturing is done differently, that management is done differently,
and so on.

Although the move of business into the Information Age raises
many ethical issues, they have received little attention from the general population, from business, or even from business ethicists.

Business via the Internet changes the relevance of location, geogra-
phy, times during which businesses are open and employees work,
how employees are used, and the like. Among the issues are: whose
laws should apply to the Internet, which crosses borders easily, what
rules and regulations should be adopted, who is to decide, and who is
to enforce them? The issues of haves and have-nots, and of the lack of
access to information and to the resources of the Internet both in
developed societies and worldwide are also of pressing concern.

The transition from the Industrial Age to the Information Age has come about without conscious direction. It resulted as technology developed and it came along as a handmaiden. Because the transition to the Information Age is in the process of taking place and the ethical issues have not clearly jelled, the task of both business and of the business ethicist in this instance is to keep up with the developments and identify problems and potential problems before they cause great harm and before they become embedded ways of doing business.

Basic Virtues of Truthfulness and Accuracy for any System of Information

Information, as generally used, stands for true knowledge in some area. Its opposites are disinformation, misinformation, and falsehood. Information is not simply data but data that represents reality. It is true and not false. Two virtues appear immediately. One is truthfulness, the other is accuracy. The virtues necessary for the Information Age are not necessarily the same virtues as are or were necessary for the Industrial Age. In the latter, efficiency became paramount. As opposed to an Agricultural Age, punctuality became important, and time took on critical importance. In the Information Age truthfulness and accuracy take on special importance. If the information is not accurate or truthful or correct, it is worse than useless. It is dysfunctional.

False information is injurious to a system built on information. So truthfulness is a necessary virtue, and the distortion of the truth, lying, and the spreading of false information are vices to be guarded against. It is not only necessary for people and governmental leaders and corporations not to lie or deceive or mislead, but it is also necessary to represent reality as accurately as possible. The enemy of accuracy is inaccuracy, which leads to disinformation and error. These two virtues or values are basic to any system of information if it is to be socially useful and economically valuable for business as well as for societies and the individuals within them.

Truth leads to the concepts of enlightenment, education, and the potential freeing of individuals and of society. As individuals learn the truth, they are empowered. The ability to limit or deny access to information carries with it issues of power, control, and possible manipulation. Not only is there the possibility of domination of citizens by government and of employees by employers, but also of one society by another, for instance through the domination of the communication resources.

As information becomes a central marketing tool, we are forced to face the harm that we can do to ourselves and to society and social relations through abuses that technology makes possible. As information becomes more and more central, we will also realize the vulnerability of networks. Unfortunately, sabotaging a corporate or national information network is easier than sabotaging its industrial network; the links are more fragile, and the interdependence greater. The need for safeguards against industrial and national espionage and sabotage is great and pressing.

To mention or raise these issues is not to solve them. But we can develop the analyses and begin better to understand the nature of information and its promises and pitfalls for individuals and for society. This is the beginning of an ethical analysis of business in the Information Age.

Information without communication is useless, and communication without information is empty. The ethics of communication shares the podium with ethics of information in the new Information Age.

Information is not useful, even if truthful and accurate, unless it is used. Hence it needs to be communicated. The communication process, which is developing at an exponential rate, is central to the Information Age. The virtues of truthfulness and accuracy carry over into communication. But there are elements of communication that pose their own ethical issues: communication of what, from whom, to whom, in what form?

A number of other virtues besides truthfulness and accuracy are important as well, such as trustworthiness and reliability. They all go together and form the basis for a smooth functioning information processing system. The application to business is part of the task yet to be done.

Changing Nature of Property Rights

Information is very different from machines and tangible products, and so requires a new conception of property and the protection applicable to it.

We can share information without depriving ourselves of its full use. It can be stolen from us without depriving us of its use. It is a form of intellectual property. But internationally we have not adequately discussed the changing nature of property applicable in the Information Age. The ease of copying software, music, books, and anything that can be put in digital form is symptomatic of a growing nest of problems. Differences of views on the nature, status, and possible ownership of intellectual property produce different ethical perspectives. Countries have sought to use traditional laws about copyright and patents, and have in the process caused a great deal of confusion. Instead of rethinking intellectual property in the Information Age, they have tried to make do with concepts and legal doctrines that were not constructed with thought of the kind of intellectual property that is emerging and that does not fit the old mold. What is fair and what is not are issues that form an important part of business ethics for the Information Age, and are issues that are especially pressing in an international context.

In this new millennium businesses must learn to integrate information and its use into new ways of doing business. Both business and those interested in business ethics must anticipate the ethical issues, or at least attempt to spot them and deal with them before they produce great harm or are so entrenched as to be difficult to change. In the process ethics plays an important role, but so do laws, government, and the general population.

We can all learn from the past as well as from each other as we move into the new millennium. The challenge of business in the Information Age is to incorporate ethics into all aspects of its activities and to act so as to make the future better for all people.

NOTES

1. See Karl Marx, Preface to First German Edition, in Karl Marx and Frederick Engels. *Collected Works*, Vol. XXXV: Marx: *Capital, Vol. I.* New York: International Publishers, 1996.

2. In his State of the Union address President Clinton called for the end of child labor—a noble and ethical end, but more difficult to achieve than to call for. And what multinationals do in the interim until all societies effectively prohibit child labor—which for many means ending widespread poverty—is a complicated issue. ("The Text of the President's State of the Union Address to Congress," *The New York Times*, January 20, 1999, A22.)

3. For a good collection of international codes of conduct see "Appendices" in O. F. Williams (ed.) *Global Codes of Conduct.* Notre Dame: University of Notre Dame Press, 2000.

4. Amartya Sen, in his *Development as Freedom* (New York: Alfred Knopf, 1999) defends the thesis that from an economic point of view capitalism in a democratic society is the most productive form of social system.

PART II

Macro-Issues

CHAPTER 10

China's Ethical Challenges after Joining the WTO

Xiaoxi Wang

China has already been admitted into the World Trade Organization (WTO). This indicates that China has already entered the tide of economic globalization. It also means that the country will be fully embedded within the intense competition of the globalizing economic sector and engaging in an invisible "economic battle" (Li and Pan 2001, 152).

In the face of China's entrance into the WTO and confronting economic globalization, China inevitably accepts various challenges. Among them, the country must also meet head-on those unapparent ethical challenges that currently lie beyond the line of vision and thought. Otherwise, China will lack economic morality and the stamina and endurance for economic development in the process of economic globalization. And what's more, it will be much more difficult for China to prevail in its economic achievements in the process of global economic integration.

THE MAIN ETHICAL CHALLENGES FACED BY CHINA'S ECONOMY

Economic globalization means that economic development will be competing in various areas, at different levels, and among diverse interests. And in the meantime, global economic integration and economic competition "is not a purely objective process" (Li and Pan 2001, 410). The national spiritual condition, especially the moral consciousness of the citizens, will directly affect the process and the efficacy of economic development after China's entry into the WTO. In fact, the competition in the course of economic globalization intrinsically involves the competition of moral quality and moral force. For this reason, an important prerequisite for strengthening economic morality and promoting economic development is to examine the discrepancies between the level of China's economic morality and that required by China's entrance into the course of globalization as symbolized by WTO. Such discrepancies include the following.

The Challenge against Barriers to Fair Competition and Former Government Provisions

Competition in the context of economic globalization should be transparent and fair. The core of the principle of economic action within the WTO's legal system is the protection of fair competition. Therefore, "most favored nation status" requires that each member's services and vendors for any other member shall unconditionally be treated as equal with any other country's services and vendors of the same sort. That is to say that as long as the imported and exported commodities and services are the same, they should be treated equally. At the same time, most favored nation status emphasizes even more that when commodities or services from any member enter within the borders of any other member, the items will receive treatment no lower than that received by the domestic commodities and services of that member state. Moreover, members are not permitted to protect domestic businesses with quotas, subsidies, or tariffs.

But the basic "fair" requirements in international economic and trade activities have not yet been fully embodied in China's domestic economic and trade activities. There still exist various restrictions on the use of products or commodities between China's different provinces and regions. For example, tools for transportation such as electric bicycles, motorbikes, and so on, are operated within the locality of their production. If you use products from other places, then you will not be able to get a license and therefore you will be prohibited from driving these bikes. This is, in fact, a kind of monopolization in a disguised form that is not only unfair but will objectively weaken the consciousness of competition, quality, and responsibility as well.

This point is even more evident in regard to China's agricultural sector. The market controls and agricultural subsidies developed naturally, prior to the country's entrance into the global arena. Now, the conflict is very apparent, including problems concerning the types and power of technology. But what is even more important to solve is the issue regarding an awareness of moral responsibility in the agricultural sector and economy. Currently, the environmental pollution and pesticides, fertilizers, and overuse or unjustified use of hormones and preservatives have made the agricultural products with already high costs lose even more of their competitiveness within China's agricultural production. If China can, in accordance with a sense of responsibility for oneself and one's customers, quickly develop organic food products that do not harm the public, then perhaps China would establish for itself a primary position within the course of economic globalization.

The Challenge for the Retail Market's Service and the Traditional Notion of Service

After China's entry into the WTO, the commodity market including direct sales, sales agents, wholesale, retail and storage, transportation, and post-sales service will be further opened. But, the current retailing and service system of commodities and service level in China cannot match those of foreign business people.

For a lengthy period of time, China's domestic and international trade operated under a disaggregated system. The coverage rate for international trade management and operational policies was low. Domestic trade and logistics were basically conducted within a limited scope, and the overall level of service for the domestic trade industry was relatively low due to the lack of standardization for operating procedures and the incomplete service system, so that most enterprises were operating at a low level, especially in terms of various practices that undermine trust, such as the crude packaging used in shipping and transport of goods, the sales of fake goods, price fixing, false advertising, and deceptive post-sales "money-back guarantees." Not only does this harm the product's market share, but it also "dispels" the potential needs of clients. As soon as tariffs are reduced on a large scale, and large amounts of goods from foreign companies or countries enter the market in China, their relatively more developed service system and their sense of responsibility toward customers will place China's businesses and goods within a position of passivity (Li and Pan 2001, 189).

The competition in commodity markets is, to a great extent, the competition of the "sense of service."[1] This is especially true in regard to the financial and insurance sectors, whose profit and future growth to a greater extent is determined by the sense of service. If the customers get a feeling of "just going through the motion of depositing and withdrawing money from the bank" or of "insurance with little assurance," it will be a fatal problem to these trades. In accordance with general contracts of service trades, 150 service sectors, including banking, insurance, logistics, tourism, telecommunications, law, accounting, commercial wholesale and retail are all considered to be open sectors, but China's openness in these areas is low, and some of these sectors have not been opened at all. China needs to be aware of the gaps that exist in the service industry and improve its "moral attitude" and moral regulations within the sector of services. While honest and moral practices sufficiently reduce expenses,[2] they also increase market competition and reduce market inefficiencies (Koslowski 1997, 25).

The Challenge for Corporate Management Principles

The main body competing within the economic globalization process is the enterprise.

> Competition does not originate out of thin air but is the struggle between two real entities. China wants to participate in global affairs and the global division of labor and thus must face international competition and must rely upon enterprises to take the lead. We must clearly understand that now international competition is not in fact competition between nations but is the competition between large corporations . . . There are no corporations as the back-up forces of nations, as there would be no way in the future within the international arena for them to seek out a more important role. (Li and Pan 2001, 222–223)

However, the competition of the enterprises is a multifaceted competition in the management and operations of enterprises. It is not only a competition of finances, technology, management, product quality, and so on, but also a competition of enterprise culture, image, and morality as well. Corporate morality, as the soul of the enterprise, is the basis and prerequisite for the enterprises to participate in international competition.

Based on the current moral situation of various enterprises in our country, most of the enterprises are more or less unfitting in terms of WTO's requirements for operational rules. Some enterprises lack a fundamental moral base and others do not even have any awareness of morality at all, producing entirely for money. For them, enterprises' wealth is narrowly understood to be materials and money, and therefore, they throw away enterprises' morality, which is not only the wealth of the enterprises, but can also help to increase the wealth of the enterprises. Some enterprises, even for immediate short-term profits, do not hesitate to harm the interests of others through cheating or deception, losing the corporate morality necessary as a force behind the future development of the enterprise. For many enterprises, the spirit of industriousness is lacking, while they have an insufficient basis of reliability and concern for its reputation. Their desire for earning money is much stronger than a sense of responsibility toward customers (Wang and Li 2001). In reality, under such circumstances, even without China's entrance into the WTO, they would have difficulty in surviving for an extended period. The numerous bankrupt domestic enterprises illustrate this point. Production without a moral conscience is "acting blindly" and "trade without morality is a type of crime against society" (Schmidt 2001, 155).

If after entering the WTO, China's enterprises still only set their sights on short-term gains and do not consider the interests of others, such short-sighted behavior will prevent China's enterprises from surviving when facing foreign companies whose "creditworthiness" is well known and whose corporate morality serves as a base for achieving profitability.

FOCUSING ON AND NURTURING BUSINESS MORALITY

In facing the intense global competition, China should possess a strong awareness of economic morality. Paying attention to morality is always more profitable than ignoring it.[3] Of course,

> the ethical terms, the pursuit of profit alone is not important but its importance lies in how the actions and pursuit for profit is conducted. Is the pursuit legitimate or illegitimate? Is it conducted through open competition or illegitimate competition? Therefore, market competition is not neutral territory in terms of morality. (Koslwoski 1997, 182)

Corporate profitability should be based on morality.

The Moralization of the Role of the Government

In the process of economic globalization, we must pay attention to the moralization of the role of the government. It can be said that many of the problems that exist in China's economy are due to the government's abuse of its authority and are created by the government excessively interfering in economic activities. The reform process of China's state-owned enterprises has been very difficult due to the enterprise's subordination to the government, in addition to the unclear divisions between the enterprise and the government's property rights, responsibilities, and interests. Similarly, administration directly interferes with the enterprise's personnel, capital, products, and operations. "Much of the obstructive force in the reform process is not due to lack of knowledge or experience, but more of it stems from control of interests, as the result of the effect of vested interests in the transition from old to new" (Li and Pan 2001, 375). The large amount of bad debt of the banks, a part of which was created by the government interfering in the bank's loan policies, make some enterprises that need money unable to borrow and those with clearly poor business or no prospects of paying back the loans able to amass large funds. The capital market is also like this.

> In terms of the authorization for public offering on the stock market and distribution of corporate bonds, there exist obvious systematic biases, in addition to a low degree of transparency and high degree of arbitrariness . . . In the market for property rights, the government has always used its administrative might to conduct "mismatched" reorganization of capital, which is not only unable to rescue those enterprises in trouble but also gives high-quality enterprises a heavy blow on their backs. (Li and Pan 2001, 364)

A business plan is often the flippant brainchild of government officials, resulting often in ineffective investment. This represents the government administration's lack of morality or even the moral depravity of the government.

The government should keep abreast of the requirements of market operations, understanding and bringing into play its function from the angle of profit maximization and profit optimization. Only when we cast away the latent consciousness and behavior of "vested interests" can we make necessary reforms to the administrative system, content and methods, and whole heartedly master the operational procedures and basic development stances of the global economy so as to concentrate on adjusting countermeasures and guiding enterprises to effectively participate in international economic competition.

Of course, the government's role is changing to macroeconomic adjustment, guidance, and service. The government should use its policies to adjust the relationships between different interest groups, motivate the different parties, and nurture the competitiveness of the entire economy. The government should also, to the greatest of its ability, provide and assist in analyzing economic data for use by enterprises in devising their market plans. Also, the government should pay close attention to the notion of "people first" to guide and adjust the structure and quality standards of products. For example, regarding China's fertilizers, in comparison to those of other countries, those with higher toxicity make up a higher percentage of the total than low toxicity, low residue, and biological fertilizers. For other types, the raw chemical composition is low, but the chaff is excessive, and the raw materials and quality of the mid-products is low with only one treatment formula, and so on. These problems not only make it difficult for China's fertilizers to compete in the international market, but it is also hard for them to survive in the domestic market. In fact, since China is an agricultural country, this problem should have been addressed a long time ago. With regard to fertilizer, the problem with the role of the government and administrative morality is more severe than issues regarding technology.

Nurturing Moral Assets and Vitalizing Production Requirements

The enterprise has both tangible and intangible capital assets. In the development of the enterprise, intangible assets are relatively more significant than tangible assets because intangible assets, such as principles of production, management methods, and corporate morality directly affect the effectiveness of the invested tangible assets in the production process. Similarly, amongst the intangible assets, corporate morality directly restricts their nature, quality, and application because the behavior of the company's employees are all affected by its principles for survival. An enterprise with a low level of morality and lacking a sense of responsibility toward its customers cannot produce high quality products and optimize profits.

Actually, any enterprise, no matter how good its facilities and how large its capital support, if it lacks a high standard of responsibility to itself, society, and others, cannot develop the use of capital, which it should have, and even wastes capital. For this reason, an enterprise lacking morality at its core will have employees who lack a sense of responsibility, making it impossible to effectively vitalize production.

Corporate morality should become an intangible asset of enterprises, and in the least, should focus on education and training to foster the moral consciousness of staff and workers and to set up a strong responsibility of production and service among these workers. At the same time, we should let the morality and a conscience of responsibility permeate various links in the production chain, making it "materialized" as positive corporate operational mechanisms and high quality products. Only in this way can we make morality an important ingredient of enterprise production itself and become a requisite for production and also become an important condition for production to function effectively and profitably (Wang 2000).

Building a Corporate Image: "Credibility is first"

To this day the competition of corporate images has already become a main force within economic competition. Not only does a corporate image directly determine the position a company has within people's minds, but it also directly affects the company's growth and future. It is often said that the corporate image is a symbol of the company's competitiveness.

The corporate image is a comprehensive conception containing rich meanings, including the company's name, the factory's features, advertising collateral, and product styles, and it also includes principles of production, cultural spirit, management system, moral environment, degree of creditability, and so on. Among them, credibility is the core of the enterprises' image and the lifeblood of the enterprise itself. In the course of economic globalization, credibility and the enterprise's survival rate are one and the same. For this reason, many companies around the world believe that when the company sells its products it is also selling its credibility, and selling credibility is even more important than selling products (*Yangzi Evening Post* 1998). Over the last few years, the main reasons for the bankruptcy of various enterprises is multiple, including lack of capital, weak technology, obsolete equipment, but the bankruptcy of other enterprises is due to the lack or loss of credibility.

The credibility is an advertisement that strikes a chord in the hearts of people. However, establishing and increasing credibility relies on the quality of products, which in turn relies upon responsible production and the honoring of service pledges.

First of all, everything is for the customer and for satisfying the customer's "human needs."[4] This is the fundamental principle for production and product design, as well as the foundation for establishing the company's credibility. In addition, after entering the WTO, China's enterprises are encountering various customers, preferences, and special requirements of customers from around the world. This itself requires an effort to understand the different types of customers to pave the way for selling products to them.

Second, a sense of responsibility toward the customer should pervade every part and aspect of manufacturing of products. For example, all products should be developed in line with a certain level of science, technology, and culture, in addition to becoming a material representation of the moral consciousness and moral sensibility of the product (Wang 2000). Even with the best technology and artistic level, high quality products cannot be produced unless the company acts out of responsibility toward the customer. A single flaw in a single aspect affects not only product quality but also contains the potential to affect and even harm the company's credibility.

Third, the service pledge is the direct way to widely promote the enterprise's credibility. Within the intense competition of international trade, the service pledge is an important measure to strengthen the degree of credibility. After entering WTO, China will follow the principle of market liberalization. Within a period of five years the quotas will be dismantled and the sales and distribution services will be further liberalized. In this way, large quantities of foreign products will enter the market that will necessarily at the same time introduce a more developed standard of service. Foreign companies in various industries within the service sector, such as telecommunications, finance, insurance, tourism, accounting, education, transportation and shipping, and so on, all adopt the service standard of "customer first." Therefore, China's enterprises must understand the "rules of the game" and the effective and systematic "service standards" to select and implement its own service pledge, thereby raising the market share of its products and services. In addition, in facing the international market, by strengthening a sense of responsibility, perfecting service standard, and prioritizing credibility, the corporate image can become victorious in the global economic battle.

Nurturing Moral Character and Strengthening Responsibility for Production, Operations, and Management

Economic competition is really the competition of economic morality. However, economic morality is not an abstract concept. Having morality come into full play in multifaceted economic competition depends on the improvement of moral consciousness and complete "permeation" of responsibility of production and management in all economic activities. Therefore, in the face of entering the WTO, China must be sober-minded and should be sufficiently prepared to respond to it in terms of morality. First, we should quicken the speed of the study of ethics and the widespread education of socialist morality so as to let people know that strengthening the moral quality of the citizens is the fundamental countermeasure to responding to the challenges of economic globalization. Second, China should excel in studying "economic requisites," which benefit the interests of different parties and can be accepted by them. At the same time, we should also construct a set of feasible production and management rules that are suitable for international economic and trade activities. Third, we should summarize the essence and key features of traditional Chinese economic morality that have been universally recognized by foreign manufacturers and managers such as "not to do to others as you would not wish done to yourself" and "to get suitable profit while doing what is morally suitable," and so on, giving play to its special economic and cultural functions so as to create for China a unique force for addressing economic competition.

NOTES

1. This "sense of service" includes a sense of responsibility to customers in the entire of the product's manufacturing and sales, including the product's design, production, sales, and post-sales service.
2. This includes the expenses of both trade parties for adopting protective measures and the losses incurred by both parties on account of counterfeiting. With high efficiency based on a foundation of trust and creditworthiness, unobstructed trade and the conservation of resources and finances simultaneously reduces market inefficiencies and lowers trade expenses.
3. Perhaps neglecting morality in production and operations will for a short time generate profits, but this would only be short-lived. It does not indicate that morality can and should be ignored or even rejected to earn higher revenues and profits. From a long-term perspective, neglecting morality is equivalent to "slow self-destruction."
4. "Human needs" here refers mainly to biological needs, psychological needs, and social needs.

REFERENCES

Koslowski, P. 1997. *Principles of Ethical Economy (Prinzipien der Ethischen Ökonomie)* (Dordrecht: Kluwer, 2001). Chinese version. *Jing ji lun li yuan ze.* Translated by Yu Sun. Beijing: China Social Science Press.

Li Heihu and Pan Xinping. 2001. *The Challenge of Economic Globalization for China.* Beijing: Social Science Document Publishing House.

Schmidt, H. 2001. *Globalization and the Reconstruction of Morality.* Chinese version translated by Chai Fangguo. Beijing: Social Science Document Publishing House.

Wang Xiaoxi. 2000. On Moral Capital. *Jiangsu Journal of Social Sciences,* 2.

Wang Xiaoxi and Li Zhixiang. 2001. Ethical Challenge of Economic Globalization for China's Enterprises. *Nanjing Journal of Social Sciences,* 2.

Yangzi Evening Post. 1998. October 28, Column 2 (A).

CHAPTER 11

Ethical Concepts of Consumption in China and the West in the Context of Globalization

Zhongzhi Zhou

The consumption culture is inextricably linked to global economic integration. As the Chinese economy is integrated into globalization, the two different concepts about consumption in China and in the West are bound to blend, as well as to collide violently. What are the features of consumption ethics in China and in the West? How do we compare Chinese and Western consumption ethics scientifically so as to reform Chinese consumption ethics for the benefit of not only economic but moral progress? These problems need to be solved properly and have become more urgent after positive enlargement of domestic demand was adopted by the Chinese government as a long-standing policy.

Historical Features and Comparisons of Ethical Concepts of Consumption in China and in the West

In China, the mainstream tends to view frugality as a virtue and luxury as a sin. Most of the philosophers and authors in ancient China advocated frugality. The most prominent representatives of this tradition are Confucius, Mozi, and Lao Tze. To completely understand this Chinese view of frugality as a virtue and luxury as a sin, we should pay attention to three factors.

First, this opinion is based on an ethical evaluation of consumption. In the ethics of ancient China, thriftiness is regarded as the ultimate virtue because it restricts human desires, while extravagance is the primary vice because it makes man want too much. Mozi, a pre-Qin philosopher, thought that frugal defines a saint, while an evil person is always consumptive. Second, this opinion is related to the stability of society and the prosperity of the country because thrift can improve the moral level of the society and make the society more stable, resulting in the peaceful rule of the country. On the contrary, public immorality can be caused by extravagance. In the process of governing the country, thrifty soil nurtures the incorruptibility that aids the country to thrive, while extravagance is the hotbed of corruption that is the prelude of perdition. As a matter of fact, it is historically evident that dynasties rose out of industry and thrift, but fell because of luxury (Zhao Xiuyi 1996). Third, this view of frugality as a virtue and luxury as a sin advocates moderate consumption. Zhou-yi, a famous philosophic book written in ancient times, believes it is good to be thrifty within measure, but bad to over-abstain from consuming. To what standard, then, should one strive to insure one's consumption is moderate? In the ancient culture of China, consumption is not only regarded as economic activity, but also as a kind of exhibition of one's ethical status. So whether one's consumption level and style is moderate depends on his ethical status in the feudal patriarchal clan system.

In spite of the fact that the mainstream Chinese culture values thrift and dismisses luxury, there are opposing opinions in China. Guanzi thought advocating luxury impels production during a business depression. In the early nineteenth century, scholars such as Tan Sitong carried forward Guan-tse's opinion. They put forward the argument that it is necessary to change ethical ideas valuing thrift in order to develop the Chinese economy. In short, throughout the lengthy history of China, the opinion favoring thrift was dominant, and the objecting voices were considerably weaker, though in them there was truth, that is, the idea that consuming demand drives forward economic development.

Historical features of the ethical opinions about consumption in the West are different from those in China. Before the modern age, ethical ideas favoring thrift were the basic tendency in Europe, but in the modern times, many changes took place and a new opinion against thrift sharply confronted the old opinion.

In ancient Greece, Aristotle made many penetrating comments about consumption. He pointed out that only proper consumption was virtuous. What kind of consumption is proper? From Aristotle's point of view, consumption in accordance with the principle of the mean is good because both excess and deficiency are vices. In the Middle Ages, overwhelmingly dominant was the theology of Christianity, in which the only way for a human's soul to keep away from evil and live in paradise for eternity is to control his desires. Asceticism, which the theology of Christianity advocated, suppresses or decreases consumer desires. As a result, opinion favoring thrift prevailed during that period. When capitalism spread, however, the ethics of consumption was rooted in economic development instead of involved in the theory of Christianity. During the transition from the neoteric to the modern times, aiming to promote productivity, different schools of thought contested if the value of thriftiness be a virtue or a vice. This contention produced two conflicting views, one of which was held by mercantilists, Adam Smith, Max Webber, and so on, who believe that ethical ideas of thrift propel production; the other one, held by Bernard Mandville, John Maynard Keynes, and so on, argues that consumption enlarges demands and luxury stimulates economic development.

The mercantilists think a strong nation depends on its silver reserve, which accumulates only through thrift and a financially safeguarded capitalist economy. They severely criticize the habit of costliness and oppose all kinds of squander and importation of luxury goods. The mercantilists' opinion of frugality won a flood of admiration from Adam Smith, though he raises his voice against mercantilism strongly in his *The Wealth of Nations*. Smith maintains that emphasizing thrift and dropping sumptuousness indeed increases social capital; it accelerates the wealth of the nation to keep down as much as possible the consumption expenses of the individuals and its government. Moreover, he stresses repeatedly that luxury is the enemy of the public while thrift the benefactor. The thrift theory of Smith, who has helped establish the classic economic system by bringing forth the theory of the "invisible hand," has had a profound effect on Western economic ideas of consumption over a considerably long period. The same attitude toward consumption is reflected in Max Weber's most famous economic work, *The Protestant Ethic and the Spirit of Capitalism*. In it, the author thinks the Protestant ethics, which legitimized capitalist acquisitiveness as God's direct will, asked men to work and save, and to wink at lavish expenditure, so that the productivity of Protestant communities came to be coupled with thriftiness. Weber concluded,

> When the limitation of consumption is combined with this release of acquisitive activity, the inevitable practical result is obvious: accumulation

of capital through ascetic compulsion to save. The restraints which were imposed upon the consumption of wealth naturally served to increase it by making possible the productive investment of capital. (Weber 1958, Chap. V, sec. 2)

Coincidentally with mercantilism, Bernard Mandeville, an English economist, presents the perspective of "private vices, public benefits," noting the advantage of a lavish expenditure and disadvantage of thriftiness. He points out, by allegorizing bees, that all walks of life are prosperous when extravagance prevails in the society but it is not so when thrift is substituted for it. To spend money extravagantly promotes public welfare in spite of being regarded as an individual vice because luxury fosters growth of social economy indirectly. John Maynard Keynes is another who objects thriftiness. He deems that what caused the Depression in 1920s–1930s is nothing but thriftiness. In the present days, Keynes concludes, the growth of wealth does not result directly from the saving of the rich people, but it is possibly hampered by saving because "the principles of saving, pushed to excess, would destroy the motive to production." He contends that the insufficient effect demand causes the increase of unemployment and leads to a vicious circle, in which "a relatively weak propensity to consume helps to cause unemployment," and the increasing unemployment, in return, brings the effect down further. Ultimately, this causes the economy as a whole to decline. Thus, proposes Keynes, governments should strengthen the macroscopic adjustment, while inducing the public to consume with moral sense (Keynes 1936).

Through the above comprehensive survey of the development of ethical ideas of consumption in China and in the West, we get a glimpse of their respective distinct features on three aspects.

Developing in Different Ways

Before the modern age, both Chinese and Western ethics of consumption laid strong emphasis on the ethical principle of frugality, which was by no means accidental because consumption depends on production. It is of historical necessity to choose the principle of frugality when material products are very scarce. Moving into the modern times, considerable disparities in ethics of consumption started to emerge between China and the West. After entering the period of industrial revolution, the growth of productivity required corresponding ideas of consumption. Consequently, opinions that seek pleasantness and preach overconsumption started to prevail in the Western world, and this tendency evolved into contemporary consumerism. On the contrary, the mainstream consumption ethics that valued frugality remained in China despite the criticism in modern times raised by some scholars such as Tan Sitong.

Based on Different Theories of Human Nature

The conception of human nature in Chinese traditional culture is different from that in the Western because of different perspectives. Western culture focuses on apolaustic aspects of human nature; especially during the Renaissance period, the enjoyable life is accentuated opposition to feudalistic asceticism. It provides cultural soil, fostering consumption opinions like Mandeville's and the contemporary consumerism. However, Chinese traditional culture places much emphasis on the ethical aspects of human nature, which controls human desire. The opinion of "keeping heaven's law, eliminating human desire," posed by the Confucian school of idealist philosophy in Sung and Ming dynasties, depresses natural human desire to the bone. This understanding of characteristic Chinese opinion about human nature underscores the belief that the principle of frugality has been the mainstream consumption ethics throughout Chinese history.

Valuing from Different Angles

In modern times, Western contentions on consumption ethics centered on the question of how to impel economic development, that is, through the ethics of frugality, or through encouraging consumption. In regard to consumption, valuing it from the point of view of both economics and ethics is necessary. It is evident that economic value of consumption is prior to ethical value in the West, while ethical value is given preference in China, as the traditional culture here is ethical.

REFLECTION ON CONTEMPORARY CHINESE ETHICAL CONCEPT OF CONSUMPTION UNDER THE CONTEXT OF GLOBALIZATION

After China's entry into World Trade Organization (WTO), more and more multinational companies and foreign corporations of small- and middle-scale have joined in China's economy in every field. If their products want to march their way into the Chinese market and win a bigger market share, they have to guide and change Chinese consumers' ideas about consumption through commercials and advertisements so that their products can be accepted by Chinese consumers. In other words, as marketing has fully developed in today's world, businesses should be concerned not only with producing what consumers want but also with keeping ahead of the consumers, creating and introducing consumption ideas, designing new lifestyles for consumers in order to achieve the goal of ethical consumption. Against the background of globalization, the meeting of Western and Chinese consumption ethics is inevitable, including dialogues, communications and adaptations as well as contradictions, conflicts, and inconsistencies. The era of planned economy in China has passed, but the ethics relating to planned economy keeps its influence in the society today. Because China has just entered the WTO, the influence of consumption ethics that reflects the new trend in modern international economy is still weak. Thus we have to enhance the theoretical study of transforming consumption ethics as well as realize such transformation under the guidance of the right values.

First of all, what are the value guidelines for modern China to achieve the transformation of consumption ethics? In the author's opinion, this value guideline should be "moderate consumption" (Zhou Zhongzhi 2001). To begin with, the analysis of the history of Western and Chinese consumption ethic shows that moderate consumption is a well-recognized principle for ideologists at home and abroad. Confucianism, the mainstream philosophy in ancient China, maintains that even austerity should be reasonable, "frugal but moderate." Aristotle, in ancient Greece, thought consumption should be under the guidance of the principle of the mean. Second, moderate consumption is the essential requirement to achieve a harmonious development of human nature. Confucianism emphasized the ethical side of human nature and people's spiritual life, which does hold some water and seemed to be noble at that time. But the Confucian school of Song and Ming dynasties overemphasized the ethical side of human nature and made it an opposing force to people's natural side, which suppressed their consuming desires, distorting their personalities. In contrast with Chinese counterparts, many philosophers in neoteric Western society attach importance to the natural side of human nature. Though it is reasonable in a sense, it pursues the sensual satisfaction unilaterally, which stimulates human desires of consumption for cakes and ale, causes distorted personality, and eventually results in the spiritual crisis of modern society. Moderate consumption can better realize the unity of man's material and spiritual life as well as a harmonious development of human nature. Third, analysis of the relationship between economics and ethics has showed that moderate consumption is the optimal choice to achieve their unity. Consumption is the ultimate goal of production as an important part of social production process, so it has a great restriction on production. When consumption demand enlarged, the economy developed. But over-consumption and wasting resources on luxuries inevitably leads to a debauched society and the backsliding of humanity which is well-grounded in Confucianism. However, overemphasizing austerity and restricting consumption with excessively strict ethical codes depress the consumption desire and have a negative influence over social development. Whether from the theoretical or practical perspective, people are required to find a balance between economy and ethics as far as consumption is concerned. This balance is moderate consumption, bridging the gap between economy and ethics (Ye Dunping et al. 1998).

Then how to understand "moderation" of consumption? Moderation requires that the consuming level be a little higher than that of frugal consumption (Li Yining 1995). This level not only meets the Chinese traditional ethos of industry and thrift, but also indicates the modern requirements and spirit that are advantageous for developing productivity, augmenting the comprehensive national strength and improving people's living standards. Certainly it is difficult to define moderation with a uniform numeric standard because of the unbalanced economic development level in each district and various individual income conditions at the primary stage of socialism in China. Thus moderation is a relative term. It should function as a principle and guideline. Furthermore, we should notice that it includes the content of moderate advanced consumption. With China's development of a socialistic market economy and its entry into WTO, consumption in credit is entering common people's economic life more and more. We should break through the consumption opinions in traditional culture that refuse to consume into debt, to accept loans on personal security for consumption, and to value the moral validity of consumption in credit according to the principle of moderation. In short, moderate consumption inherits and develops Chinese traditional consumption ethics and is also an inevitable choice for China to develop market economy and integrate into the world economy.

Second, Green Consumption representing advanced consumption ethics should be introduced and popularized in modern China. The concept of Green Consumption, as a great reform in consumption, is based on the fundamental idea of unification and harmony between man and nature, breaking through traditional anthropocentrism. The problems of the ecological environment become sharper and sharper with the rapid development of science and technology, the speedy expansion of manufacture scale, and the prompt increase of consumption. In general, the direct objects human beings consume exist in the form of labor results, but the ultimate objects are primitive natural sources. Common property is the transformation of natural sources. The continual increase of consumption is sure to stimulate the development of productivity, putting more pressure on nature. However, the bearing force of nature is limited. Once the pressure is beyond the critical point, the ecological balance will be destroyed, and human beings will also be punished by nature. To keep the ecological equilibrium and ensure the sustainable development of society, we must control the increase of manufacture properly and the unilateral increase of consuming demands in some consuming fields. We must change some traditional ethical opinions on consumption to make it. For example, some people think consumption is only concerned with financial ability; "people with money can consume whatever and how much they want." In the process of consuming, people should consider not only the producing ability, but also whether the products are advantageous to the ecological environment. The consumption beneficial to the ecological environment will finally be propitious to the sustainable development of the society, and thus ethically correct, and vice versa, even though it can momentarily meet human demands in utility.

Of course, Green Consumption must be understood in an appropriate and comprehensive manner. It is not an unbalanced view to regard Green Consumption as a requirement to reduce and restrain consumption. The contents and styles of consumption are diversiform; some refer to the problems of ecological environment, while others do not. The latter type of consumption should be encouraged instead of reduced so that it can stimulate economic development. Even for the former type of consumption, reducing and restraining are not the only ways to solve the problems of ecological environment, but changing the contents and styles of consumption can also make some difference in unifying humanity and nature. History and reality have showed us that only in the almost united frame of economy and ethics can people solve the problem of green consumption better.

Lastly, we should evaluate consumerism objectively. Consumerism has been a kind of lifestyle, cultural attitude, and concept of value existing widely in Western developed countries since the middle twentieth century. Coming from Western ideology, consumerism is a basic doctrine indicating that the first requirement of individual self-satisfaction and happiness is occupying and consuming material products. As Chinese economy integrates into the wave of globalization, consumerism will inevitably spread early or late in China, affecting ethical ideas about consumption. How to evaluate consumerism? Different scholars have made evaluations that are dissimilar or even opposing each other with equal harshness from diverse angles. The supporters think that it is a requirement for economical development with great productivity. This view sees consumption as an appealing lifestyle, which changes the purchase and use of goods into a kind of religion from which people get spiritual satisfaction, thus putting it beyond reproach. The deprecators argue that consumerism cannot bring happiness to life because it encourages people to overconsume, thus regarding consumption as a sin and a hypocritical desire that distorts humanity. It also leads toward the inverse direction of the neglecting of the ecological environment. Marcuse and Fromm of the Frankfurt School, and Daniel Bell, the author of *The Cultural Contradictions of Capitalism* (Bell 1978), are well-known representatives of this opinion, criticizing consumerism in modern Western society. From the point of view of the author of this paper, consumerism has advantages and disadvantages. Consumerism pushes the economic development of Western society. Two-thirds of America's economy is pulled by domestic demands, which attribute to consumerism in great measure. On the other hand, it is an evident fact that consumerism has caused the crisis of individual spiritual life and abnormal personality apparent in Western society.

From the comparison between Chinese and Western ethical opinions on consumption, we can easily find that consumerism is connected closely to Western culture, involving the comprehension of human nature. Consumerism is not suitable for the situation of China, for Chinese culture is different from the West. However, taking into account that China is still at the primary stage of socialism, with a lower developing level of productivity, and needs to stimulate economic development through expanding consumption, we had better deal with the problem of consumerism carefully and seriously while yet also resisting and rejecting it. Chinese consumption at present has reached the level of moderate livelihood at most, much lower than that of Western developed countries. In some areas of China, people can only dress warmly and eat their fill. Therefore, on the whole, it is not good timing to advocate objecting to consumerism at present. In other words, objecting to consumerism will be more appropriate in the future rather than at present. But this does not mean that in all districts, for all people, consumerism need not be criticized now.

Owing to the unbalanced economic development in China, the economic development of some districts has reached a high level. Among the people who have become rich first, there does exist the trend of consumerism that should be examined. Moreover, people at different ages have different opinions and understanding of consumption. Most middle-aged or elderly people value frugality, while a lot of young people, going after fashion, have a far greater consuming level. Therefore, even if one should object consumerism in general, one should mainly focus on the younger generation of change the attitudes.

REFERENCES

Bell, D. 1978. *The Cultural Contradictions of Capitalism*. New York: Basic Books.

Keynes, J. M. 1936. *The General Theory of Employment, Interest and Money*. London: Macmillan.

Li Yining. 1995. *Ethical Issue*. Shanghai: Three Jointed Press.

Weber, M. 1958. *The Protestant Ethic and the Spirit of Capitalism*. New York: Charles Scribner's Sons.

Ye Dunping, Gao Huizhu, Zhou Zhongzhi, and Yao Jianjian. 1998. *On Dialectical Relations Between Ethics and Economics*. Shanghai: Shanghai Education Press.

Zhao Xiuyi. 1996. On Frugality. *Studies on Mao Zedong and Deng Xiao Ping Theories*, 4.

Zhou Zhongzhi. 2001. Ethical and Economic Evaluations of Consumption in Contemporary China. *Business Ethics: A European Review*, 10(2), 92–96.

CHAPTER 12

Ethical Evaluation of the Income Distribution in China According to Its Five Income Sources

Jianwen Yang

GENERAL REMARKS ABOUT THE ETHICS OF DISTRIBUTION

Income and wealth distribution is an essential dimension of economic activity. It is not only an important economic factor that enables the continuation of economic production and human society, but it is also a basic stimulus to fierce ideological battles among human beings. Historically, the prosperity and downfall of dynasties, changes of regime, social progress, cultural evolution as well as ideological upheaval are all closely related to shifts in the distribution system. Therefore, evaluating distribution from an ethical perspective has become, in itself, an important test for the harmony and unity between economy and ethics. On this basis, distribution has an intrinsic relationship with ethics.

In line with the principles of Western economics, the processes and states of affairs of distribution are the results of the contribution labor makes to the creation of products and wealth, for which labor pays the price of forgoing leisure time. In other words, labor endures disutility or suffering while making this contribution. Therefore, the reasonable distribution of income and wealth among labor becomes a critical issue for both economics and ethics: economics describes and analyzes the actual ways of distribution while ethics examines how the distribution should be shaped. Evaluating from the ethical perspective, the issue is how to distribute income and wealth in such a way that it accords with people's ethical standards, which is the meaning of distribution ethics in this article.

More specifically, focusing on personal income, distribution ethics deals with the questions on how the equality principle should be applied to income distribution and to what extent the actual income distribution reflects the ideal of equal distribution. Therefore, if the equality principle has been fully implemented in its economic meaning (namely that every member has gained the same net income from society), it has moved toward, although not reached, the ultimate ethical concept of distribution. In fact, equality in terms of net income (which, for the sake of simplicity, may represent the social and economic conditions of the individual) does not account for inequalities in terms of natural conditions, that is, for example, of disabilities. For instance, from the same amount of income a disabled person may draw a lower level of well-being than a "normal" person does. It is therefore believed that society should do more for disabled people than normal people in order to eliminate the unequal conditions given by disabilities. Consequently, distribution ethics in its full sense aims at making everyone's ultimate condition as equal as possible. Undoubtedly, this goal of equal treatment is highly ambitious because it stipulates to overcome not only social and economic, but also natural inequalities (Xia 2000).

It can be concluded from the earlier remarks that the ultimate ethical concept of income distribution emphasizes the equalization of distribution results as well as distribution conditions. However, as a matter of fact, it is difficult to fully implement the ultimate concept of distribution ethics. This problem occurs not merely because the equality standard of distribution falls into the category of ethics, but because different interest groups as well as different social classes have different ethical standards and thus, different equality standards. What is more important is that distribution ethics itself is shaped by historical conditions. In different historical phases, distribution ethics has been endowed with different connotations and has also been influenced and constrained by different factors. Hence it is difficult to judge whether income distribution is equal or not by one agreed upon set of ethical standards. It also explains why people often reach different or even contrasting ethical appraisals of the same pattern of income distribution. However, in any case, the ultimate concept of distribution ethics aims at the equalization of both the results and the conditions of the income distribution, although in different times people may disagree and have various types of ethical standards and measures of income distribution.

FIVE TYPES OF INCOME OF CHINESE RESIDENTS IN THE TRANSITION PERIOD

Since reform and the open-door policy were adopted, Chinese residents' income sources have become more and more diversified. Some are reasonable and some are irrational, even illegal. Nevertheless, the formation of those diversified income sources can be mainly attributed to two reasons. First, the development of the market economy has liberated people from the planned economy and offered people more room for free choice. Consequently, it is possible for people to create more sources of income. Second, the economic transition has brought about changes in people's value concepts and value orientation. In particular, some people have fallen prey to the fetish of money in the conflicts between old and new ideologies as well as ideologies at home and abroad. Putting it more specifically, there are five types of income sources nowadays in China.

The First Type of Income is Based on Labor and Basic Elements

Distribution according to one's labor is the basic mode of income distribution in China. Therefore, income from labor[1] is the primary income source for Chinese workers. In recent years, along with the deepening of reform, one's labor combined with various basic elements has been proposed as the fundamental mode of distribution at the 15th National Congress of the Communist Party of China. As a result, income from basic elements—scarce resources that play a role in production[2]—becomes another important income source. Correspondingly, the person who owns and inputs those basic elements can obtain relevant payment. For instance, after their basic requirements are satisfied, many people save a large sum of residual wealth and deposit it into banks in the form of savings and thus gain interest income, which is the payment of money capital. Another instance is that through hard work and effective management, some private leaders and proprietors of private enterprises have achieved proceeds that can be categorized as the payment for these entrepreneurs' talents after excluding the payment for workers' work and other basic elements. It should be pointed out that although, in China, land has begun to be regarded as a production factor, land rent, that is, the income from land, can only be collected by the government. It cannot become a source of personal income because the land is owned by the country, not by individuals.

The Second Type of Income Comes from Aid

To put it more specifically, the second type of income is not gained through people's own efforts, but provided by the government in the form of social insurance and transfer payments. These payments are designed to ensure the basic living standard of people below the poverty line as well as to deal with some consequences of disasters such as floods and earthquakes. This income constitutes the income source of those people living below the survival line and is, in general, constrained by certain conditions. However, social welfare is enjoyed by every citizen and usually works as an invisible income, an example being charitable activities organized by the government for people living in regions hit hard by natural disasters.

The Third Type of Income is Unexpected and Risky

One distinct feature of the source of the third type of income is its huge uncertainty and unpredictability, which mainly includes three basic income forms: (1) speculation income or risk income, the price of which is great risk as taken in speculation on the stock market or the real estate market; (2) lottery income, which does not involve a huge risk but is very random with an extremely low chance of winning a prize; and (3) income from market fluctuations. Because the market is the place where people execute transactions, fluctuations in the market greatly affect the income of those involved in the transactions. For instance, when the market is suddenly in a state of oversupply, the commodity price declines, and consumers virtually obtain an invisible income (i.e., saving expenses); in the opposite situation, suppliers will receive an income instead. In another instance, the occurrence of inflation will affect residents' income on the whole. As a result, people's actual income will decline somewhat. In particular, in an inflationary spiral, the degree of the decline of actual income will be even more obvious.

The Fourth Type of Income Comes from Power and Administration

The source of the fourth type of income can be called "power income," which is an important cause for the widening income gap. It includes two kinds: (1) reasonable monopoly income that refers to securing the market share by relying on one's own strength (advanced technology, economies of scale, etc.), and (2) policy income. In China, policy affects income significantly. This kind of income, which falls into three categories, mainly refers to extra proceeds achieved by exerting the power of government or privilege. The first category includes policy income on the whole, benefiting one group in the short term while doing good to the whole in the long term. For instance, one may mention the policy "allowing some people to become rich before others and then all the people can become rich" and the policy "coastal areas should develop first and then can help the inland areas develop too." The second category covers the exclusive policy income of a group. For instance, the local government protects the interest of local residents through administrative divisions and economic obstruction by noneconomic means. The income gap here represents the short-term interests of a group. The third category is self-regard privilege income. This includes extra income obtained by trade or financing, which relies on a privilege. This type is distinguished from the fifth type of income because the fourth type or power income refers to legal yet irrational income.

The Fifth Type of Income Comes from Illegal Activities

The source of this type of income differs substantially from the other four types because it is obtained through illegal means. While this income source also existed in the planned economy, it is now on the rise in the current period of transition, causing confusion among many people. It results from corruption of government officials, making and selling of fake goods, smuggling, prostitution, and so on. Only a small number of people usually benefit from this source of income. However, it not only harms economic development, but also restricts social progress.

ETHICAL EVALUATION OF THE FIVE TYPES OF INCOME GAINED BY CHINESE RESIDENTS

In the following, the five types of income are analyzed from the ethical perspective. The types are ranked in the order of their legitimacy as perceived by citizens, that is, the first type is considered most legitimate, the fifth least legitimate.

First, the history of economic development shows that other basic elements besides labor also play an important role in economic development. In addition, the demand for commensurate rewards and compensation by the person who owns these basic elements has gradually been deemed a reasonable demand. In a socialist market economy, labor and basic elements also have both economic and ethical features. This is manifested in the fact that labor and basic elements that achieve income are calculable and can be rewarded. Workers can make free choices (e.g., about the profession or the work organization) according to the amount of payment. It is not only helpful to the self-adjustment of economy, but also facilitates the smooth development of humanity (Hayek 1997).

However, in the process of China's actual economic development, people have not fully acknowledged the first type of income. For, on the one hand, the stipulation and actual implementation of the evaluative standard of worker's wage income cannot always reach the requirement of objectivity and fairness. On the other hand, people have doubts about the way and manner some owners of capital have secured their capital. Notwithstanding, essentially, the doubts are related to the "system vacuum" caused by progressive reform and will definitely vanish as reforms continue to deepen. Therefore, the first type of income will not trigger any conflicts of ethical judgment.

Second, from the perspective of different social levels, it is very likely that those people who depend on labor income alone have difficulty surviving due to various influences. Under these circumstances, the government's transfer payments and social insurance also have the function of stabilizing society, both checking the possible development of hostile psychology toward society due to changes in some groups' conditions, and also ensuring that the ethical concept of the poorest people does not become distorted. People at other social levels also acknowledge this difficulty out of a sense of fairness and altruism. For it is apparent that absolute egoism will not only trigger turbulence in the society, but also endanger people's own benefits in the long run. In addition, social welfare is a kind of general revenue benefiting the whole. Although everyone pays for it, the benefits received are much more than the costs.[3]

Therefore, people generally acknowledge the second type of income. Based on this general understanding, income of this type can be considered to be supported by both ethical and economic considerations. However, at present, major problems remain. Although poor people have received support from social relief programs, they still ask why they are unluckily poor (despite their hard work or willingness to work hard) while others are rich. Moreover, the government is ineffective in the actual implementation for granting income on this level. As a result, there are conflicting ethical views on what is fair. In fact, these conflicts manifest themselves in negative behaviors such as drinking, complaining, gambling, or idling about. Some people become hostile to society and fall prey to engaging in illegal activities. An ethical view gains ground that is encapsulated as follows: "The one who has money is dad and the one who has milk is mom."

Third, a distinct feature of the income of the third type is the view that some people's high incomes, gained instantaneously, have been generated either from other people's high losses or from the total loss of many people. Objectively speaking, economic activity that aims at gaining profits is not only the objective demand of the market economy, but also a rational activity in line with people's pursuit for more income. However, in terms of ethics, the pursuit of benefits and the securing of wealth can stem from very different motivations such as greed or care or other factors. Regarding the third type of income, conflict in people's distribution ethics becomes more evident. On the one hand, when people dare take risks and also bear risks that others cannot bear in securing income, they are usually highly praised for their courage and insight. On the other hand, the risk-loving attitude may increase uncertainty overall and thus expose the risk-averse people to risks as well. As a result, some people become rich overnight while others lose everything.

When the uncertainty exacerbates, people's good nature may vanish completely. Then people only struggle for life just like animals living in nature. If this condition cannot be changed, people even go so far astray as to believe in fatality. For instance, in recent years, certain religious ceremonies such as the worship of wealth deities have become popular at the ribbon-cutting ceremonies of businesses in several large cities in southern China. These emerging phenomena indicate that people are losing their identities in the ever-changing market. Therefore, in a period when money worship becomes more and more prevalent, the drastic fluctuations in the market may very possibly trigger a crisis in belief among people.

In particular, China's market economy is not perfect, and the fluctuations in the market are somewhat induced by some people's manipulation, which arouses more dissatisfaction and leads to further deformation of people's ideas. A case in point is the launching of the securities market originally aimed at creating a new and "good" way for economic development. Its creation is also an objective demand of economic development. Therefore, ethical and economic considerations should go hand in hand. However, in reality, some big stockholders viciously manipulate the market so much that numerous smaller stockholders believe the securities market is "a machine for big fish to eat small fish and for the rich to make money from the poor."

Some people even think the market itself is set up for the rich to earn more money. Although this idea is not widespread yet, it at least indicates the changes in people's ideas concerning distribution ethics, changes brought about by the third type of income, which is closely related to the market in the transition period. Moreover, the changes will become even more prominent along with China's progressive reform.

Fourth, a core ethical issue in economic development is the dispute about equality and efficiency. Therefore, the fourth type of income can be distinguished at two levels. The first level focuses on issues about equality and efficiency in income distribution, concerning the macroregional policy of the government or the income gap caused by the legal monopoly of enterprises. This kind of distribution objectively aims at enhancing efficiency, although it is also inherently somewhat unfair. Fair distribution should treat every region, every department, as well as every industry equally. All preferences, both man-made and natural preferences, indicate unfairness and thus will affect the enthusiasm of other regions, departments as well as industries.

Since the 1980s many policies in China have greatly emphasized efficiency, the different development strategies among regions, the investment policies favoring the southeastern coastal area, or the distribution policies allowing some people to get rich first, to name a few. Not surprisingly, the results have stimulated new social and economic conflicts, regional differences, and disparities between the eastern and the western regions as well as created a wealth gap among different people. As a result, some people began to wish back the time before the reform, while other people started calling for equality. From the ethical perspective, the exclusive pursuit of efficiency will force the society and individuals to aim at realizing the greatest profit as the only goal, which will encourage egoism. Society will end up lacking a human face.

Without fairness to coordinate and check efficiency, the efficiency-first market will be very relentless, keeping out mutual help, cooperation, unity, and harmony, and instigating tensions and conflicts among people. For instance, nowadays some hospitals do not save dying people, which totally contradicts the medical ethos. Sometimes people just stand aside and let criminals commit their deeds without trying to stop them. These phenomena clearly indicate a decline of ethical attitude and behavior. By stressing efficiency excessively, harmony in the market economy is being reduced. However, from another angle, the prevalent ethical concept of equality is not necessarily correct either. Although some people recall the old idea of absolute equal distribution, it belongs to the past and will not come back again. At present, the income gap caused by the fourth type of income is prevalent, and people's ethical views about this gap conflict sharply. Along with the economic development, though, there is hope that this conflict will disappear slowly and be replaced with a new and better concept of distribution ethics.

In addition to the first level concerning macro-regional policies and legal monopolies of enterprises, at the second level there is total self-centeredness, lacking a complete and long-term concept of ethical distribution. Although some residents in particular regions gain income derived from regional policies, it is at the price of irrational costs assumed by other regions and people. Moreover, these costs cannot be compensated for by policies for all. In addition, this type of income "from power and administration" has the effect of "restraining power" in the society and will also corrupt people's ethical view that might be favorable to the formation of a positive socialist spirit. This type of income has actually fallen into the trap of money worship, which is irrational, though not illegal, and disapproved by many people. This problem has developed before our eyes on a grand scale. While the law, in principle, cracks down on illegal activities, there is no court of ethics to try legal yet irrational activities. Although, in recent years, the phenomena such as hitting the jackpot through immoral activities and official profiteering have been prohibited, they cannot be fully eliminated and are barely restricted in the real world. As time passes, this type of income will substantially increase people's dissatisfaction with society, causing anger and thereby triggering a crisis of distribution ethics (Gao 2001).

Fifth, a large amount of facts indicate that the major reason for the phenomenon of an unfair gap between the rich and the poor lies in multiple wrongful activities for getting quick money—such as rent seeking of power, asking for bribery relying on power, making and selling of fake goods, corruption, tax dodging and evasion, prostitution, drug smuggling—the source of the fifth type of income. Because it is beyond ethical acceptability and disregards the restrictions of traditional ethical standards, this fifth type of income radically distorts the people's concept of distribution ethics (He 1997).

The critical factor here is the psychological and mental impact of this type of income on the population. While people have long believed that through arduous work and justified means people can get rich, the nouveaux riches who have earned money quickly and through illegal means seem to prove the contrary. While some people may still continue to work hard and believe in work as the only way to get rich, others may reflect upon their deeds and realize that one needs to obtain power first in order to get rich. By taking risks one will become richer, thus encouraging a philosophy of worshiping only money and power. For others, they will give up their self-control and begin to act in a hostile manner against the society. This hostility not only leads to gearing against the rich who use illegal means, but also leads to misinterpreting the rich who use justified means. These three ethical groups all exist in the current society, but they belong to different social classes. Generally speaking, the first group of people is prevalent among intellectuals equipped with technology, ability, and innovative ideas. The second group is often found among government officials and leaders of state-owned enterprises, and the third group includes mainly workers, farmers, and unemployed people with little education. It goes without saying that these different concepts of distribution ethics clash and influence each other. Moreover, they may have far-reaching consequences on the evaluation of all types of incomes in China's changing society (Xu 1998; Ye et al. 1998).

NOTES

1. It mainly refers to regular wages and other subsidies paid to workers for their labor.
2. It includes land, capital (money capital and physical capital) as well as entrepreneurial talent besides labor.
3. In fact, the benefits here should be called social benefits while costs refer to private costs. One important feature of the second type of income is that it has strong positive external effects.

REFERENCES

Gao Zhaoming. 2001. On the Crisis of Moral Belief in the Transition Period. *Zhejiang Social Sciences.* Vol. 1.

Hayek, F. A. 1997. *The Constitution of Liberty.* University of Chicago Press (1978). Chinese version translated by Deng Zhenglai. Shanghai: Shanghai Hong Kong Joint Publishing House.

He Huaihong. 1997. *Contractual Ethics and Social Justice.* Shanghai: Shanghai Hong Kong Joint Publishing House.

Xia Weidong. 2000. What Business Ethics Studies. *Jiangsu Social Sciences.* Vol. 3.

Xu Xiangyang. 1998. *China's Puzzlement in the Transition Period.* Beijing: Huaxia Publishing House.

Ye Dunping, Gao Huizhu, Zhou Zhongzhi, and Yao Jianjian. 1998. *Evolution and Adaptation of Business Ethics.* Shanghai: Shanghai Education Publishing House.

CHAPTER 13

Business Corruption in China's Economic Reform and Its Institutional Roots

Dajian Xu

During the past 20 years, China's economic reform has achieved great success. The building of the market economy stirred up people's enthusiasm for production and made economic organizations more active and efficient. As a result, the national economy boomed and the living standard rose quickly. But, at the same time, there also emerged all types of business corruption in China. These corrupt practices indicate that a great part of the private income produced by economic efforts is not obtained by the creation of the nation's wealth, but by the infringement of the rights and interests of certain people, "hindering personal economic efforts from becoming activities with a private rate of return close to the social rate of return." These kinds of corruption are not only producing social injustice, but also thwarting sustained economic growth in China and threatening the strategic implementation of the country's modernization.

This essay tries to set forth that the main cause of business corruption now dominating China lies in the imperfections of the current market system in the country. Therefore, further reforms in the system and the property rights arrangements are required. These reforms need the moral values that support the market economy but are incompatible with traditional Confucianism. So Western formal institutions should be built up by introducing advanced cultures suitable for these institutions to assimilate China's traditional cultural heritage.

Business Corruptions in China's Economic Reform

One of the hot spots in Chinese society in recent years is the problem of all kinds of business wrongdoing characterized by fake and shoddy products,[1] jerry-built projects,[2] deceitful advertisement and promotion, contract double-crossing,[3] falsified certificates, accounts and profits,[4] and the like, producing a crisis of confidence. Falsehood and deceit have already spread throughout the areas of business management such as production, marketing, personnel, and finance. While business cheating has happened in ancient and modern times, in China and other countries, at all times and in all lands, the business cheating prevailing in China at present is, it can be said, second to none, be it in width and depth or in species and quantity, especially concerning fake and shoddy products, business chain debt, avoidance or repudiation of debts, and falsified accounts.

These immoral business activities will inevitably generate grave results. They have already affected the operation of the national economy seriously, not to mention the harm they have brought to the nation and individuals. First of all, the fake and shoddy products greatly increased the transaction costs of consumption and suppressed the consumption demand. Second, when there was an excessively high avoidance of debt repayment, banks were reluctant to grant loans; and the falsified accounts of listed public companies made the stock market overcast and suppressed investment demand. Third, contract cheating and lack of confidence significantly increased the transaction costs of enterprises; and all these atrocious behaviors have obviously affected the sales of products and the will of investing, which has made it extremely hard for enterprises to operate.[5]

The direct result of these problems is the low efficiency of the national economy. As reported, China has paid the costs of approximately 585.5 billion yuan annually for the lack of confidence: this includes direct costs for dodging repayment or repudiating debts of about 180 billion yuan; direct costs for contract cheating of roughly 5.5 billion yuan; costs for fake and shoddy products of at least 200 billion yuan; and the added financial costs caused by chain debts and cash trading amounting to approximately 200 billion yuan.[6]

In the long run, these business wrongdoings, if not brought under control, will not only endanger sustained growth of the national economy, but can also ruin the reform of the market economy and even poison the national spirit leading to the decline of the nation.

The Defects of the Formal Institutions

The causes of business cheating of all kinds mentioned earlier are various. But one thing is certain that these "dirty pools" are not produced by the market economy. Theoretically, the essence of the market economy is trading and competing on an equal footing, and its normal operation needs a dual moral foundation: protection of the property rights of the trading subjects and wide-ranging trustworthiness in the market.[7] However, the essence of business cheating is infringing upon others' property rights and breaking trust, thereby undermining the foundation of the market economy. Therefore, the real market economy disallows business cheating. Historically, there are fewer business cheats in a mature market economy. As some scholars have pointed out, the market economy does not only naturally produce business cheating, but it also creates an atmosphere of trustworthiness.

In fact, the primary cause of business cheating is the unsound state of the current market economy in China. There are two main defects in China's formal institutions: one lies in the economic system and the other lies in the judicial system.

Economic reform to address these defects has taken a kind of systemic transformation. In its process there inevitably exist remanents of the planned economy, mainly the institution of examination and approval by government. Business corruption is thus rooted in an institution of the system, which is not yet eliminated by the systemic transformation. For example, dodging repayment or repudiating debts has, to a large extent, resulted from the present financing system that embodies the institution of examination and approval by government. As it was just pointed out, dodging repayment or repudiating debts is one of the main causes of bad assets for the state-owned banks, and therefore must relate to bank loan behavior. According to an analysis of the bad assets of Chinese state-owned banks, a large part of the bad assets belongs to so-called voluntary bad assets or the loans known by banks as nonperforming when they were granted. But why did the banks grant these loans when they knew clearly that they could not get the money back? The cause lies exactly in the intervention of and approval by the local governments. The banks were not only irresponsible in granting the loans, but also did so specifically to gain advantages from the local governments. So dodging repayment or repudiating debts in China was encouraged by the present financing system to a large extent.[8]

The institution of examination and approval by government has two characteristics: first, it results in a kind of monopoly, which will inevitably bring about corruption for lack of competition or restraint; second, the institution provides power without responsibility, which means the person who has the power to examine and approve does not have to bear the responsibility for the results of the examination and approval and thus does not have to think twice before making decisions.[9]

The institution of examination and approval by government was originally a tool, in the planned economy, of the government for administering the economy and allocating resources. Through this institution, almost all management decisions, from the establishment of an enterprise over the grant of a loan and the allocation of material resources up to the use of enterprise personnel, had to get approval by the government. The fatal defect of this institution, based on the assumption of a "rational person," is that the lack of correspondence between power and responsibility is ultimately unable to obligate people effectively. The case in point, par excellence is the so-called soft binding obligation of "being responsible for the profit but not for the loss." In the current process of economic reform, in order to build up modern business enterprises with "clearly established ownership, well defined power and responsibility, separation of enterprise from administration, and scientific management," the institution of examination and approval by government must be reformed and transformed into a means of macro-control of the national economy instead of remaining a tool of direct management by the government. Otherwise, it will not only hinder the allocation of resources by the market as well as harm the allocative efficiency of the whole economy, but it will also become a monopoly of privileges in the market economy and a hotbed of business corruption. As a matter of fact, the institution of governmental examination and approval currently practiced in China has not brought about the complete separation between government functions and enterprise management. According to a report, "the institution of governmental examination and approval practiced at present is complex and irregular," "the government control is too much, too concrete and too much abused" so that "70 percent or more of the social resources are still allocated by government."[10]

The unsound state of the rule of law is another primary cause that results in business cheating. The rule of law is the most important formal institution that defines and protects the property rights of trading subjects, and therefore it is the core of the market system. Since beginning economic reform and opening to the outside world, China has already established a whole system of laws and regulations according to the market economy and made great progress in the economic realm. However, for several reasons along with the fact that China has had only a relatively short period of experience with the market economy, the present situation of the rule of law in the economic realm is not satisfying. Now and then, the laws are not being observed and strictly enforced, except for laws in some areas, which are imperfect and cannot restrain business cheating effectively. The fact that fake and shoddy products and chain debts are so rampant must be accounted for to the legal circumstances prevailing now in China.

To illustrate the weak and incompetent rule of law, we may take the example of the practice of "beating counterfeit." According to the discussion of "Beating Counterfeit" on July 29, 2001 featured on the program "Everybody Can Speak Out" by the Shanghai Television Station, the experts and representatives of the public expressed the following opinions:

1. The strength of the present laws against making and selling counterfeits is far from sufficient. For example, according to the current law, consumers who have bought counterfeits can only get reimbursement of the prices of the counterfeits. The punishment of the person who makes and sells counterfeits normally consists of the confiscation of the counterfeits and a fine of double or triple the value of the counterfeits, while the profit from making and selling them exceeds by far this kind of punishment.

2. The transaction costs of consumers' beating counterfeit are so high that most of the victims are reluctant to take legal action. For example, if one wants to appraise the quality of a bottle of wine, one has to pay the fee of 150 yuan; and for a battery of a mobile phone, one must pay a fee of 200,000 yuan and even go to Beijing!

3. As the activities of making and selling counterfeits are too rampant, the enterprises are reluctant to tell the methods of discriminating the genuine from the counterfeit. They are afraid of losing customers who would learn that counterfeits exist and could be made even better than the originals. This would impair the beating counterfeit actions of the law-enforcing agencies.

4. Regional protectionism often makes the law-enforcing agencies ineffective and the companies' personnel for beating counterfeit helpless.

Based on this analysis, the following efforts must be undertaken in order to make the institutions of the market economy more effective and eliminate business corruption. First, the institution of the examination and approval by government must undergo a serious reform; the functions of government have to be transformed; the enterprises are to become real business enterprises with the power of decision making; the order of fair play must be developed; and business corruption caused by the monopoly of power has to be eliminated. Second, supervising systems of information networks such as the bank credit information system and the business trust information system should be established quickly in order to keep immoral behavior of enterprises and individuals on record and prevent them from hiding any longer. Third, current laws and regulations should be revised and improved, supervising systems of law enforcement should be established, strict and fair law enforcement should be strengthened, and business corruption should be severly punished, all of which is of paramount importance for reconstructing moral business behavior. Finally, in order to guarantee strict and fair law enforcement across the country, an effective system should be set up to break regional protectionism.

THE DEFECTS OF THE INFORMAL INSTITUTIONS

There is no doubt that, in addition to the formal institutions, the informal institutions also contribute to cheating in business of the various kinds mentioned earlier. Informal institutions mainly consist of customs and morality that is accepted by the society. They support and complement formal institutions, without which the formal institutions will be less efficient and perhaps even cease to exist except in name. Their binding force, while less strong than that of formal institutions, is generally embodied in the public opinion that is based on public conscience and carried by moral education in both families and schools. Additionally the activities of the news media publicize and supervise people's opinions.

From a superficial point of view, the deficiency of the informal institutions lies primarily in a decline of the moral climate of society in recent years. But, in my opinion, this decline is rather the result of a loss of belief and trust due to the transformation of the economic system, since China has not developed the morality suitable for a market economy. On the one hand, instead of being appropriate for a modern market economy, Confucian ethics with its core of "loyalty and filial piety," based on ties of blood and affections and upholding the feudal autocracy, is part of the problem of immoral behavior in the market economy because it cannot face the transformation of the economic system. On the other hand, the ethics characterized by "utter devotion to others without any thought of oneself" and "submitting oneself to all the arrangements of the organizations," which is based on the tradition and build up of the planned economy, is in fact no longer held true by the people since it is not suitable for the market economy.

Facing this kind of "crisis of confidence" caused by the transformation of the economic system, the present moral education in China is unsatisfactory. As numerous facts show, families pay much greater attention to intellectual education than to the moral education, which is so essential to cultivate the moral character of a person, while education in schools tends to place intellectual education above all and to preach morality without any link to reality, which is of little benefit to youngsters.

As a result, moral preaching is becoming a sort of window-dressing of enterprises and thus the object of the public's disdain. On the one hand, people insist on personal moral perfection without compromise. On the other hand, they are blatantly opportunistic in this embryonic market, without any respect for contracts, even making light of the concept of social justice. It goes without saying that, far from providing support to the binding function of the formal institutions, such moral conditions in the informal institutions are exactly one of the basic reasons that business cheating is so rampant in present China.

Compared to moral education in families and schools, the situation of supervision by news media and public opinion is much better. In recent years, many news media in China such as the television programs of CCTV, the newspapers such as *Southern Weekend, Chinese Youth Daily,* and the magazines such as *Finance and Economics, Sanlian Life Weekly,* and others have greatly contributed to the advancement of the morality suitable for the market economy by making the public aware of immoral business activities. However, the effectiveness of this endeavor is challenged by those who profit from the old ways. Above all, due to the deficiencies of the rule of law and the attacks and repression by vested interests, the news media and their employees are exposed to great pressure and even encounter illegal treatment or assassination.

It follows from the analysis just explained, that within the informal institutions, too, the morality suitable for the market economy should be studied and developed in order to eliminate current business corruption in China.

To do this, first of all, it is essential to recognize that in the market economy all transactions are equal, its basic moral principle requires one "not to violate the rights and interests of others" and to pursue "win-win" strategies, and its moral basis lies in the property rights of the trading subjects, which are to be clearly defined and well protected.

Second, the traditional, narrow view that conceives morality essentially as altruism and self-sacrifice must be modified. This view, which still prevails in moral education in China today, isolates morality from law (*"ius"*) by relating it only to "lofty morality" that is supposedly irrelevant to law, but not to basic morality, which is the foundation of law. Roughly speaking, the principle of basic morality is justice or "not violating the rights and interests of the others," which is the basic principle of law, while the principle of lofty morality is "self-sacrifice," which is not the principle of law. Without a doubt, one basic goal of the market economy is to seek personal gain in a proper way. If one contends that the essence of morality is altruism and self-sacrifice, one implies that the search for personal gain necessarily conflicts with morality. This would not only deprive the law of moral support, but, under the impact of the market economy, could also create an anemic lofty morality. Conversely, if one emphasizes the basic morality of "not violating the rights and interests of the others," one not only provides the law with a powerful support, but also lays a solid foundation for the lofty morality. Consequently, most people would no longer think of morality as just a preaching device that is divorced from reality. Therefore, it is crucial to emphasize the importance of basic morality in the market economy.

Third, in order to establish the moral principles of the market economy of not violating the rights and interests of the others and pursuing win-win strategies, the rights and duties, or rather, the proper personal interests of the trading subjects must be clearly defined. Hence self-interest as motivation cannot be rejected completely, as it is foundational for proper personal interests. In fact, while self-interest can lead to immoral business activities, as a motivator it not only belongs to human nature but is also a motivational force of economic development throughout the history of human beings. Therefore, the correct way to approach the motivation for self-interest is to control it and make it beneficial to both social progress and personal gains by emphasizing the basic morality and the establishment of the strict rule of law, rather than to try vainly to eliminate self-interest by preaching lofty morality.

CONCLUDING CONSIDERATIONS

Among various views about the main causes of business corruption or the crisis of confidence, there are particularly two predominating in

China today. The first position, held by some philosophers and ethicists, claims that the crisis of confidence stems from the impact of the market economy on people's ideas. This economy generates an extreme inflation of selfish desires among some people, weakens their ideological self-renewal, and causes the decline of public morality day by day. Therefore, the primary task to overcome this crisis is the reconstruction of morality, preferably with the integration of traditional Confucianism.

The second position is taken by most economists and lawyers who see the primary causes of the current crisis of confidence in China as lying in the institutional and juridical defects. These institutions fail to provide effective binding against business cheating. The problem cannot be resolved by moral preaching because the conditions of widespread fraud and unfair competition make deceit profitable and greatly impair honesty. It follows that one should primarily concentrate on the reform of institutions and laws in order to overcome the problem.

With regard to these two positions, I submit the following considerations. First of all, the binding forces of institutions, law, and morality are all necessary for preventing immoral business behavior. On the one hand, without the binding strength of institutions and the protection by law, morality becomes anemic. It cannot prevent the "dirty pools" of the few with no conscience and is unable to stem the increasing tendency of people to follow their wrong impulses, since they are unwilling to suffer from unfair competition. On the other hand, the institutions and laws that protect the rights and interests of the people are themselves based on some moral values. They cannot be set up to function properly without the support of these moral values. Even high transaction costs, which should deter wrongdoers, cannot prevent a large number of immoral activities.

Second, to eliminate business corruption the reform of formal institutions is more important than strengthening informal institutions through the enforcement of morality. This is not only because social existence determines the social consciousness and the economic foundation determines the superstructure, as Marx stated long ago, but it is also because the moral development in China will hardly break through traditional Confucianism without the advanced culture of formal institutions as its foundation, Confucianism being, on the whole, incompatible with the market economy that is characterized by transactions and competition on an equal footing. If one examines the relationship between the defects of China's current institutional culture and the characteristics of Confucianism, one cannot help thinking that there are countless links between traditional Chinese Confucianism and the current business corruption in China.

Without a doubt, traditional Confucianism is a culture of familism characterized by a patriarchal system and lacking a spirit of the rule of law. Its ultimate goal is to attain the stability and prosperity of the family and society through a set of formal and informal institutions, which emphasizes and supports the centralization of state power and the obedience to this power. Although this institutional culture supports normal behavior of people, maintains the social order, and keeps the stability of society under the condition of a certain productivity, it lacks the restraint and balance of power, it hinders innovation and progress, and inevitably it is becoming the root of corruption. Thus, it is no longer suited for modern large-scale and rapid production.

In conclusion, in order to restrain the current business cheats in China and ensure the country's modernization, one must get to the roots of corruption and keep reforming both the formal and informal institutions. Because traditional Confucianism is essentially incompatible with the market economy and related to the institutional defects that lead to current business corruption, it cannot directly provide the moral foundation for the market economy. Rather, formal institutions of the market economy have to be built up by introducing advanced cultures suitable for these institutions, including Marxism, to assimilate China's traditional cultural heritage.

Notes

1. There are countless reports on fake and shoddy products. See, e.g., *The Newspaper of Digest* (Shanghai), November 22, 1998 and *Sanlian Life Weekly* (Beijing), 2001, 3–4.
2. See note 1.
3. *Xinhua Net*, March 6, 2002; *Global Times*, October 6, 2001.
4. *Chinese Economy Times*, February 8, 2002.
5. *Chinese Operation and Management*, March 11, 2002; *Chinese Youth Daily*, March 25, 2002.
6. *Chinese Youth Daily*, March 25, 2002.
7. Dajian Xu. *Business Ethics*. Chapter 2. Shanghai: Shanghai People's Publication, 2002.
8. Ping Xie. "The Bad Capital of the State-Owned Banks." *Sanlian Life Weekly* (Beijing), 5, 2002, 23.
9. *Southern Weekend*, November 23, 2000.
10. *Southern Weekend*, November 23, 2000.

CHAPTER 14

Rules, Roles, and Moral Disparity: The Problem of Corruption

George G. Brenkert

INTRODUCTION: THE PROBLEM OF MORAL DISPARITY

Business ethics has often focused on determining general ethical principles for business and how they can be applied within situations of general compliance. Much less frequently has it examined cases involving widespread noncompliance with widely accepted moral views. Nevertheless, such cases are well-known and crucially related to issues in business ethics worldwide. They are an example of what, more generally, I call "moral disparity." There are several features of this phenomenon. First, these cases occur when people act in ways at odds with what an office, role, or position is held to require. Second, the various ensuing ways of acting are widely viewed as not morally appropriate (at least in themselves), even though some (even many) may still feel justified engaging in them. Finally, I will assume that moral disparity is undesirable if not morally wrong. It is a condition that we should seek to reduce, if not eliminate.

One prominent example is bribery. The point has been made many times that bribery is considered illegal, if not immoral, in every country around the world. Nevertheless, bribery is practiced in every country around the world. Other examples from within business might include employees simply doing nothing on a job they are hired to do, or marketers deceiving customers regarding their products. Examples outside business involve athletes cheating through taking performance-enhancing drugs, or spouses betraying each other. When these examples are cases of moral disparity, we confront widespread forms of behavior divergent from what the offices or roles involved are supposed to require. Obviously there may be variations from country to country, as well as within countries, with respect to how widespread such behaviors are.

What are we to make of these situations? It is a question that has been asked many times. Some of the responses look to the causes of moral disparity. For example, in the case of bribery, some of its causes are said to be poverty or powerlessness, on the one hand, or unconstrained and unaccountable power on the other hand. If these are indeed its causes, then perhaps means can be found to curtail bribery. Though these discussions are important, I do not intend here to consider this approach to moral disparity.

Instead, I want to briefly survey several other responses to moral disparity in a business context with the aim of recommending one kind of response that I believe requires more attention by business ethics than it has received. My theme will be that there is an important ethical issue regarding how people see themselves vis-à-vis the roles they inhabit and the rules and relations that define those roles, which is at least as important in addressing problems of business ethics as looking to the principles that ethicists have worried about, or the forms of enforcement and incentives that managers have focused upon. In particular, there are important normative issues regarding the relevance of personal considerations and relations as they relate to the rules and expectations that define these roles and positions. If we are to address the significant issues that arise regarding moral disparity as it pertains to business, then this important normative issue also needs attention.

Three Responses

Three standard responses to cases of business moral disparity involve enforcement, incentives or enticements, and normative moral principles.

First, some contend that in as much as relevant legal and moral rules are being violated in these cases, they are simply examples of moral breakdown. Accordingly, some sort of legal and/or moral enforcement is required in order to get people to do what they ought to do and what they nominally know they ought to do. Thus, laws and codes of ethics, and so on are proposed. This is a compliance response. It is an important response. Still, when levels of moral disparity are high, it is an inadequate response, for it assumes that this phenomenon is simply (or primarily) a failure of obedience. For example, though there are any number of laws that protect various forms of intellectual property, these laws are (in various ways and extents) frequently and widely broken (both in the United States and outside the United States). Enforcement alone is a failure. Instead, something else is going on that needs to be addressed.

A second (related) response to moral disparity focuses on incentives. The people involved simply do not have the proper enticements to lead them to do what they ought to do in the roles they occupy. The problem is one of aligning incentives or enticements and the motivations of the people with the principles they should follow. This is an economic response. Much of agency theory is an attempt to construct some coordination of enticements so that people will do what they are supposed to do.

Again, there is also much to say on behalf of this view, though it too has its own serious limitations. We can not always align one's moral duties and one's enticements. This might be a nice thing to happen. However, theoretically and practically it is implausible to think the proper set of self-interested incentives or enticements which will always motivate the appropriate moral behaviors might be developed.

A third response contends that in cases of moral disparity people must not really know (or understand) the proper moral principles or values that should guide them. Perhaps the principles (and the theories associated with them) do not give sufficiently clear guidance. Thus, we need to examine these principles, to show the guidance they provide, and to convince people of their justification. Accordingly, we must attempt to identify the correct moral principle (or principles) and educate office holders regarding them. This is the response of the ethicists.

This response is also an important one. Many people experience a great deal of unclarity about morality and moral principles. They need to be convinced of the justification and the importance of basic moral principles. Still, the efforts along these lines have not obviously had much effect to date on the problem of moral disparity.

Though there are limitations to each of these responses, each one of them is also a correct and very important response. People do need to be punished for failures to obey various laws and rules. They also need education regarding those rules and principles. Finally, the motivations and incentives of people must be such that they can support behavior according to those principles. As such, each of these alternative accounts has implications for action, on the part of people in business and business ethicists regarding moral disparity.

Nevertheless, I believe that each of these responses neglects an important normative feature of the offices, roles, or practices involved.

Business ethicists need to address this issue more directly. Both this normative aspect of offices and the preceding responses are required to attack moral disparity.

OFFICES AND THE PERSONAL OR IMPERSONAL

The normative feature of offices, and so on, in question concerns the place that personal or private considerations play within the context of the rules and expectations that define those offices. I wish to pursue this issue by considering the case of corruption as an instance of moral disparity.

I propose that, in accordance with the general framework of moral disparity, corruption be understood to be (1) the misuse or violation (or that which leads to it) of various rules, norms, or justified expectations that (at least in part) define an office, role, or practice, within an organization in ways (2) that are intended to benefit the private interests of individuals (or even organizations) engaged with that office or organization.

Several things should be noted about this view. First, corruption, so understood, is not the same as immorality in general. Second, the private interests benefited may be quite narrowly circumscribed or viewed more broadly to include family, relatives, and friends. Third, corruption is a broad phenomenon that includes bribery, fraud, kickbacks, and so on. Finally, the offices or roles defined by the rules, standards, and expectations, may be explicit and formal, or may be implicit and informal. What is crucial is that these rules (etc.) have a general nature related to activities designed to fulfill or accomplish some end(s) or purpose(s) of the offices and/or organization of which they are a part outside the private benefits of the particular officeholders.

Now instead of simply focusing on the nature of offices or positions themselves, I want to consider three normative views people take of those positions when they occupy them. Depending upon their views, people treat these offices differently. The resulting forms of behavior may lead to corruption and, when widely followed, moral disparity.

One such view is that any position or office in an organization is an opportunity for self-enrichment or self-protection (including one's friends and family). In accordance with my assumption, just mentioned, this is not, however, what the formal rules (at least) that define the office prescribe. Still, this self-focused view might be part of a general social view that this is what one does in business (or governmental) positions. For example, Banfield attributed such a view to the villagers of Montegrano, a small southern Italian city, in his study of the moral basis of this city: "Indeed, official position and special training will be regarded by their possessors as weapons to be used against others for private advantage" (Banfield 1958, 88f; italics omitted).

On this view, an office is viewed as simply subject to the individual. Any more general notion of an office as defined by rules or norms transcending this or that person's interests is rejected. For a person to occupy an office, then, is not to commit oneself to anything beyond his interests, even though he may take an oath of office, or agree to discharge certain functions of the office. Such individuals do not view themselves as bound by the rules defining that office.

This does not mean that these officeholders do not adhere to any rules. But if they do, those rules are to be distinguished from the rules that define the office. In addition, these other rules prescribe the subordination of offices to officeholders. Of course, if people take this position, there will be bribery and corruption. And the more widespread this view of offices is, the more widespread will be the bribery and corruption. The effect of this normative stance renders organizations weak and ineffective.

A second view, at the other extreme, is that one must subordinate oneself to the office or position. Since the rules and expectations that define such offices are not self-interpreting this view is ultimately that one is to follow the rules as interpreted by one's superiors on the job. Accordingly, this is a view in which obedience to both rules and supervisor is primary.

On this self-absorption view, the individual is wholly subordinate to and identified with the office. Officeholders simply do what they are told. And since one who strictly obeys is viewed as not fully responsible for resulting actions, officeholders in this sense even may be said to enjoy a form of freedom: they do not have to bear the full responsibility for their actions.

Once again this normative view of offices and their rules does not obviously render moral disparity or corruption impossible. Questions of corruption might still arise, since an officeholder might be directed by a superior to engage in activities that violate the rules of that office. Or a person might seek means involving personal considerations that undercut the office's rules, which fulfill the ends of that office. Only if an officeholder were held to morally justified rules for an office that were independent from the officeholders would this view escape from questions of corruption.

Further, in as much as this view involves the subordination of oneself to one's office, it also crucially raises the issue of the nature of a moral agent. Those who defend this view appear to hold that moral agency requires (or at least permits) high levels of obedience to authority, which may diminish officeholders' responsibility for their actions. As such, this view does not offer us a way to reduce corruption or moral disparity.

A third normative view is that offices are defined by various rules pertaining to the end or object of that office and that these rules apply on the basis of various objective or impersonal determinations related to the purpose of the office. These rules are not defined through personal relationships of the officeholder, though personal relationships may play an important role in their fulfillment. In such a position one has various duties, which one must fulfill and to which one views oneself as committed, but within the bounds of a critical moral stance.

Obviously, there may be degrees of commitment to one's office, from notions of a calling (Novak 1996) or profession (Tawney 1948), at one end of a continuum, to less invested views of oneself and one's role, at the other end. Clerks, administrative assistants, and low-level employees may view their roles with much less commitment than those in a profession or calling, though this need not be the case. Occasionally, we learn of, for example, a traffic officer who enthusiastically directs traffic and maintains the rules of the road in his area.

This is, clearly, a very different view from the first two views. It involves a different understanding of oneself and the roles one occupies. On this view, the individual is subject to the office the individual occupies, but not wholly subject to it. This is a bounded view of officeholding. The office occupant owes his office not only his industry but also his judgment (Emmet 1966, 204). As such, one is subordinate to the office, but not wholly subordinate. Further, the means of realizing the rules and practices that define the office do not undercut the office, nor does their use by officeholders.

The relation of the personal and the official in holding roles, positions, and so on, is a central issue here. Those who urge officeholders simply to follow the rules of an office face the problem that such rules may not be complete and may be short-sighted. Personal connections may be required to supplement the office's rules or to circumvent obstacles that such rules unwittingly erect. But those who urge the primary importance of the personal in office occupancy raise the problem of the subversion of that office.

Accordingly, this normative sense of office occupancy requires that one have an understanding of the job, what its point is, and within what frameworks its rules can be bent or even broken. Several years ago, a prominent American business advertised that its employees were encouraged "to break a few rules." This was not meant to encourage their engaging in corruption, but rather to promote their helping customers. Such an approach means that employees or subordinates must be trusted. Superiors must be confident and not defensive. They cannot seek wholly to control every action of every employee.

The preceding sketches three different normative responses to an office, role, or position. The first sees the role in an instrumental manner. It serves the ends of the jobholder. The second views the jobholder as serving, with little qualification, the ends of the job as interpreted by those in authority. Here the jobholder is the instrument of the job. The third view seeks to place boundaries on the extent to which the jobholder or the job is to be viewed simply instrumentally. It offers, I have suggested, the most defensible relation of a moral agent and an office.

In taking this third view, a jobholder is supposed to accept and act by various rules that are defined in terms of the ends or purposes of the job. These rules are of a general nature and apply to everyone in a similar manner. Hence, this third view also suggests that the personal is to be subordinated to the official in the execution of a job. There are two limitations here. First, there may be formal and informal rules that permit personal aspects to coexist with the formal features of the job. The limit on these is that they must not undercut (but promote or be indifferent to) the purposes of the position. The second is that if the job itself is characterized in a manner that contravenes other moral standards, the individual may be justified in opposing (in some manner) what the rules of the job prescribe. This is, again, the bounded nature of the position.

THE FIVE E-CONDITIONS

Enforcement and enticements (incentives) are important ways (I have agreed) of reducing moral disparity and corruption, but they will not themselves foster the preceding third view of offices or roles. Instead, embracing, enabling, and ensuring conditions must also be drawn upon.

Embracing conditions include providing that roles or offices, and the system within which they are embedded, have a purpose of which officeholders may approve, if not esteem. The reasons for approval (and esteem) might be varied. The assumption here is that those reasons do not simply promote the officeholder's own self-interests. Still, this is compatible with the demand that the role and its system work, in the long run, on behalf of the enlightened interests of the participants. This is part of what it takes to get people invested in the roles they are asked to occupy.

A second embracing condition is clarity with regard to what an office or role involves. If one does not know what a position requires, one cannot be said to have embraced it. This second embracing condition applies to the explicit rules that define the office as well as the more implicit rules. This condition clearly involves a certain level of trust on the part of the potential officeholder since, given the implicit and customary rules that are involved in offices or roles, one might not be able to gain this knowledge until on the job.

Enabling conditions also are several in number. One enabling condition might be referred to as that of moral distance, or the viewing of the situations one faces in terms of objective, general considerations or standards, rather than immediate, personal features of those situations. This condition may, of course, impede various moral responses. For example, with globalization, a person may not see or live near the people his or her decisions affect and, consequently, may have a reduced level of moral sensitivity to them.

On the other hand, moral distance has an important and positive function when it comes to fulfilling the rules that define the role one occupies. As an officeholder, one has to be able to distance oneself from others in order to make various moral determinations. This depends, of course, on the supposition that such moral determinations are of a public or social nature involving general considerations. Granted the importance of moral distance for officeholding, this condition should not be confused with that of moral indifference. Moral distance is intended here to foster fair treatment of those people with whom officeholders deal, rather than to suggest a lack of concern with those individuals.

A second enabling condition is that a person who occupies a role or office successfully must know not only the office's rules, but also the ends or purpose they are supposed to further, such that a person may use his or her judgment regarding the application of those rules.

A third enabling condition is that one must be able to be confident that the determinations one makes regarding the rules of a particular position or office will not be undercut by others (superiors or outsiders). Such confidence is not simply a predictive matter, but also a question of trust in the behavior of others toward the ends and purposes of the particular office. A recent well-known book by Fukuyama (1995) speaks of the importance of trust in the development of large organizations in different societies. Though he does not directly relate this to issues of moral disparity and/or corruption, surely there is a rather direct connection.

Finally, ensuring conditions include those of openness and transparency. It is often said that corruption is practiced in the shadows and that it cannot be announced. This is only partially correct. When corruption becomes rampant, its results (and even procedures) may become quite apparent. Still, corruption does largely take place because it can occur quietly and nonpublicly. Something like "Gyges' ring" is in operation. Gyges' ring refers (you will recall) to a shepherd in Plato's *Republic* who discovers a magic ring that allows him to become invisible (Plato 1968). With the power of invisibility, he decides to murder the king, seduce the queen, and take over the kingdom. One of the points of the story has to do with the view that people do what is right simply because of outside pressures. However, a related point is the importance of transparency and openness in morality. We are social beings and absent exposure to others more generally, to their approval and disapproval, we may not follow the rules that define our roles, or be the moral beings we are. Of course, some have interpreted this to mean that those who do what they should do because of the pressures that arise through transparency are not really acting morally. Though I cannot argue the point here, I believe this to be an overly narrow understanding of the nature of moral action.

Business Implications, Challenges, and Conclusions

The upshot is that the problem of moral disparity and corruption can only partially be attacked through the creation of enforcement means involving laws and codes of ethics (compliance efforts), attempts to devise systems of incentives or enticements, and/or pronouncements of universal moral principles. This is not new, though this does not mean that these responses are unimportant.

However, in addition to these undertakings, business ethics must also look to the important notions of officeholding and rule following within organizations. It is of little use to proclaim the importance of universal rules, if the occupation of offices and rule following itself are themselves in question. A central focus must be the conditions that promote the bounded form of officeholding and rule following I have noted. The problem of moral disparity and corruption is one of the respect of, or adherence to, various roles or positions people occupy in the form of the respect for the rules and expectations that define those positions. This requires arriving at appropriate relations of the personal and impersonal, as well as public and private considerations, within the three additional "E-conditions" I have sketched. Addressing moral disparity in this manner should also have the twofold desirable effect of, on the one hand, providing content for the more general principles business ethicists identify, and, on the other hand, helping produce more productive, efficient, and moral organizations.

However, my argument is not one simply on behalf of following rules, since rule-bound behavior can be inappropriate, enervating and even deadly in some circumstances. People may follow rules in different ways. One undesirable result may be a system that is slow, bureaucratic, and unimaginative. Accordingly, it is important that people inside and outside an organization have an understanding of the point of the rules, but also the limits of self-interpretation.

There are opposing forces in society presently affecting moral disparity and corruption. On the one hand, the anonymity of modern society promotes situations that encourage moral disparity. So does the vast disparity in wealth that occurs in most societies.

On the other hand, international nongovernmental organizations (NGOs) and intergovernmental organizations (IGOs) encourage measures that seek to redress moral disparity by providing greater information and transparency regarding the actions of businesses and their members. Interestingly, the Internet (that great source of information) may both discourage and encourage moral disparity. And free markets, to the extent that they operate with open rules and broad social understandings, may promote decisions focused on the merits of exchanges. In this way, dubious exceptions for other more particular and arbitrary reasons may be reduced and with them moral disparity. In this sense, the popular phrase, "think globally, act locally," is a radical call for a kind of society that reduces corruption and moral disparity. If people think globally, they will be less inclined to make exceptions for themselves (and those related to them), but more prepared to abide by the general aspects and conditions of the positions they occupy, as I have portrayed earlier. And this, I have contended, would be a contribution to the reduction of both moral disparity and corruption.

REFERENCES

Banfield, E. C. 1958. *The Moral Basis of a Backward Society*. New York: The Free Press.

Emmet, D. 1966. *Rules, Roles and Relations*. Boston: Beacon Press.

Fukuyama, F. 1995. *Trust*. New York: The Free Press.

Novak, M. 1996. *Business as a Calling*. New York: The Free Press.

Plato. 1968. *The Republic of Plato*. Translated by Francis Macdonald Cornford. New York: Oxford University Press.

Tawney, R. H. 1948. *The Acquisitive Society*. New York: Harcourt, Brace, and World, Inc.

CHAPTER 15

Confidence in the Financial Reporting System: Easier to Lose than to Restore

Georges Enderle

In the aftermath of the collapse of Enron and Andersen with its far-reaching repercussions, we have realized how crucial it is for the functioning of the economy to have confidence in the financial reporting system. When the numbers in the financial statements are not "honest," the users of these statements are misled: investors cannot make informed decisions; employees cannot trust their employers; business partners cannot collaborate effectively; competitors cannot engage in true competition; government cannot collect fair taxes; financial markets cannot operate properly; the public loses confidence in business; and business loses its legitimacy. Those in charge of financial reporting, both the providers and the certifiers, not only violate their professional duties and lose their integrity, but also jeopardize the whole financial reporting system.

After the Enron and Andersen debacle and the series of further corporate scandals there is no doubt that financial reporting is a serious problem, not only in the United States but in other countries as well. It becomes an even more formidable and pressing issue as globalization advances. In this chapter I first describe the key features of the financial reporting system in the United States. Second, I discuss the concept of confidence in financial statements. Third, I explore three sets of crucial factors for the loss of confidence, exemplified by the Enron and Andersen case. Finally, I conclude with an outlook to restore confidence in the financial reporting system. The reference

to Enron and Andersen is not meant to be an exercise of finger pointing. It rather serves as a backdrop and illustration for discussing a
more general problem, which can occur in other countries, including
China.

The essay attempts to show that business ethics, when facing complex issues such as confidence in the financial reporting system, should
limit itself neither to the questions of institutions and rules (to be set
at the macro-level) nor to the questions of individual and organizational behavior (at the micro- and meso-level). Rather, it needs to
embrace a three-level approach that pays due attention to the
indispensable roles and responsibilities of persons, organizations, and
systems (see Enderle 2003). Questions of the ethics of financial and
nonfinancial reporting and implied concepts of the firm are further
discussed in Enderle 2004.

Characteristics of the Financial Reporting System in the United States

The modern financial reporting system has become a highly complex
system, encompassing three kinds of actors: the *providers* of financial
statements; the *certifiers* who attest the truthfulness of the statements;
and the *users* who make their decisions based on this information.
Reporting is supposed to follow certain regulatory and legal rules,
both in the spirit and the letter, in order to provide a common understanding of the statements, regardless if they are looked at from the
perspective of the provider, the certifier, or the user. Nevertheless, it is
also influenced by individual interpretations.

Within the company, the provider of financial statements is corporate management aided by management accountants. They prepare
the financial report of the company, often certified by internal auditors, and submit it to the board of directors whose audit committee is
in charge of examining it. When reviewed by this committee and certified by the external auditor, the board publishes the report to the
owners of the company and, in case of publicly listed companies, to
the public. Moreover, rated companies are continuously monitored by
credit-rating agencies. In order to supervise the certifiers, there are
other actors in place: the Public Company Accounting Oversight
Board (replacing the Public Oversight Board POB in 2002), supposed to monitor the accounting industry; the Security and Exchange
Commission (SEC) to enforce all accounting rules; and the legislators
in charge of the political supervision. Finally, the users of financial
statements: investors, be they institutional investors such as pension

funds or small investors; creditors lending money to companies; and governmental agencies collecting taxes. The actors in charge of setting the regulatory rules are the states Boards of Accounting, the Financial Accounting Standards Board (FASB), the SEC, and the International Accounting Standards Board (IASB).

Financial statements are also particularly crucial in the investment industry. In order to raise funds, firms issue new securities including initial public offerings (IPO), which, through the intermediary services of underwriting firms, are sold to investor firms. In this process, investment analysts play an essential role. By their research and recommendations and backed by their employers (investment banks and research firms), they exert considerable influence as to what extent the issuance of securities benefits the issuers, the intermediaries, and the clients.

What Is Confidence?

Confidence in financial statements means that we can rely on trustworthy or honest numbers, which adequately reflect real processes and states of affairs and are generated by people who are motivated by the knowledge that they are being trusted and by a moral commitment[1] to honor this trust. This definition includes the following components, indicating the critical points where confidence can be violated (see also Hausman 2002).

1. The users of financial statements relate to "trustworthy" numbers, which are essentially comprehensible, although to some extent they may need some interpretation. It is through the numbers, and not other kinds of information besides these numbers (which might be useful without being essential), that the "substance" of the business has to be clearly conveyed. Therefore, to the extent that financial reporting fails to get across this substance, confidence is undermined.

2. Generated in accordance with appropriate rules of financial reporting, the numbers should adequately reflect real processes and states of affairs of business. This means that the providers must apply the rules properly; otherwise they act with a lack of competency and impair the confidence in the financial statements. However, they should not be blamed for inadequacy, if the rules themselves are inappropriate. In this case it is the responsibility of those who set the rules, namely the regulatory and legal agencies in collaboration with the professional bodies of accountants and investment analysts, to establish and enforce appropriate rules and thus prevent the loss of

confidence. It goes without saying that, through serious professional training, the providers of financial statements must thoroughly know the rules and their application procedures in order to establish and maintain confidence in the reporting system.

3. In addition to honest numbers and adequate rules and procedures, confidence requires trustworthy people. They are not only competent in their fields, but also know that they are being trusted and have a moral commitment[2] to live up to this trust. This personal component for maintaining confidence in the reporting system is indispensable because individuals always have some discretionary space for decision making. They have to decide whether or not they want to comply with the spirit and the letter of the rules and, within the given set of rules, which course of action they want to choose. In order to make such decisions, they need to be not only technically competent, but also ethically responsible and can therefore fail in either respect. Here is the place where professional ethics (of accountants, investment analysts, and others) comes into play. Of course, there are many more factors, some of them mentioned earlier, which determine the level of confidence in the reporting system. But, however elaborated the system or the so-called mechanisms (a highly misleading term by the way), they cannot completely eliminate the discretionary spaces of individuals, all the more because financial markets and international business are of great complexity and develop at high speed.

In short, confidence in financial statements depends on all three components: the numbers, the rules and their application, and the individuals who are supposed to follow the rules and provide the numbers. If one or more of them fail, confidence is undermined and will eventually collapse. Thus recipes for failure include believing merely in numbers, following only the letter not also the spirit of the rules, and disregarding the importance of trustworthy people.

It may be useful to conceive confidence in the financial reporting system as a "public good" (see Enderle 2000). The public good in economic terms is defined as a good from which nobody can be excluded (nonexclusivity) and that can be consumed by any actor without reducing (or impairing) its consumption by other actors (non-rivalry). Honest and dishonest people and organizations alike benefit from (or "consume without using up") the confidence in the financial reporting system. Only if a reasonable level of confidence exists, however complex the system may be, can the system function at all.

Besides the question of consumption, there is also the question of production of confidence as a public good. By far more difficult, the production and maintenance of confidence require collective efforts by all actors participating in the system since individual efforts alone, though indispensable, cannot produce and maintain public goods. Consequently, its erosion, often perceived very late, is a failure not only of individuals but also of the whole group. Therefore, the easiness of consuming and the difficulties of producing confidence can explain, to a great extent, why the loss with its snowball effects is much easier than the restoration of this public good.

LOSING CONFIDENCE

I now turn to three sets of crucial factors that have led to serious damages of the financial reporting system in the United States. They were caused by the misbehavior of Enron and Andersen with the complicity of other organizations and individuals.

Corporate Failings in Financial Reporting

The first set of factors, illustrated by Enron, concerns the providers of financial reports. In all companies, providers include both the organization as a whole and individuals within it. Individuals range from the board of directors to senior managers and management accountants through to anybody in the company who is involved in the reporting process. Based on Enron's financial reporting, its share price rose from below $10 in 1991 to $90 in August 2000 and then fell to less than $1 in December 2001. Obviously, investors, lenders, rating agencies, opinion leaders in the business press, and others believed in Enron's numbers until its share price peaked in mid-2000 and most of them kept a high level of confidence in Enron until mid-2001 when the share price was still above $40. However, from October 16 to November 8, the price cascaded from over $32 to below $10, accompanied and partially caused by the following events: Enron reported a big third-quarter loss. The *Wall Street Journal* described $1.2 billion reduction in Enron shareholder's equity. The *Journal* also reported that Enron executives made millions from partnerships. Chief Financial Officer Andrew Fastow was replaced. The SEC elevated informal inquiry to formal investigation. Enron reduced its previously reported net income dating back to 1997 by $586 million, or 20 percent.

What went wrong? There is no doubt that the problem arose long before Enron's share price began to fall. Based on investigative reports, congressional hearings, and other investigations, it is possible to identify some key factors.

With regard to *financial reporting*, Enron's report (the "Powers Report"), commissioned by a special Enron Board-appointed committee before December 2, 2001 and published on February 2, 2002, concludes that many transactions apparently were designed to accomplish favorable financial statement results, not to achieve bona fide economic objectives. In addition, reported earnings between September 2000 and September 2001 were $1 billion higher than should have been reported. What the report does not say, according to *Financial Times* (*FT* 2/4/02), are several other accounting practices: Enron bolstered profits by booking income immediately on contracts that would take up to ten years to complete. It shifted debts into partnerships (Special Purpose Entities or SPEs) it had created, using them to manipulate its accounts. It masked poorly performing assets by rapid-fire deal making. It also employed an aggressive tax avoidance strategy with the result that only in one year did Enron pay federal tax at all, just $17 million in 1997. For sure, not all these activities were illegal (see for a thorough assessment, Benston et al. 2003).

As for *the role and behavior of individual employees*, Enron's report states that CEO Kenneth Lay had the ultimate responsibility for taking reasonable steps to ensure that the officers reporting to him performed their oversight duties properly. It also says that Enron employees (including A. Fastow and M. Kopper) involved in the partnerships were enriched by tens of millions of dollars they should never have received (*FT* 2/4/02). But it does not add that many Enron employees who invested in 401 (k) retirement plans were not allowed to sell their stocks and lost their earnings.

Regarding Enron's *corporate culture*, seemingly a shining example for outsiders over many years, it turned out to be quite ruthless and reckless (*FT* 4/9/02). On the one hand, Enron was presented as a visionary, innovative, and dynamic company with the core values of respect, integrity, communication, and excellence. On the other hand, Enron's code of conduct (regarding especially conflicts of interest) was suspended in the late 1990s. The company's true interest lay in "performance," that is in actions that boosted its bottom line and ultimately its stock price. Enron engaged in aggressive accounting and financial manipulation, designed to conceal losses and make its operations highly profitable. "There were no rewards for saving the company from a potential loss . . . There were only rewards for doing a deal that could outwardly be reported as revenue or earnings" (*FT* 4/9/02). In fact, a culture of fear was established, enforced by the powerful "Performance Review Committee" (PRC). Its nominal purpose was to grade Enron employees on how well they had followed the company's core values. "But former employees dreaded the PRC because they believed that PRC was based solely on how much paper profit they had booked for the company that year" (*FT* 4/9/02). It goes without saying that such an environment represses unpleasant messages and critical questions, making whistle blowing almost impossible. Only very few employees, in particular Sherron Watkins, had the moral strength to stand up and warn the CEO, although to no avail. Given Enron's culture, one can wonder why so much confidence was placed in Enron and its board and top executives.

Dependent Auditing

The second set of factors relates to the certifiers of financial statements, exemplified in the Enron situation by Arthur Andersen and its employees. First, a few facts. Andersen, one of the Big Five accounting firms, with 85,000 employees in 84 countries and revenues of $9.3 billion in 2001, has found itself at the center of the Enron scandal because of its failure to detect questionable bookkeeping. Throughout the 1990s until 2001, Andersen provided Enron both auditing and consulting services (for $25 billion and $27 billion in 2001, respectively), which was a common industry practice. Among the Big Five, consulting generated a substantial part of their U.S. revenues and non-audit fee income (particularly from consulting) tripled industry-wide over the last five years while audit fee income remained approximately at the same level (*FT* 3/5/02). This practice was justified by the accounting industry on the grounds that, by providing different kinds of services to the same clients, the service costs could be reduced, the consulting interests and the auditing interests could be kept separate, and the industry's self-policing through the Public Oversight Board would be effective.

However, evidence suggests that Andersen did not keep those conflicting interests separate. Rather, it succumbed to the temptation of aligning with Enron and pursuing their common corporate interests to the detriment of independent and truthful auditing. As Enron's report says, Andersen did not fulfill its professional responsibilities in its audits of Enron's financial statements, or its obligation to bring concerns about Enron's internal controls to the attention of Enron's board (*FT* 2/4/02). Moreover, David Duncan, the lead auditor of Enron, organized the disposal of thousands of Enron-related documents shortly after learning that Enron had received request for information from SEC. On January 15, 2002 Andersen admitted the shredding of documents, was convicted of obstruction of justice in June, and dismantled itself by October.

To conclude, it is fair to say that the audit profession's slogan of "independence in appearance and in fact" was violated by Andersen and its employees involved with Enron. The audit firm and individual auditors violated the principle of independence by having direct and material indirect financial interest in the client. Moreover, the principles of integrity and objectivity were disregarded as well. In sum, the undermining of confidence was caused by a combination of several factors: grey areas were interpreted against the spirit of the law; established rules were violated; some rules themselves were deficient; individual auditors failed in their professional duties; and a deficient corporate culture provided the wrong support to the employees.

Biased Investment Analysis

The third set of factors concerns the investment banks. Although they are not at the center of the Enron scandal, they contributed, in varying degrees, to the misleading appearance of Enron's financial statements. In the period of 1999–2001 a large number of prominent investment banks were underwriters, agents and/or advisors for Enron, "greasing Enron's money machine" (*Wall Street Journal* 2/14/02, Cosimano 2004). These banks were: Citibank/Salomon Smith Barney, J. P. Morgan Chase, Credit Suisse First Boston, BNP-Paribas, Deutsche Bank, Merrill Lynch & Co., Goldman Sachs Group, Bank of America Securities, and Lehman Brothers.

Since an analysis of the role and responsibilities of investment banks in the Enron debacle is beyond the scope of this paper, I only highlight a few general aspects with regard to financial reporting. As intermediaries, investment banks are supposed to be honest brokers between companies that want to raise funds and investor firms that look for profitable return on their assets. They not only manage investments, but also often provide investment analysis for issuing securities. An impenetrable "Chinese Wall" within the company is supposed to separate these two kinds of services. Investment analysts and their employer firms, as with the individual auditors and audit firms, should be committed and adhere to independent and objective research and recommendations.

However, there is an enormous amount of pressure for financial results particularly on the sell-side analysts. Issuing firms are interested in being analyzed and presented to the investors in the most favorable way. Investment banks share this interest to some extent because their commission is tied to the profit of issuance. Moreover, the underwriting itself, that is the brokerage process, can be very beneficial to the banks. For instance, when an IPO is underpriced, bought, and quickly resold at a much higher price, tens of millions of dollars can be reaped (see Loughran and Ritter 2004). This clearly conflicts with the interests of the investors who want to buy the equities at a realistic price. In addition, not only investment banks as organizations, but also individual financial analysts face serious conflicts of interest that can be exacerbated by the culture of their employers (for instance: bonus system linked to investment banking revenue; issuing only favorable research in order to capture lucrative investment banking deals; stock ownership of client companies). Thus they have no incentive to remain objective and issue a hold or sell recommendation if this is what the situation warrants.

In sum, financial reporting by investment analysts and their employers is exposed to serious conflicts of interest with far-reaching consequences. It would be short-sighted to expect from individuals and even companies to resist those enormous pressures to produce biased numbers and recommendations. Without a fair and effective regulatory framework in line with the rapid developments of financial markets, the very functioning of these markets is at stake. Confidence in the investment industry is being undermined and can eventually collapse because investors, not willing to be deceived and harmed, will withdraw their assets.

Conclusion: Restoring Confidence in the Financial Reporting System—an Outlook

Since the crisis of confidence has affected the financial reporting system as such, restoring confidence cannot be achieved by individual actions alone, however heroic they might be. In order to fix this highly complex problem, collective efforts, too, are needed because confidence is rightly considered a public good, its absence a "public bad."

In conclusion, I would like to indicate several recommendations. First, *the regulatory framework* needs to be strengthened. Accounting rules should cover all assets and all liabilities and provide clear guidance particularly for revenue recognition, asset valuation, and earnings management. New standards for investment analysis should ensure that the provision of independent and objective research be humanly possible without heroic behavior on the part of the providers. Conflicts of interest between auditing and consulting services of the accounting firms and between investment management and research in the investment banks should be prevented at the regulatory level, not only at the company and individual levels. Moreover, the self-policing system of the accounting industry through the POB needed to be replaced by an independent and powerful body of the SEC, the Public Company Accounting Oversight Board (PCAOB). Also, closer cooperation with international institutions, particularly IASB, is imperative.

Although such a regulatory reform is crucial for restoring confidence in the financial reporting system, it would be naive to believe that new "mechanisms" alone could solve the problem. To follow the spirit, not only the letter, of the rules and to put "substance over form" can only work in conjunction with the moral commitment of the individuals and companies.

Second, *corporate governance and corporate culture* are key factors determining the quality of financial reporting. Only the board of directors has the power to check misconduct by executive management. Directors must be independent, rely on a strong audit committee, and assume personal responsibility for truthful financial reporting. Given the important roles of top executives and the professionals in law, finance, and human resources departments, they should be subject to a meaningful risk analysis and be involved, along with line personnel, in compliance and ethics programs. The culture of the company must reflect its commitment to truthfulness, consistency, transparency, and accountability.

Third, the role of *professional associations*, especially of accountants and investment analysts, should be enhanced in providing professional competence for designing and implementing regulatory standards and in training professionals. Professional ethics should be an essential part of the curriculum.

Fourth, in any work environment *individuals* still have some space of freedom. Normally, they can choose among different courses of action. In any case, they can embrace, keep distance from, or reject the rules and standards set up by the regulatory bodies, their own employers, and professional associations. Therefore, individuals cannot avoid the decision whether or not they want to honor the trust given by their fellow human beings. Without such a moral commitment, confidence in financial reporting is not possible.

Notes

I acknowledge my gratitude to my colleagues Tom Cosimano, Jerry Langley, Tim Loughran, Pat Murphy, Paul Ralser, Frank Reilly, and Norlin Rueschhoff as well as to my MBA students Dixon Braden, Todd Foote, Eileen M. Murphy, and Chris Reeves. An important issue, not addressed in this essay, is the public mandate of the commercial banks (see Cosimano 2004). Of course, I bear full responsibility for my text.

1. Here "moral commitment" is understood in a "modest" sense, namely to live up to the ethical principle of honesty in providing adequate financial statements while being supported by the culture of the employer organization and the regulatory framework. Not requested in this context is "heroic behavior," that is to take a bold ethical stand against a prevailing misleading organizational culture and a deficient regulatory framework.

2. See note 1.

References

Benston, G., M. Bromwich, R. E. Litan, and A. Wagenhofer. 2003. *Following the Money. The Enron Failure and the State of Corporate Disclosure.* Washington, D.C.: AEI-Brookings Joint Center for Regulatory Studies.

Cosimano, T. F. 2004. Financial Institutions and Trustworthy Behavior in Business Transactions. *Journal of Business Ethics,* 52, 179–188.

Enderle, G. 2000. Whose Ethos for Public Goods in a Global Economy? An Exploration in International Business Ethics. *Business Ethics Quarterly,* 10, 131–144.

———. 2003. Business Ethics. In: N. Bunnin and E. P. Tsui-James (eds.), *Blackwell Companion to Philosophy.* Oxford: Blackwell Publishers, 531–551.

———. 2004. The Ethics of Financial Reporting, the Global Reporting Initiative, and the Balanced Concept of the Firm. In: G. G. Brenkert (ed.), *Corporate Integrity and Accountability.* Thousand Oaks: Sage, 87–99.

Hausman, D. M. 2002. Trustworthiness and Self-Interest. In: T. Cosimano, R. Chami, and C. Fullenkamp (eds.), *Managing Ethical Risk: How Investing in Ethics Adds Value. Journal of Banking and Finance,* 26: 9 (2002), 1767–1783.

Loughran, T. and J. Ritter. 2004. Why Has IPO Underpricing Changed Over Time? *Financial Management,* Autumn, 5–37.

CHAPTER 16

Speculation and Insider Trading as a Problem of Business Ethics

Peter Koslowski

The stock exchange is the central institution of mediation between the supply of and demand for capital. What is proper conduct in the capital market, and what does justice in exchange and in pricing mean in the stock exchange? One of the key questions of proper conduct in the capital market is debated heatedly as the problem of insider trading, an issue that receives great attention in the debate about the business ethics of the capital market. The *Zweite Finanzmarktförderungsgesetz* (Second Law on the Improvement of the Financial Market) prohibits insider trading in Germany as of August 1, 1994. In the debate within schools of economics and law, there is, however, no agreement on the question of whether insider trading is detrimental or not.

INSIDER TRADING AS A FOCUS OF THE ETHICAL QUESTIONS OF THE STOCK EXCHANGE

The question of the ethical economy of the capital market and of the admissibility of insider trading is threefold. It is first the question of the institutional ethics and economics of the institution "capital market," which is part of the ethics and economics of the larger cultural sphere and the societal subsystem or concrete order of life "market economy." It is thereby a question of economic law, too. The ethical economy of insider trading is secondly a question of organizational ethics regarding the organizations' policies, culture, and conduct, and thirdly a question of personal ethics, the organizations and individuals working within the rules of the game "stock exchange."

The system of obligations arises from the nature of the matter in three respects. The obligation is derived from the purpose or teleology of the institution, from the idea of justice, and from the prerequisites of legal safety. The purpose of the sphere of culture and law in question, the idea of justice, especially of formal justice in the sense of the principle of equality, and the demands of certainty in the definition of law and in jurisdiction define the obligation of ethics and of law. According to Radbruch, the idea of law arises from the purpose or teleology of the sphere to be ruled, from the principle of formal justice, and from the principle of safe legal procedure (Radbruch 1973, 114).

The Nature and Function of Stock Market Speculation: Bearing Uncertainty

Applied to the question of the ethics and legislation of the capital market, one must judge the problem of insider trading from the criterion of the purpose or teleology of the institution of the capital market, from the criterion of formal justice or equal right of all participants in the capital market, and from the criterion of legal safety and stability.

The teleology or function of the institution of the capital market within the order of the economy is the following. The capital market fulfills two tasks in which it resembles the credit market. Like the latter, the capital market functions as the transfer process, in which savings are transferred into investment, and as the transformation process, in which investment of different terms of time periods are transformed into investments of long-term ownership titles or securities. The transfer of savings and the transformation of time periods are accomplished in the capital market for shares not by the financial intermediaries of banks but by the securitization of the loans, by their marketability in the stock exchange, and by the existence of speculative trading of securities. The function banks fulfill in the credit market is exercised in the stock exchange by other institutions, namely by the control of the issuing of new shares effected by the stock exchange administration or by government, by the marketability of shares and securitized loans, and by professional and amateur speculation about future prices of stock.

Investing in shares in the capital market is—compared to deposits in banks—an investment of higher risk. The stock market serves as the means to allocate investible funds to companies according to price differentials reflecting the expected risk and profit of the companies taking part in the stock exchange as they are seen by the market participants. The prices of shares reflect the assessment of return and risk.

Shareholders are investors bearing as owners the full risk for their invested capital. Given full publicity about the past and present record and the future strategy of the corporation, the price of its shares is formed in the market according to the assessment of the past and present performance and of the future expected return and risk.

In an ideal market, each share would have a fixed market price. Hardly any trading would take place, since the price would be the same for everyone at every period of time. In reality, however, there are huge trading volumes in the existing modern capital markets. According to Friedman, the annual trading volume on the New York Stock Exchange, for example, is normally nearly one half of the total value of listed existing shares (Friedman 1987, 323). Friedman explains this huge trading of shares by the different risk assessments of investors but does not mention the differentials in the intended duration of investment and the contingently changing decisions to disinvest shares. Shares are permanent or at least long-run investment. The ownership title they define remains constant, but their actual owners change in time. The periods of holding shares can be transformed at low transaction costs compared to other ownership patterns. The transformation is made possible by the marketability of shares in the stock exchange. That shares be marketable requires in turn that the supply of a given share find a demand for that same share at any given moment in time, even if the originally intended time periods of investment in this share do not coincide between the buyer and seller. The transformation of different periods of investment is done by trading. The supply and demand for shares, their marketability, are enormously increased by a group that, in the division of labor, professionally trades stock, the group of professional speculators.

Professional speculation creates trading volume by adding supply and demand of shares in the stock exchange that exceed the volume that would exist in the absence of speculation, when investment in shares is effected for returns from permanent investment only. Speculation is that sort of economic activity that tries to gain profit from differentials between present and future prices of stock. The speculator speculating à la hausse ("bull") assumes that the future price of a share will be higher than its present. Speculation à la baisse ("bear") speculates that the price will be lower. The bullish speculator tries to make profit by buying shares today and selling them in the future. His investment decision does not concentrate on the expected return from dividends but on the differential between future and present stock value of the share. The division of labor in the stock market between those concentrating on the returns and capital value of the stock, the investors in the proper sense, and those concentrating on the differentials of fluctuations of stock value in time, the speculators, makes sure that the investment in shares can be liquidated at any given moment of time (Röpke 1926, 708). The speculation in shares increases the marketability of shares and, thereby, the transformability of time periods of capital investment in the stock market. Professional stock market speculation decreases the risk not to be able to transform the periods of investment and disinvestment in shares and thereby renders an important service to the economy.

Speculation bears part of the uncertainty about future random changes of investment periods and increases the investor's independence on the time horizon of the other investors, of their time schedule for their investment or disinvestment in stocks. The profits from speculation are the price that the nonspeculative investors must pay to the speculators for their provision of the additional trading of stocks. Professional speculation—besides having other more problematic aspects—is the intelligent gambling for profit that produces the side effect that the trading of stock is increased and the transformation of investment periods facilitated. Speculation on the spot market for stocks resembles the speculation in futures in its effect on the increase in the trading of stock.

The speculation in the forward market for commodities, currency, or stock enables the hedging of prices for those commodities and stocks whose producers or investors do not want to speculate but to calculate with predictable prices for future goods. Speculation in futures serves as an insurance on future prices for the nonspeculators. In the same manner, the increase in trading by speculation in stocks in the spot market is an insurance for those who want to be free in their decisions about the time period of their investment in shares. The spot market speculation in stock assures the nonspeculative investors that they will be able to find demand for their shares whenever they want to disinvest them. In the forward market, the division of labor between the speculating and the hedging market participants stems from the fact that some people must speculate so that others can calculate with ascertained or certain future prices. In the spot market for stocks, the effect of speculation is not the complete insurance of future prices but the assurance that the time periods of investment in stocks will be transformable in the future by selling or buying in the stock market.

The assurance of time transformability of shares through speculation in the stock market is economically advantageous only if speculation is not interested in price fluctuations of stock and, therefore, does not increase in the fluctuations of stock prices over time.

Speculation is most profitable when its price anticipations are correct and when it acts contracyclically under negative elasticity of demand for stock on market expectations. It is not very profitable when it follows the market expectations with positive elasticity, and it is not profitable at all when it is wrong in its prediction about future prices. There is, therefore, a built-in tendency in speculation, brought in by the profit motive, to anticipate future price-changes of stock correctly, and there is a motive to speculate in such a way that stock market fluctuations are suppressed by the higher profitability of contracyclical speculation.

The thesis that speculation in the spot market for stocks absorbs uncertainty about future transformability of periods of investment contends that it is the function of speculation in the stock market to reduce an uncertainty of the market participants that cannot be made up for by other means. The risk of return and bankruptcy can be calculated approximately by the market, the uncertainty about future periods for which investors want to hold their investment cannot be calculated by means of the calculus of probability. It can only be speculated about it.

That the contribution to the common good by reducing uncertainty justifies professional speculation means in turn that speculation which does not reduce an otherwise, that is, by other means than speculation, irreducible uncertainty is not economically and ethically justifiable. Speculation is justified as the absorption of uncertainty, where there is no other way to handle it. Where uncertainty can be reduced by less costly means than speculation, this means should be used. Where speculation does not really reduce uncertainty, it is not justified.

Insider Trading as Pseudo-Speculation and Agiotage

In the case of insider trading in the stock exchange there is no real uncertainty, since the facts of the insider information are already known uncertainty can be reduced by less costly means, that is, by the publication of the insider information to the public. The insider produces no real good and renders no service to the stock market participants that could not be produced by the simple publication of the insider fact by the corporation affected. The insiders' speculation is a sort of pseudo-speculation, since the speculating insider does not bear uncertainty but a pseudo-uncertainty about the facts of his insider information. The insider still bears some risk—the takeover could fail to take place in the end although the insider was told so, the effects of the journalist's recommendation for a share could be less strong than he or she anticipated, and so on. The insider's risk is, however, much lower than that of the other speculators acting in the same market.

Profits from professional speculation are the remuneration for the productive effect of absorbing uncertainty. Where the speculator's effort is not productive, since he or she bears only pseudo-uncertainty, it does not carry the legitimization to earn profit. The insider speculator absorbing only pseudo-uncertainty is not entitled to the profit arising from his or her insider trading. Analogous to gambling, the speculator plays with marked cards by reducing the element of chance and uncertainty inherent in speculation only for himself and not for all players. The inside speculator is playing the game with less uncertainty than his or her co-speculators, and the profit he or she derives from playing the game with marked cards does not correspond to his or her economic performance and productive contribution.

Arbitrage, Speculation, Agiotage

The productive result of insider trading speculation is neither arbitrage nor true speculation but agiotage. Arbitrage is the productive effort to earn profit from equilibrating price differences in space. The arbitrageur makes profit by lowering the price differential between different places at the same time. When the level of the interest rates for credits is low in Tokyo and high in Rome at the same date, it is profitable arbitrage to borrow money at low interest in Tokyo and to lend it at high interest rate in Rome. The arbitrageur reduces the differential between the prices at different places and equilibrates price levels between two places by removing an oversupply in one trading place and reducing a shortage—in our case a shortage of credit—in the other. Arbitrage creates welfare effects by equilibrating prices between different markets at one moment of time; speculation is the equilibration of prices at the same market place between different moments of time. Speculation is, so to say, arbitrage between points of time, not between points of space. Both arbitrage and speculation render the service of equilibrating prices to the economy.

From arbitrage and speculation, agiotage must be distinguished. Agiotage designates the activity of making profit by raising a mere surcharge (*agio*) on a given good or service without adding value to it. The price difference between the shares bought and the shares sold is just the surcharge or agio levered by the agiotageur. The insider is an agiotageur who, although he or she buys at time t and sells at time $t + 1$, adds no value to the goods traded, that is, shares, since the information on which he or she bases the profit was already there at time "t." The distinction between arbitrage in space and arbitrage in time or speculation as value-adding economic activities on the one hand, and agiotage as surcharging without value creation on the other, permits us to classify insider trading as mere agiotage and to distinguish it from the other value-adding activities in the stock exchange, that is, as arbitrage and speculation over time.

Insider Trading and the Fiduciary Relationship

Insider speculation as mere agiotage, like reselling the same good without ameliorating it and without rendering a productive contribution to the community by the reselling, violates the nature of the matter of speculative trading. This holds true even in circumstances in which the insider trading is useful to a third party. Take the case of a firm that plans a takeover. The management or one of the shareholders can tip an insider trader to buy stock of the company to be taken over in the near future. The insider will earn an extra profit from this tip, the tipping company can stretch the buying out of the stock over a longer time period and probably acquire the stock at a lower price. Thus, the tippee or insider trader is informed by the tipper, the firm, in the firm's own interest and is induced to buy stock at the insider's profit. The insider trader renders some service to the economy, namely to the firm that plans the takeover. This service, however, could also be achieved when the acquiring firm buys the stock itself or an agent buys it on its behalf under a contract of acting on behalf of the firm. The firm planning a takeover need not use the means of tipping an insider trader and, thereby, using an ethically questionable means for an end that can be reached by ethically and legally admissible means. The existence of cases where insider trading is in the interest of a third party, the tipping manager or shareholder, does not refute the thesis that insider trading is mere agiotage and not productive speculation. The tipping company has the knowledge on which the insider trading is effected and could spread it or, if this damaged its business, can withhold it and act for itself by buying out the stock over time itself.

The example of insider trading by an insider buying stock for his private account in the interest of a third party demonstrates that insider trading cannot be judged unethical on the grounds only that it breaks a fiduciary duty (Moore 1990). In many cases, it does so and is then unethical on the grounds that it is an offence against the fiduciary duties. In quite a few cases, it is, however, the very person that constituted the fiduciary relationship who proliferates the insider information to another who trades in his private interest. The arguments in favor of insider trading claiming that insider trading improves the allocative function of the market by distributing information about stocks are based on the fact that insider trading is not only in the interest of the insider trader or agent, but also can be in the interest of the principal.

Again, neither the advantage of the inside trader nor the advantage of the principal nor some small allocative effect of the insider trading on the price formation in the stock market can be a justification for insider trading when its unethical character is due to the violation of the nature of the matter of speculation in the stock market, when it does not serve to reduce uncertainty.

Insider Trading as Perverse Incentive

The conditions under which speculation in the stock market is productive and conducive to the common good by bearing uncertainty are not only violated by the detrimental effects of insider trading when it occurs; rather, the detrimental effects are intensified through perverse incentives that are furthered by legally allowing insider trading. The intermediaries in the financial markets have strong incentives to invest in the search for insider trading opportunities, if insider trading is allowed. Instead of searching for the correct anticipation of the future in speculation, they will look for insider information about a future that is not really future but already present. They will be negligent in doing proper speculation and distract their attention to insider investment opportunities.

Since the insider investment opportunities are augmented by random price fluctuations and high amplitudes of these fluctuations, the incentives of insider trading further induce the financial intermediaries to support price fluctuations instead of suppressing them. Additional „perverse" incentives to increase, instead of decrease, uncertainty for the other market participants are thus created by the legal admittance of insider trading.

Insider Trading and the Duty to Ad hoc—Publicity

Insider information is unproductive information since its general availability is hindered only by intentionally holding it back from the market. The use of the insider information does not have an advantageous effect on the economy since it is not arbitraging between places or speculating between time periods.

Where trading is only agiotage or making surplus but not arbitrage or speculation, the buyer or seller is not entitled to hold back his information and to derive profit from his knowledge about future price changes. Since the insider has not invested in productive but in unproductive knowledge, he or she is not entitled to a profit derived from the lead in knowledge that has been unjustly acquired over the competitor or is of unproductive character.

Detrimental Effects of Insider Trading on Allocation, Distribution, and Stability

Insider trading reallocates resources from speculation to pseudo-speculation, from spreading knowledge to withholding it. There might be a minor effect of spreading knowledge to the stock exchange by the stock purchases of insider traders and some beneficial effect in the temporal extension of stock purchases in case of takeovers supported by insider traders. These beneficial allocative effects are, however, far outweighed by the misallocation of resources in the search for unproductive insider information, by the perverse incentives of insider trading to increase price fluctuations and to destabilize the stock market, and by the problematic distribution pattern resulting from insider-trading gains.

The perverse incentives of insider trading lead to questionable insider investments and profits. The problematic insider capital gains, their short-termism and so on, result in a socially destabilizing and economically and ethically questionable distribution of income. The concern of the public about the income distribution derived from insider gains cannot be simply dismissed as envy. Not so much the resulting distribution as the repercussions of it on the incentive structure and the allocation of productive effort in the financial markets should be the concern. Since allocation and distribution cannot be separated, huge profits from insider trading direct resources to their use in insider trading. All three economic criteria, allocation, distribution, and stability, require the suppression of insider trading. The arguments from allocative efficiency, from distributional justice, and from economic stability of the capital market coincide in the judgment derived from the nature of the matter, from the nature of the capital market, that the participants in the capital market have the duty to engage in productive investment and uncertainty bearing and not in the pseudo-speculation of insider trading.

Sixty-five years ago, Nell-Breuning asked the question of whether the stock exchange needs speculation in shares or whether it could work without it (Nell-Breuning 1928, 54). The analysis of insider trading demonstrates that the stock market can work without pseudo-speculation but that speculation plays an indispensable role in bearing irreducible uncertainty. One can conclude that the nature and function of speculation in the stock exchange requires the strict suppression of the pseudo-speculation of insider trading, of bearing bogus uncertainty. The principle of equal justice in the legitimization of norms demands the equal right of access to information for all shareholders and speculators and therefore rules out that management or single shareholders give insider tips to third parties. Finally, the principles of economic and legal safety and stability require that insider trading be prohibited because of its perverse incentives effects. The price fluctuations in the stock market must not be augmented by forms of speculation that are not justified by the function of the capital market to bear and transform risk and uncertainty.

BIBLIOGRAPHY

Friedman, B. M. 1987. Capital, Credit and Money Markets. Vol. 1. In: *The New Palgrave. A Dictionary of Economics*. London: Macmillan, 320–327.

Koslowski, P. 1982. *Ethik des Kapitalismus*. With a Comment by James M. Buchanan. Tübingen: Mohr Siebeck. First edition 1982, sixth edition 1998. English version in: Koslowski, P. 1996. *Ethics of Capitalism and Critique of Sociobiology*. Two Essays with a Comment by James M. Buchanan. Berlin: Springer (Studies in Economic Ethics and Philosophy, Vol. 10). Chinese version: *Zi ben zhu yi lu li xue*. Translated by Y. Wang. Beijing: China Social Sciences Press.

———. 1988. *Prinzipien der Ethischen Ökonomie*. Reprint 1994. Tübingen: Mohr Siebeck. Chinese version in 1997: *Jing ji lun li yuan ze*. Translated by Yu Sun. Beijing: China Social Sciences Press. English version in 2001: *Principles of Ethical Economy*. Dordrecht: Kluwer.

———. 1997. *Ethik der Banken und der Börse* (The Ethics of Banking and the Stock Exchange). Tübingen: Mohr Siebeck.

Moore, J. 1990. What is Really Unethical about Insider Trading? *Journal of Business Ethics*, 9, 171–182.

Radbruch, G. 1973. *Rechtsphilosophie* (Philosophy of Law). Stuttgart: Koehler, 8.

Röpke, W. 1926. Spekulation. In: *Handwörterbuch der Staatswissenschaften*. Fourth edition. Vol. 7. Jena: Gustav Fischer, 706–710.

von Nell-Breuning, Oswald. 1928. Volkswirtschaftlicher Wert und Unwert der Börsenspekulation (Economic Value and Nonvalue of Stock Exchange Speculation), *Stimmen der Zeit*, 114, 46–56.

CHAPTER 17

The Problems of Declining Birth Rate and Aging in the Japanese Welfare State and Its Implications for Business and Economic Ethics

Koichi Matsuoka

CHANGING PATTERN OF ECONOMIC DEVELOPMENT: JAPAN'S EXPERIENCES IN THE LATE TWENTIETH CENTURY

Economic development produces positive values and, at the same time, causes negative effects. This pattern in the Japanese society is characterized by two dominant trends: (1) the declining birth rate as the result of an increasing number of young people who do not want to get married or who postpone marriage (EPA 1992, 23; EPA 1994, 12); and (2) the increasing numbers of aged people in the total population as a result of the rising level of income and medical care (EPA 1994, 13).

Today the Japanese society has reached a matured stage. When, in the 1970s, Japan faced an economic crisis created by OPEC, rising energy costs compelled her to create a high technology industrial structure to produce "light, thin, short, and small" products (Sawa 1993, 6). As a result, the percentage of added value produced by service, information, and software industries became much bigger than that produced by industries manufacturing material goods (ibid., 11).

In the 1990s, however, the Japanese economy was seriously disturbed by the collapse of the so-called bubble economy. It heavily affected the high technology industries, which were the core of the manufacturing industry. Asset deflation, which means a sharp decline of the value of assets, dramatically reduced the level of people's consumption (EPA 1999, 123; EPA 2000, 193) and therefore disrupted their lives in general. Due to such a rapid transformation of the economy, consumers shifted their habits away from mass consumption and waste toward saving resources and taking care of the global environment. They now tend to control mass consumption guided by the principle of thrift.

Over the last 30 years, the Japanese economy has steadily continued to transform, going through the following three stages: In the 1970s, Japan pursued the goal of establishing a big welfare state with big government that put priority on fairness while neglecting efficiency. In the 1980s, in accordance with Reaganomics and Thatcherism, she aimed at becoming a big economic power with a lean government. In the 1990s, she tried to abandon the goal of a welfare state with a high level of consumption and the belief in gross national product (GNP) (Sawa 1993, 11–19).

Economic Development and Declining Birth Rate

Since the mid-1970s, the maturing society in Japan has constantly shown a declining birth rate. In 1999, the rate was 1.34 children per couple, which means that the simple replacement of the population is impossible. A similar sharp decline can be found, more or less, in all advanced countries. However, particularly in Japan, it causes many difficult problems. Although the decreasing rate is expected to move toward a more balanced level, it is important to introduce some suitable policies to support young couples who wish to have children.

In Japan the declining birth rate is a result of women choosing higher education, the rising rate of obtaining nondomestic jobs, the increasing number of non-married women, and the delay in starting reproduction. Because of "equal opportunity" to participate in all activities, women's employment will naturally increase (EPA 1994, 55; JCO 2001, 7–9). But both work and care of children should be maintained. Therefore, the following policies are being promoted:

- Multiple opportunities of employment suitable for women.
- A system that allows employees to leave work for child care.
- A supporting system that allows women to return to work after giving birth.

- Externalizing domestic work in order to free housewives.
- Creating satellite offices to bring work places closer to home.
- Promoting work at home (JCO 2001, 288).

As Japan produces fewer and fewer children, the remaining children are now being brought up in the atmosphere of excessive indulgence. They do not learn how to control themselves, often causing bullying and violence to each other in classrooms as well as outside of school. Conversely, because of the declining ability to educate children in family and neighborhood communities, the isolation of children from relatives, communities, and friends, and uncertainty of an income that is only based upon the work of the husband, parents often illtreat their children.

The Advanced Welfare State and the Problem of Aging

Aging is a natural result of people's efforts and government's economic policies to attain a more affluent life. In Europe, where a high economic standard of life has been reached, countries have been facing the problems of an aging society. Developing societies like China will enter into a similar situation. The population explosion in the world may be resolved along with economic development because higher education of the younger generation tends to decrease the number of children.

In the stage of old age, many problems arise simultaneously: retirement from work; worsening health conditions; and being bereaved of a spouse (EPA 1994, 57). It is therefore essential to assuage the older generation's worries; and even for the younger generation, it is increasingly important to develop a lifestyle that will be conducive to living for a long period of time in the aging stage.

Human destiny can be shaped by the intersection of negative and positive images. The aged life may often carry negative images of a decaying mind and body, illness, bedridden life, dementia, scarce income, isolation, and so on. But, life after retirement can also be seen as a period to regain the energy, to enjoy less mental pressure, and to open a new life. These are sources of positive images. Only a small number of people tend to see the aged stage with the negative images of being left behind the times or losing the opportunity of self-actualization. One may hope people make life plans, according to which they can enjoy the aged life positively.

However, aged Japanese of both genders are reported to invest most of their leisure time in domestic sightseeing, gardening, and eating out. As happens in Western countries, after retirement, people tend to lose their drive and not utilize the opportunity for a new life. Without a doubt, aged people are actually inclined to lose energy and ambition. They tend to avoid working and making an effort in the final years of life. Japanese men, who have usually devoted all their working years to their work places, tend to feel isolated in retirement because they have not established connections in their neighborhood community. Women, on the contrary, have often built human relations in the community, which is especially possible for housewives.

In Japan, the process of industrial development, because of the isolating conditions of industrialization, has destroyed intimate human relations in the neighborhood community and in family life. People only devote themselves to human relations at work. Of course, the industrialization and marketization of society have had positive consequences as well. But undeniably they have produced negative effects such as human isolation. Japan was able to create prosperity, but this prosperity failed to satisfy all the needs of the people. How can this trend be reversed?

Here, we should discuss the role of the family. The declining number of children and the fostered tendency of aging have seriously destroyed the traditional system of family, which had been composed of aged parents and a young couple. Such a traditional type of family has been transforming into a family composed of a single generation and its children as economic development tends to spread cultural change over the whole society. Not surprisingly, the decreasing number of family members changes the functions of the family including the traditional caring system of the aged parents.

Since 1980s, the "hotelization" (see website in references) of the home and the individualization of the family have progressively been fostered in Japan. In the field of consumption, so-called McDonaldization (see website in references) has become dominant, meaning that people increasingly go to "fast" food shops catering homogeneous food like hamburgers. Moreover, people especially of the young generation economize, and thus replace their family life, by shopping in "convenience stores." One significant effect of the globalizing market is the ensuing homogeneity of consumption life.

In rural areas, many young people have abandoned their villages, leaving their aged parents to a lonely life. Economic development inevitably produces depopulation in the countryside and overcrowded societies with homeless people in the cities.

The biggest factors causing uneasiness to aged people are illness and living costs, including medical costs, bodily troubles being especially onerous. Aged people increasingly seek employment to supplement their income. But it is not an easy task to supply varied opportunities to work in which aged people can hope to maintain their familiar current or similar jobs. They seek work that does not require heavy responsibility and prefer jobs in which they can practice their hobbies and use their knowledge. Thus they do not want to look for new jobs, but want to get work in which they have some experience. Aged people cover their livelihood with public pensions and earnings of their work, but also need private pensions and savings.

The care for aged people demands several policies (EPA 1994, 152):

1. Continuation of normal life: aged people enjoy their lives in the same environment as normal people do.
2. Respect for the personalities of aged people.
3. Self-determination: aged people want to be cared for according to their own will.
4. Vitalization: aged people do not want to be left alone, but thrive when stimuli for various activities is provided.

Such policies require the services of home helpers and visiting nurses, which should be supported by public budgets and, because of their restrictions, also by private market-based organizations.

SOCIAL CHANGES CAUSED BY THE INFORMATION REVOLUTION: TOWARD A KNOWLEDGE SOCIETY

In order to cope with the problems of declining birth rates and aging one should consider the advantages of the information revolution. In the twentieth century the industrial society developed toward a uniform system of mass production and consumption and is gaining a multidimensional knowledge across industries in the twenty-first century. Companies have become knowledge organizations, which has transformed a producer-centered society into a citizen-centered society. Therefore, the Japanese industrial society should remodel itself toward a new diversified and decentralized system. For example, the employment system with its three traditional characteristics of life long employment, seniority system, and in-house trade unions is now changing toward more flexibility. Without "*keiretsu*" (i.e., a business group of closely interrelated companies of different industries), the work style is becoming open through the information network

(Kumon 1995, 346). Workers begin to move from company to company as free persons.

In the knowledge society, there are "netizens," that is, citizens who mutually communicate through the Internet (Kumon 1994, 84, 210, 213; EPA 1995b, 5; Kizaa 2001, 287; Etzioni 2001, 506). They can exchange information and do research on the Internet. For example, they can experience electronic shopping, electronic libraries, electronic services of public administrations, and VOD (video on demand). In this way, new communication patterns have been so widely created that traditional communities with their local autonomy are facing a new frontier. In Japan, a new wave of restructuring the local autonomy system is developing (System 1999, 14).

The information revolution is producing positive changes in many fields (EPA 1995b, 6): expanding the spaces of activities for the aged and handicapped people; providing better communication with people in society through e-mail; opening up new frontiers for medical care through electronic ways of diagnosis and treatment; meeting individualized educational needs and developing multiple educational systems beyond the traditional uniform school system; communicating outside the family with members of the local community through mobile phones (which, though, may destroy intimate family conversations). As a result of these information networks, various types of communities are now emerging.

An important factor for the creation of a new society is the public sector when it uses the information revolution for public communication. Close communication between public administrators and citizens can foster transactions across areas of life and generations, which can generate new local community systems. In this respect, there is no gap between developed and developing countries. Leaders can be found, for example, in Japan, China, Singapore, and the United States (Etzioni 2001, 458; System 1999, 19–22).

On the one hand, the information revolution makes people's lives affluent. On the other hand, people face excessive and rapid transformations in many areas of life. They have to cope with drastic changes in the economy, their employment situation, and new technology, which causes the so-called digital divide between people over 50 years of age and the younger generations (JCO 2002, 131–132).

It should be honestly reported that several phenomena of deterioration in Japan's society are found in noneconomic areas of life as well. The quality of school education in particular is declining. Cramming with information, school refusal, bullying, disorders in the classroom, and the leveling down of academic achievement are quite common all over Japan. Therefore, calls for teaching young people autonomy, self-responsibility, and creativity can be heard throughout the community. Moreover, Japanese people are facing a moral crises. People's desire to pursue an affluent life and grab "more and more" undermines their moral lives. Crimes are committed not only by "children," but also by business persons with higher education.

The trends of a decreasing and aging population and the information revolution have put the Japanese economy and society in a turbulent situation, which is completely new in Japan's history. This experience is also radically new for all developed and many developing countries because they all have followed this path of increasing numbers and quantities in every area of life. China too will face the same situation in the near future. Since no comprehensive answers to these problems exist, one has to learn by trial and error.

Changing Business and Economic Ethics and Human Involvement of People

In conclusion, it seems necessary to pay attention to ethical problems in the transformation mentioned earlier. The maturity of Japan's national economy with the declining birth rate and the increasing ratio of aged people leads to changes of business and economic ethics in various dimensions. As ethics sets the guidelines for goodness and competitiveness of economic behavior, it inevitably fluctuates, due to the transformation of the national economy. So, generally speaking, ethics is being transformed toward a system of "market-oriented" ethics.

This reform of ethics comes with the maturity of the Japanese economy, signaling the turning point of mass production and mass marketing of commodities that had generated rapid economic growth up to the 1980s. Currently Japan is suffering from the hardship of "global deflation," that is the lowering of the general price level caused by rapid economic development in China and Southeast Asian countries, the decreasing costs arising from the global information revolution, and the global over-supply of goods and services. In such a situation every corporation is strongly motivated to explore technological innovation not only of production, but also of marketing. Consequently, the traditional system of business and economic ethics needs to change itself in many important areas. Although the Japanese economy remains characterized by a traditionally high level of innovation not affected by global deflation, the so-called *Keiretsu*-oriented way of doing business among corporations has recently become unstable and been abolished. Now the companies try to increase the speed and efficiency of transactions and expand globally.

However, ethical problems related to the integrity of information have occurred quite often. For example, many companies are not honest enough to provide accurate information about the kind and quality of commodities they deal with. They tend to violate accounting laws and hide information that should be disclosed in order to enable "informed consent" in economic transactions. All these ethical requirements are subsumed under the ethics of "compliance," which is increasingly asked from companies to follow the rules of the market economy.

Along with such trends, the declining birth rate and the rapid pace of aging are inevitably generating additional changes in traditional corporate ethics, especially with regard to human resource management. Historically, three main pillars of corporate ethics enhanced the power of Japanese companies: (1) lifelong employment; (2) the promotion system according to the duration of employment; and (3) labor unions restricted to individual companies. However, the decreasing number of young workers reversed the age structure of the labor market toward a small portion of young workers and a big portion of older workers. Global competition forces companies to lay off workers, and consequently workers move from company to company. These trends undermine the traditional promotion and reward system based on the duration of employment. Workers are now increasingly rewarded according to their abilities. Along with this, fostering workers' mobility across companies weakens the traditional role of trade unions in individual companies to support workers' rights. Because the loyalty of workers to their companies is decreasing, companies need to create a new ethical system to motivate ordinary workers. Traditionally, the workers in a company had a sense of belonging to the same community where a notion of mutual help instead of crude competition existed, which was called "corporate groupism." But now a strong sense of individualism prevails among workers in Japanese companies. It makes work ethics, in an individualistic sense, more liberal and cosmopolitan, which is suitable for global market competition.

In addition, such a trend of workers' individualization corresponds to the ethics of restructuring national welfare policy in order to establish the public pension system by deregulation and lean governments at both the national and local levels. Ethics does not only concern the efficiency of economic activities but also welfare and other aspects. Nevertheless, the ethical transformation now taking place in Japan is nothing but a move toward market ethics. Japanese people and business leaders earnestly call for the urgent implementation of market ethics based upon individual freedom. This can be regarded as an inevitable way, at this developmental stage of Japan's economy, to approach an economy with a human face. In order to reach such a final goal, it is necessary to establish the ethics of a human economy in which the potential power of human beings is used in human ways.

As a consequence, all human beings should be trained in the following three skills (The Institute of Moralogy 2001, 107–108): work skills, human relation skills, and management skills. These skills should be based upon basic mental power, the consciousness of autonomy, self-discipline, flexible and general culture, information skills, foreign languages, and cross-cultural adaptability. These requirements contain several historically new and radical tasks for Japanese people, their economy, and society. For instance, information skills and international languages are rather new in their everyday life. In order to expand their business and communication in Asia, Japanese will need to learn the Chinese language in addition to English as the first international language.

It is fortunate to find guidance from classical wisdom that provides great energy:

Realize oneself, know others, and respond to changing situations.
Try to engage human beings of all generations in human ways.
We start from a similar character, but reach different goals through education. (Uno 2001, 523)

Bibliography

Economic Planning Agency (EPA). 1992. *White Paper of National Life in Heisei 4.* Tokyo: Japanese Government.

———. 1993 *White Paper of National Life in Heisei 5.* Tokyo: Japanese Government.

———. 1994. *White Paper of National Life in Heisei 6.* Tokyo: Japanese Government.

———. 1995a. *White Paper of National Life in Heisei 7.* Tokyo: Japanese Government.

———. 1995b. *Development of Multi-Media and National Life.* Tokyo: Japanese Government.

———. 1996. *White Paper of National Life in Heisei 8.* Tokyo: Japanese Government.

———. 1997. *White Paper of National Life in Heisei 9.* Tokyo: Japanese Government.

Economic Planning Agency (EPA). 1998. *White Paper of National Life in Heisei 10*. Tokyo: Japanese Government.

———. 1999. *White Paper of National Life in Heisei 11*. Tokyo: Japanese Government.

———. 2000. *White Paper of National Life in Heisei 12*. Tokyo: Japanese Government.

Ekins, P. (ed.) 1990. *The Living Economy*. Translated by Shigeki Maruyama et al. Tokyo: Ochanomizu Shobo.

Etzioni, A. 2001. *The New Golden Rule*. Translated and compiled by Y. Nagayasu. Kashiwa-shi, Chiba-ken: Reitaku University Publishing Company.

Furuta, Takahiko and The Seibu Department Stores (eds.) 1993. *The Shock of Decreasing Population*. Tokyo: PHP.

Galbraith, J. K. 1996. *The Good Society*. Houghton Mifflin.

Hotelization. See: http://homepage2.nifty.com/t-tamai/kichokouen%20o%20kiite.html

Japanese Cabinet Office (JCO). 2002. *White Paper of Aging Society in Heisei 13*. See: http://www.fri.fujitsu.com/hypertext/fri/cyber/hotkey/did/did.html. And: http://www.asahi-net.or.jp/cn2k-oosg/ddividel.html

Japanese Cabinet Office (JCO). 2001. *FY 2000 Annual Report on the State of the Formation of a Gender Equal Society*. And: *Policies to Be Implemented in FY 2001 to Promote the Formation of a Gender Equal Society*. Tokyo: Japanese Government. See: http://www.gender.go.jp/e-vaw/index.htm

Kanamori Hisao, Shimada Haruo and Ibe Hideo (eds.) 1992. *Economic Policy for an Aging Society*. Tokyo: University of Tokyo Press.

Kizaa, Joseph M. 2001. *IT Society and Information Ethics*. Translated and compiled by M. Ohno and Y. Nagayasu. Tokyo: Nihon Keizai Hyoron Sha.

Kumon, Shumpei. 1994. *Information Revolution of America*. Tokyo: NEC Creative.

Kumon, Shumpei. 1995. *Informational Civilization*. Tokyo: NTT.

McDonaldization. See: http://geocities.co.jp/CollegeLife-Club/8202/book.html

Okuma, Nobuyuki. 1975. *The Theory of Life Reproduction*. Tokyo: Toyo Keizai Shinpo Sha.

Prime Minister's Office. 1998. *The Present Status of Gender Equality and Measures*. Tokyo: Japanese Government. See: http://www.gender. go.jp/english-contents/plan2000/1998/index.html

———. 1999. *The Present Status of Gender Equality and Measures*. Tokyo: Japanese Government. See: http://www.gender.go.jp/english-contents/plan2000/1999/index.html

———. 2000. *FY 1999 Annual Report on the State of the Formation of a Gender Equal Society*. And: *Policies to Be Implemented in FY 2000 to Promote the Formation of a Gender Equal Society*. Japanese Government. See: http://www.gender.go.jp/english-contents/plan2000/ 2000/ index.html

Sawa, Takamitsu. 1993. *Economic Ethics of a Maturing Society*. Tokyo: Iwanami Shoten.

Sawa, Takamitsu. 1997. *Challenges to Japan.* Tokyo: Nihon Keizai Shinbun Sha.

Stiglitz, J. E. 2002. *Globalization and Its Discontents.* Translated by Chikara Suzuki. Tokyo: Tokuma Shoten.

System Community's PFI Project. 1999. *Local Community and Information Systems.* Tokyo: Patent Sha.

Takemura, Shinichi. 1998. *Sensitive Network.* Tokyo: Iwanami Shoten.

The Communitarian Network. See: http://www.gwu.edu/ccps/

The Institute of Moralogy. 2001. *Management Theory Towards Triad Goodness.* Kashiwa-shi, Chiba-ken: Hiroike Gakuen Publishing Section.

Uno, Tetsuto. 2001. *New Interpretation of Analects of Confucius.* Tokyo: Koudansha Gakujutsu Bunko.

Yashiro, Naohiro. 1999. *Economics of Decreasing Children and Aging.* Tokyo: Toyo Keizai Shinpo Sha.

PART III

Perspectives of Corporate Ethics

"Moral Reticence": Corporate Management's Tendency to Avoid Addressing Ethical Issues

Lanfen Li

MORAL RETICENCE: A PROBLEM NOT TO BE IGNORED

Corporate morality is the rationale for the practice of enterprise management. Corporations encounter critical questions when they begin operations: How should the corporation behave and which types of actions should be adopted? Corporate morality is a principle and standard for behavior that directly takes corporate practice as its goal and functions by providing both limitations and incentives. Only an enterprise that understands how and why a particular thing should be done, can be considered a self-conscious enterprise. This type of enterprise, by clearly understanding its position amongst different social relations, obligations, and management choices, can effectively achieve its future development objectives. In other words, corporate morality is the behavior necessary for the enterprise's survival and growth and to maintain its relationships with social relations and the public order itself. It also functions as a kind of self-reflection, sensibility, evaluation, and action in regards to the social responsibility it has committed to and is obligated to carry out.

Corporate morality is the structural linchpin linking together business performance and ethical relations. Within the company, it builds a type of shared value system, shaping a cohesive workforce. In addition, it helps to create a type of corporate image and one-of-a-kind corporate philosophy for those outside the company. However, many revealed facts indicate, to the contrary, that within corporate management, there exists a large degree of immoral activities, including deferred payments on expenditures, loans, and taxes (76.2 percent), breach of contract (63.2 percent), manufacturing and sales of fake commodities (42.4 percent), in addition to information falsification, quality and price misrepresentation, and trademark and intellectual property infringements (*China Youth* 2002). Surprisingly, even some enterprises that are dedicated to public welfare or charitable projects cannot refrain from falsifying their accounting ledgers and not reporting bad debt. Such phenomena greatly interfere with the development of enterprises and create an even greater disruption to public order, impacting the quality of people's lives. An even more unbearable fact is that a number of business leaders and corporate managers simply ignore or evade public censure and consumer criticism.

We identify moral reticence, whether in attitude or behavior, as a modern problem in enterprise management. Moral reticence can appear as a lack of direct discussion and engagement with the issue of morality, or it could be an evasion of morality, tacit conformity to immorality, or an abandoning of moral responsibility. Accordingly, the moral reticence within corporate management can be comprehended as the enterprise's disinterested posture regarding fulfilling its obligations and social responsibilities. This attitude is revealed when managers or supervisors reveal within their behavior or management style a lack of understanding and recognition of ethical issues, or when they fail to respond to or simply dodge the calls for social responsibility from the public. Moral reticence is also represented as a lack of self-awareness and sense of conscience regarding moral action within day-to-day business operations.

Considering the numerous choices regarding management positions on corporate values, the posture of moral reticence within corporate management can also take on many different forms. One such form is the clamorous refutation of the need for morality by those who hold that the enterprise's growth is all that counts. For example, providing quality-certified products to customers is a fundamental work ethic and ideal of professional morality for corporate management. However, some managers, possibly upon learning about product flaws, intentionally cover up or are unwilling to promptly reveal relevant information to the public (such as the recent incidents involving Panasonic notebook computers, Mitsubishi all-terrain vehicles, and many Chinese flu medicine containing PPA [Phenylpropanolamine]). There are also enterprises that hold an attitude of "moral evasion," in which it is believed that the behavior of enterprises is neutral and hence can only be judged by factual evaluations and non-value judgments. For example, some enterprises borrow legal "camouflage" or methods to encroach upon certain public shared knowledge and traditional values. When the enterprise's fundamental interests are not directly impacted, they usually don't heed negative public opinion (such as one American genetic engineering company that in the face of nationalist protests in Thailand stole the already registered DNA mapping of Thailand's jasmine rice).

Some enterprises hold morality in high esteem, and they recognize the fact that the behavior of enterprises should not turn away from morality and must bear certain social responsibilities. However, they hold reservations in regards to enforcing other enterprises to fulfill their social obligations. The management of enterprises may hold an attitude of "disinclination" out of a concern that "the efforts to fully respond to the public's requests may lead to unprofitable and endless debates with those who can never be satisfied" (Pratley 1999, 114). For example, now some enterprises have introduced Total Quality Management (TQM). However, in order to raise the public's awareness of the enterprise, the management may be more inclined to use an objective (i.e., nonmoral) certification process, such as ISO-9000 quality management standard as a selling point while passing over the ability of TQM to uphold moral standards. Therefore, "they lack power to appropriately use moral language to solve the necessary issues of responsibility for product circulation and environmental protection" (ibid., 114). Pratley outlines the posture by management of "moral reticence" as follows:

1. producing moral amnesia;
2. holding a narrow understanding of the concept of morality: management avoids discussing the issue of morality, viewing the issues as nonmoral ones having to do with daily management operations;
3. applies pressure on the management level: the inability to more openly articulate moral aspirations will in the end bounce back and affect the managers (i.e., the lack of discussion on morality will aggravate moral pressure);
4. neglect of moral abuse: resistance to certain standards can lead to moral reticence and vice versa, thereby producing a type of culture of moral neglect;
5. decline of moral standards: the sustained existence of moral reticence within the management of quality can mock those who are responsible for maintaining moral standards because moral standards are often viewed as intervening from outside.

Enterprises, the Public, and Society: Three Factors Leading to Moral Reticence in Enterprise Management

A theoretical study of moral reticence in enterprise management can only be achieved by identifying reasonable explanations for its main causes.

Self-Centeredness and Rationality: The Inner Factor

As an economic institution, any enterprise that wants to subsist and develop invariably attaches the greatest importance to maximizing its profits or interests. This inevitably leads to the widespread adoption by managers of the dual principles of self-centeredness and rationality. We may safely say that it is self-centeredness that leads enterprise man-agers to place their enterprise's prosperity and development as the top priority, while the public expectation of the enterprise fulfilling its social responsibility is regarded as an extra burden on their production cost. In this sense, self-centeredness of an enterprise makes it inevitable that managers consciously choose the latter when caught between morals and profits. Likewise, it is rationality that leads managers to regard maximizing the profits or interests of their shareholders as their irrevocable responsibility, thereby holding a position of indifference to or completely ignoring the criticisms coming from the general public. Considering these, it is no wonder that such managers deliberately omit in their corporate policy making the moral values or moral requirements imposed by society.

In summary, the self-centeredness and rationality of an enterprise act as a type of double-layered shelter from the adoption of business morals, the result of which may be the desertion of the much-needed morals. Morals in enterprises, then, could become either harmful or excessive, for they would both decrease the competitiveness of an enterprise and be completely rejected by the management level for the reasons mentioned earlier, and be considered a kind of luxury too dear to be paid off. The moral behavior of an individual enterprise may be possible, but should never be followed, for such behavior would disturb the market competition mechanism and destroy price information as a result (Koslowski 1997, 214 and 181).

Expectations and Criticisms: The Outer Pressure

Criticisms, expectations, and other pressures from society and the general public in terms of the enterprise's moral behavior and social responsibilities could often make enterprise managers psychologically tense and morally reticent as a consequence. When the public concern for the moral behavior of an enterprise becomes sufficiently strong; when the gap between the public expectation and managers' self-definition of responsibility is too wide; and when organizations (trusted both by the enterprise and the general public) and effective channels or ways of communication and negotiation between the enterprise and the public cannot be found, managers would usually display a mentality of evasion or reticence, or could behave in an uncooperative manner. Even if an appropriate organization existed, it is possible that the managers would view it more as a disadvantage than as a way of constructive communication because of the existing or potential harms to their enterprises.

It cannot be denied, however, that poorer enterprise performance and the managers' subsequent moral reticence could be the result of irrational or overly radical demands by the public on the enterprises' moral responsibilities. There are also instances of enterprises choosing to be morally reticent on the premise that their confrontation with the public would produce negative feelings on both sides, thus worsening the already touch-and-go relationships between them. And some managers prefer such a moral stance because they believe that the outcome of such dialogues with the public is too unpredictable a fight and too difficult to win.

The Lack or Absence of Trust During Society's Transformation: The Social Factor

Anthony Giddens believed that trust is a type of structure. The structure of trust falls into two categories: interpersonal trust and institutional trust, with the former referring to trust between people familiar with each other and the latter to that of a system or mechanism that assists in simplifying the complexity and uncertainty of the environment. For instance, loans and property rights belong to institutional trust characteristic of the market economy (Giddens 1998, 51–52). Unfortunately, the system needs to be much improved in present-day China, where outstanding debt, "triangle loans" or multiple-way loans, as well as the vague definition of property rights, are painfully widespread. The lack or absence of trust creates ill consequences: greater costs in business transactions, the shrinking of market share, and the impossibility of profits for enterprises.

The transformation of society in China could be compared to a huge wave of unskilled laborers moving out of their traditional outdated tribes, who, unable to quickly adapt themselves to the new environment, fall into groups with conflicting interests and find all friendships, emotions, and obligations quickly absent from their lives. In this conflict, those who profited first, more often than not, were those people and enterprises on the margins that could easily take advantage of the opportunity to advance to the second arena of social activity. Their success, frustratingly, was due to rejection by their original social groups because of their failure to observe rules, fulfill promises, and behave honestly. In other words, those people or enterprises that were not honest initially gained profits during this transformational period. It is true that such individuals and enterprises have not been in the mainstream, but they have indeed shocked the integrity of the moral system and directly contributed to the lack or absence of systematic or intuitional credit. Without a doubt, moral reticence in enterprise management is another case showing the absence of such credit.

Enterprise Performance and Social Responsibility: The De-Structuring of Moral Reticence in Enterprise Management

The rational analysis of the reasons for moral reticence does not prove its rationality but rather serves to rationally dismantle the effective paths enterprises take in choosing moral reticence. It is not difficult to discover that in dismantling the structural reasons for moral reticence, the two major issues to address are performance standards and social responsibility. Therefore, improving the system of enterprise performance standards and corporate social responsibility is an effective means for dismantling the corporate management syndrome of moral reticence.

The stance of moral reticence as adopted by corporate managers seeks to reject society and the public's right to monitor the enterprise's social responsibility. The understanding of corporate social responsibility and performance standards by the enterprise and the public are divergent, thereby leading to one of the main causes for moral reticence.

The Chinese word for "performance" is comprised of two characters: *ji* (achievements) and *xiao* (effects or results). We can evaluate enterprise performance as the result of the development of the enterprise behavior (*ji*), in addition to the effects, benefits, and value of the enterprise's behavior for itself, the public or society (*xiao*). The former tends to reflect the status of and prospects for the enterprise's development or the results of its corporate actions. The latter tends to show the value of its development or the meanings of its actions. Combined, these together indicate the real condition of the enterprise's growth. Therefore, performance standards indicate the level of development for a certain enterprise for a given period of its business operations. Evaluation standards, as an effective system for supervising modern corporate management performance, have already been adopted in developed countries within the West for many years, and now is an important means for many enterprises within the market economy to appraise, supervise, direct, and improve themselves.

The standard of evaluation has changed in accordance with different definitions accepted during different eras, such as the sales profit margin, which was considered a key index in the 1960s. In the 1970s, investment yield became the primary index for corporate performance, and in the 1980s, the financial indices of the ratio between projected and actual profits, investment yield, and cash flow garnered international acceptance. At the same time, a number of multinationals started to look carefully at several nonfinancial indices, such as productivity, market share, and relations to host country governments. In the 1990s, nonfinancial indices became more and more important, and currently, the accepted indices for multinationals include market share, product quality, delivery efficiency and reliability, sensitivity and adaptability, employee morale, innovation, and customer satisfaction. Therefore, in the evolution of enterprise performance standards, there is a tendency toward adopting business-based standards, regardless of whether they are financial or nonfinancial in nature. In reality, nonfinancial factors, such as relations, culture, morale, and innovation, which are not incorporated into accounting balance sheets, play a valuable role in evaluating enterprise performance. We can even predict that in the new economy and era of technology, the survival and success of an enterprise will become more and more dependent upon exactly those factors not found in the legers. In theory, business-based performance standards have three major flaws:

1. It is difficult to conduct a complete assessment of the enterprise including various social and environmental factors since the evaluation standard primarily covers only the enterprise itself.
2. Most of the evaluation criteria are used by the management for projections, thereby diluting a focus on strategy, making it difficult to promote sustained performance.
3. Since the performance criteria focus on profit as the vital result of business operations, it is difficult to make an appropriate and reasonable valuation of the enterprise's state of business operations.

In reaction to the flaws discussed earlier, a number of Western academics have constructed new theoretical models after critical analysis of the business-based performance standards. For example, Andre de Waal (de Waal 2002) has developed a multi-tiered pyramid-shaped system of standards to evaluate business organizations. The base of the pyramid is comprised of multiple and complex performance standards of the enterprise's current performance. The middle tier includes targets of the enterprises, such as revenues, profit margin, and customer satisfaction. The tip of the pyramid includes the "ultimate standards," reflecting the reasonable application of environmental resources and opportunities to reach the objective of sustainable development. Here, the ultimate objective is not purely the pursuit of economic benefits, but rather, strategic planning that results in sustainable development. In addition, T. Cameron (quoted in Meng 2002) in the United States outlines four important methods for evaluating corporate performance. They are as follows:

1. the successful achievement of the enterprise's goals, often referring to the sales of products or services;
2. the enterprise's successful acquisition of what it needs from the environment, mainly involving scarce resources;
3. the successful resolution of the enterprise's internal issues; and
4. the satisfaction of strategic benefactors, including consumers, employees, and shareholders.

The last item indicates that the wishes of the public and society are important to the evaluation of corporate performance, thereby affirming the feasibility of social responsibility serving as a criterion for corporate performance.

Social responsibility can be interpreted broadly in terms of economic, legal, and moral responsibility. For example, Stephen Robbins (1991, 124) asserts that corporate social responsibility does not just indicate legal and economic requirements, but means the social responsibility that enterprises assume in their goal of long-term benefits to society. In a narrower sense, social responsibility may only indicate moral responsibility, but the main issue today is that economic and legal responsibility are not sufficient without moral responsibility. How can enterprises assume social responsibility? This can be decided by the rights that enterprises enjoy. Archie Carroll (quoted in Meng 2002) notes that the rights-responsibility relation is the basis for pointing out the social responsibility of enterprises. Keith Davis shares Carroll's view that social responsibility should match social rights, with the "iron law" referring to the principle that those who do not exercise rights responsibly toward society should be deprived of those rights (quoted in Zhou Zucheng 2000, 39). Emil Durkheim, who believed that the economic functionality of enterprises is not the ultimate goal, but only serves as a means to achieve the goal, also reinforces the social and moral responsibilities of an enterprise. According to Durkheim, social life is a combination of various wills and desires and should be harmoniously united to work toward a common goal (Durkheim 2001, 18). The nature of the modern enterprise is in fact a team or a long-term contracted collective. In the management of an enterprise, the value of certain resources relies on other related resources and the cooperation of those who share common interests. Any unilateral or opportunistic action can cause harm to the other party's interests. Any standard of evaluation for enterprise performance that aims to include aspects concerning social responsibility should at least include the following:

1. Equal job opportunity.
2. Guarantee and improvement of working and living quality.
3. Protection of consumer rights.
4. Protection of investors and creditors.
5. Protection of ecology and the environment.
6. Help to promote the stability and development of the community.

Only by developing this type of dynamic and transparent standard for enterprise evaluation to replace the static and opaque system can the moral reticence problem be solved within corporate management. These standards will enable the conditions for total, healthy, and sustained development of enterprises.

REFERENCES

China Youth. 2002. April 15.

de Waal, A. A. 2002. *Quest for Balance: The Human Element in Performance Management Systems.* New York: Wiley (2002). Chinese version translated by Wang Kaihu. Shanghai: Jiaotong University Press.

Durkheim, E. 2001. *Physique des moeurs et du droit.* Paris: Presses Universitaires de France (1950). Also *Professional Ethics and Civic Morals.* Translated by Glencoe C. Brookfield. Illinois: The Free Press (1958). Chinese version translated by Qu Dong and Fu Degen. Shanghai: Shanghai People's Publishing House.

Giddens, A. 1998. *Modernity and Self-Identity. Self and Society in the Late Modern Age.* Stanford, CA: Stanford University Press (1991). Chinese version translated by Zhao Xudong and Fang Wen. Beijing: Joint Publishing Company.

Koslowski, P. 1997. *Principles of Ethical Economy*. Dordrecht: Kluwer (2001). Chinese version *Jing ji lunli yuan ze*. Translated by Yu Sun. Beijing: China Social Sciences Press.

Meng, Jianmin. 2002. *Remarks on Chinese Enterprises' Performance*. Beijing: China's Finance and Economics Publishing House.

Pratley, P. 1999. *The Essense of Business Ethics*. New York: Prentice Hall (1995). Chinese version translated by Hong Chengwen et al. Beijing: Zhong Xin Publishing House and Prentice Hall.

Robbins, S. P. 1991. *Management*. Third edition. Englewood Cliffs, NJ: Prentice Hall.

Zhou Zucheng. 2000. *Management and Ethics*. Beijing: Qinghua University Press.

CHAPTER 19

The Necessity and Prospects of Promoting Ethics in Chinese Enterprises: Experiences of Dazhong Transportation Group

Xiuhua Zhou

The opening up of China to the outside world over the past 20 plus years has brought remarkable achievements in the transformation toward a market economy and unprecedented development opportunities for Chinese enterprises. However, these changes have generated not only opportunities, but also risks. Various defects of the rules and the functioning of markets have caused different types of disorder such as triangle debts, weak trust in enterprises, tax evasion, and the influence of money on public authorities. Given all these facts, a serious examination of the situation is called for: while establishing the market rules, is it necessary to set up an ethical "barrier" for having the economy catering for the normal needs of human beings? Indeed, the growth of the modern economy has proved the supporting function played by ethics in the maturation of a market economy. Now that China has entered the World Trade Organization (WTO), Chinese enterprises, as the main body and beneficiary of the market economy, have to shoulder the task of establishing the ethics of that market economy. The construction of ethics in Chinese enterprises has became an imperative task.

The Necessity and Urgency of Promoting Ethics in Chinese Enterprises

1. *With China's accession to the WTO, Chinese enterprises have been exposed to and integrated into the global economy, which provides a critical moment for them to recognize the ethics of a market economy.* One of the fundamental functions of the WTO is the establishment of rules to ensure that all WTO member countries can do business and compete in an open and fair global environment. The essential prerequisite for Chinese enterprises to participate is to obey the international economic rules and the market ethics implied in them. Unfortunately, the biggest problems for Chinese enterprises and the Chinese are a lack of rule consciousness and a weakness in ethics. The operation of the market economy over the past 20 plus years has witnessed the introduction of several fairly perfect policies, laws, and regulations, along with two unresolved issues. First, do the functionality and the morality of the rules themselves match international norms? And second, is the cultural support of ethics sufficiently forceful to effectively enforce obediance to these newly created and reasonable rules? Today, Chinese enterprises, facing not just a domestic market but a global one, undoubtedly will be excluded from international competition unless they obey the international rules and, most importantly, the ethics of a market economy. Therefore, it is an urgent task to promote ethical attitudes such as sincerity and fairness in order to improve the functioning of the market economy and to successfully join the global economy.

2. *Currently, most commodity markets in China have become buyers' markets (i.e., where supply exceeds demand).* Chinese enterprises not only need to build ethics in order to compete in the international arena, but also in the domestic one. With the continuous booming of the socialist market economy, China has entered an age of abundant commodities. The sellers' market has gradually changed into a buyers' market. As the focus of competition among enterprises has moved to services, fake and inferior products will be eliminated sooner or later. Chinese enterprises have come under increasing pressure to offer first-grade products with first-rate service. This is the essence of Haier's success. Its perfect and considerate after-sale service has yielded both more customers and better returns. People are willing to pay a higher price for a better service. The sale of reputation has taken priority over the sale of products. Without a strong corporate ethics, Haier could not have established itself in an unassailable position in the electrical home appliances market. Undoubtedly, corporate ethics is important even in domestic markets.

3. *After the opening up of the economy and its concomitant confusion and trials, social values are becoming more reasonable, and the whole society is paying more attention to the building of professional ethics, social ethics, and family virtues.* The opening up to the outside world has not only brought significant reforms in the national economy, but also has diversified people's notions of virtues. After experiencing much confusion, hesitation, and pain, the whole society is calling for a return to ethics. People have come to realize that noneconomic factors including ethics are the main driving forces of growth in the market economy. The ethics of self-discipline plays a role of equal importance as mandatory policies and laws in the operation of the market economy. Since market economic activities are a kind of social behavior relating to consumers, the natural environment and the social order, they need ethics to fill a regulatory role. The main agents of the market must abide by professional ethics before they can well fulfil their posterior duties. Therefore, it becomes a kind of objective demand to extract from practice the ethical norms that both manufacturers and business people should obey. In this process, one can establish the existence of ethical standards in all areas of business, including investment, manufacturing, sales, and other services. Meanwhile, to create a better social environment for the promotion of professional ethics, China has recently made great efforts to foster social ethics and family virtues, advocated in part by President Jiang Zemin. According to the president, all components of the economy should be filtered through ethics before they assume their roles in the market economy. It is an effective way to reduce destructive behavior in market operations.

4. *China's listed companies and outstanding private enterprises should take the lead in transforming themselves into respectable ethical organizations.* The companies listed on the stock exchange will undoubtedly act as the primary leaders among Chinese enterprises seeking ethical excellence. With scientific decision procedures, sound financial conditions, and smooth financing channels, they provide good examples of successful Chinese enterprises. Yet private companies, an emerging economic force in recent years, have also been investigated by many economists because of their open-mindedness, sharp market awareness, and flexible operation mechanisms. Their achievements and potentials should not be underestimated. Since China's entry to the WTO, the enhancement of the competitiveness of national brands has become the basic objective for the country's economic growth in the future. Therefore, outstanding Chinese listed and private companies should not shirk their responsibility to compete

in the international arena. First, they have a solid basis, and, second, they face an urgent task to narrow the gap between themselves and famous international corporations, not only in terms of economic indicators but also in terms of corporate culture and ethics.

THE USE OF GOOD CORPORATE CULTURE FOR THE PROMOTION OF ETHICS IN CHINESE ENTERPRISES

The systematic development of business and economic ethics in China throughout Chinese enterprises needs the joint efforts of government, enterprises, citizens, and others and involves multiple aspects such as restructuring the political system, changing governmental functions, establishing market regulations, building corporate ethics, and improving attitudes and behavior of citizens. Given this broader context and having discussed the necessity and urgency of promoting ethics, in Chinese enterprises, it is fruitful to observe the ways in which Dazhong Transportation Group has accepted its responsibility to contribute to the consolidation of ethical business. Based on my long-term experiences with this company, I would like to show the crucial role that corporate culture plays in enhancing corporate ethics.

General Remarks

As the twenty-first century is an era of both cultural management and cultural success, the building of the corporate culture is a major way to strengthen the promotion of ethics in Chinese enterprises.

Since the management theory of corporate culture took off in the 1970s, it has had a wide impact throughout the world. The success stories of Japanese enterprises told the world that corporate culture could consist of motivational resources and the coherence of the organization while technology need only be a platform. The vitality of an enterprise is quite limited without a strong corporate culture. As a matter of fact, this knowledge not only benefitted Japanese companies but also worked well for many outstanding enterprises around the world, such as General Electric Company (GE) and British Aerospace Ltd. (BAE).

In the late 1980s, Chinese enterprises began to realize the importance of corporate culture. Now that the building of corporate culture is sweeping through every corner of the Chinese nation, there are many famous Chinese corporate names such as Haier Group, Huawei Technologies, and Legend Group. Several years ago, the managerial personnel of our company traveled to the North and the South in order to get first-hand experiences of the corporate cultures at Haier and Huawei. These cultures not only embody their distinguishing features, but, more importantly, they also reflect the fine tradition of Chinese culture and the advanced culture of humanity in their emphasis on virtues like fairness, self-respect, universal love, honesty, and sincerity, which are powerful moral resources that hardly can be overestimated.

Just as individual values define the ethical standards of a person, so the values of an enterprise determine the ethics of the enterprise. The decisive part in the building of a corporate culture is the definition of the core values of that enterprise, which correspondingly determines the ethics it abides by. Therefore, the development of the corporate culture will undoubtedly be the main channel for the promotion of ethics in Chinese enterprises.

Core Values and Code of Conduct at Dazhong Transportation Group

After the study visits in 1999 at Huawei in Shenzhen and Haier in Qingdao, the decision-making body of Dazhong reached a clear understanding that, compared with those advanced corporate cultures, Dazhong still had much room for improvement and urgently needed to develop and perfect a more coherent and focused corporate culture in order to strengthen the ethical fabric of the company. Through systematic research, analysis, and planning over almost two years, the core values of Dazhong Transportation came into being, summarized as "all for the community." This means providing the customers of Dazhong with warm and satisfactory services, repaying the shareholders of Dazhong sound returns and creating a happy life for the employees of Dazhong. Based on these values, the core code of conduct was formed accordingly: "Enjoy and respect your work and be honest and trustworthy in your work!" When reading these guidelines, one might take them for mere slogans. But when riding in any of the familiar mint green taxi-cabs, one may experience these values directly.

"Respect the passenger!" The passenger who rides in a Dazhong taxi enjoys a series of standard services which, in order, include polite wording, selection of the best route, visibility of the taxi odometer, issuance of the receipt when reaching the destination, and, finally, notification of the passenger about lost items and other things.

"Offer warm service!" The passenger can enjoy not only the good service itself, but also emotional satisfaction, which involves four service concepts: politeness, self-restraint, sincerity, and comfort. Through appropriate manners and direct eye contact, the driver will create a favorably polite impression on the customers. The driver's ability to control mood and behavior demonstrates his self-restraint. Providing honest services to the passengers such as assisting them out of difficulties offers the driver an opportunity to show sincerity. And comfort is not only expressed through a clean cab and safe driving, but also by the individual appearance of the driver. Dazhong Transportation continues to specify these concepts in more detail and to integrate them into its culture.

Faithfulness is the soul of business. As the market economy is based on trust, good will lays the foundation for every enterprise. It is embodied in the service commitments of the Dazhong taxis that provide the best services and take care of customers' complaints with unwavering friendliness. The eight service commitments the company promises to society are the following: sound car appearance; well-functioning air-conditioner that is used according to the passengers' wishes; clean seat covers; ticket machine in good condition and taxi fares settled as required by the passengers; clean and neatly printed fare receipts; clean uniform of the driver in service; no smoking for drivers in the cab; and mobile phones prohibited for drivers. If any of these eight commitments is violated, the passenger has the right to refuse to pay the fare. A measure of Dazhong's seriousness of these commitments is that in the past six years Dazhong taxis received 10,855 complaints and paid a compensation sum of 615,682 yuan (approximately US$75,100).

In order to better understand the honest service of Dazhong, one may consider the story "Choice," which is included in Dazhong's Mission Statement.

When you face a choice like this, what do you do? A passenger rode in a taxi at 3 p.m. and told the taxi driver that he wanted to go to Pudong International Airport (ca. 50 km in the east out of Shanghai) in order to purchase an air ticket and fly to Shenzhen. On the way to the Pudong airport, the driver was informed that there was a flight at 6 p.m. with still available seats or, on the other hand, one could fly from Hongqiao airport (ca. 18 km in the west of Shanghai), but seats were not surely available. Many drivers would choose to bring the passenger to Pudong International Airport, since the driver could get a taxi fare of some 150 yuan (or US$ 18) and the passenger wouldn't miss the airplane. But Yutong Zhao, a driver of Dazhong, made a different choice.

He put the interest of the customer first and gave the passenger the phone number of the information service at the Hongqiao airport. The customer called the airline from the taxi and learned that there still was a free seat. With no further ado, Zhao changed the direction and drove to the Hongqiao airport. Upon the arrival, the taxi meter showed a fare of 95 yuan. But Zhao only took 50 yuan for the ride because, as Zhao explained, he, as a driver of Dazhong, couldn't accept the additional money since the detour was not the passenger's fault. The customer was deeply touched by Zhao's words and they cordially shook hands.

When the individual interest of the driver conflicts with the interest of the passenger, employees of Dazhong will choose the latter without second thoughts. Although Zhao made less money, the passenger will bear this experience in mind and recommend Dazhong taxis to his relatives, friends, and colleagues. But this should not be limited merely to a financial calculation. The example of Yutong Zhao illustrates the ethics of honest services and shows the important role corporate culture can play in promoting corporate ethics.

As Dazhong Transportation faces fierce competition, especially after China's entry to the WTO, the building of corporate ethics is all the more imperative. The success story of Dazhong proves that the building of corporate culture is one effective means to develop corporate ethics. Chinese enterprises will gradually strengthen their corporate cultures and enhance the development of corporate ethics in China.

APPENDIX: ABOUT THE COMPANY

Dazhong Transportation Group Co. Ltd., until 1999 known as Shanghai Dazhong Taxi Co. ("Dazhong" means many people), was established on December 24, 1988 with a 65-million-yuan bank loan. In July 1992, it was reformed into a Sino-foreign joint stock company and its A shares and B shares were listed on the Shanghai Stock Exchange in summer 1992. With ten years of continued efforts, the company has developed rapidly with its main operations in private and public transportation and tourism, along with activities in the high-tech industry, financial and industrial business, properties, and trade. The net asset return rate has averaged at more than 10 percent. At the beginning of the twenty-first century the core business was shifted from traditional transportation services to modern passenger traffic and modern logistics. Website: www.96822.com.

CHAPTER 20

The Moral Values of "Joint-Forces Culture": The Example of Xuchang Relay Group

Farong Qiao

China, a developing country, is experiencing large changes in its enterprises, as they transform from the traditional model to modern types. With China's entry into the World Trade Organization (WTO), China's enterprises have reached an even deeper level of reform. Facing economic globalization, the companies are asking themselves how they should build their own corporate culture and—what is even more challenging—which moral values they should adopt to shape such a new culture. Extensive investigations have been undertaken to explore appropriate ways to build up corporate cultures of integrity for all employees. The following analysis of the development of a "joint-forces culture" in an old, state-owned enterprise (SOE) may illustrate these endeavors.

THE MEANING AND FUNCTION OF THE "JOINT-FORCES CULTURE" IN A BUSINESS ORGANIZATION

Henan Xuchang Relay Group, a Chinese model enterprise, has implemented a "joint-forces culture," which has become a distinctive characteristic of the organization and an essential part of its innovative management. The joint-forces culture is a corporate philosophy whose key values are "joint forces." It is the core, the essence, and the cornerstone of its corporate culture, which shapes the organization's code of conduct and guiding value judgments throughout the management process.

It regulates complex organizational relations which integrates the company's internal and external resources, forms a strong force of cohesion and guarantees the realization of values by individuals, the enterprise, and society. The joint-forces culture guides corporate policy and decision making and directly impacts the company's performance and plays a key role in the company's survival and whether or not the company can achieve its growth objectives.

Therefore, the joint-forces culture, as the company's management principle and philosophy, is key to the company's prospects for growth. The joint-forces culture, composed of material, spiritual, and behavioral factors, forms an organic whole. It influences the entire enterprise and plays a central role in all aspects of the enterprise. The joint-forces culture, as the enterprise's "platform for values," influences the enterprise's entire chain of value creation, guides and ensures the cohesion of its logistics, manufacturing, sales, and customer services.

To begin with, in more concrete terms, the joint-forces culture's innovation breaks through the traditional management philosophy, permeating the enterprise's value-creating process. As the symbol of the modern business enterprise, it is characterized by an open, pragmatic, and cooperative attitude, overcoming conservative management concepts and succeeding in building a collaboration-oriented enterprise. For instance, in the past, a product comprised a production line in which a business was fully in charge of producing and selling a product, from the research and development of hardware, software, and technology to the post-sales services. As a result, divisions within the company were isolated entities, unable to communicate and share information with each other. Even worse, management and employees did not collaborate efficiently. Large amounts of resources were wasted because of basic, simple, and repetitive work, slowing down the development of the company. Moreover, under the influence of today's market economy, the relations between enterprises have tended to become less antagonistic and more collaborative and better coordinated. Xuchang Relay Group has involved the suppliers, customers, and even its competitors into the process of value creation for customers and society. It has adopted a strategy incorporating cooperation and competition, leveraging mutual advantages, and building powerful alliances, thereby transforming the Group into an open and dynamic system that can generate extensive synergies with the external environment in order to speed up the development of the Group.

Second, the joint-forces culture can lead to the adjustment and integration of internal resources and the value chain of the enterprise. Promoting the joint-forces culture and building up its strength lie in the foundation of forming the enterprise's core competitiveness. The enterprise's internal value chain includes three aspects: value of selection (detailed market analysis, target market, product position), value of supply (research and development of products and services, manufacturing of products, price setting, distribution, and sales), and value of communication (sales, marketing, and advertising). The enterprise should integrate human resources, products, technologies, services, and other resources into the main business flow of its value chain, shed or release itself of nonessential business resources, and ensure that it cannot be easily copied by competitors, thereby rendering the enterprise uniquely more competitive while enhancing its profits.

In the third place, the joint-forces culture helps the enterprise to better draw on external resources, which integrate the enterprise with its external value chain. In addition to the company's internal value chain, the company must strive for a competitive edge through suppliers, marketing channels, and final customers. In the future, the social division of labor will be increasingly differentiated, and the coordination and communication between industries will become more important. The value customers obtained from the final product is the organic sum of the value created by every organically united activity in the value chain. Thus the external value chain is an indispensable component of the enterprise, to which the inner value chain is closely related. As a matter of fact, the more integrated and united the inner value chain is, the stronger its influence on the external value chain. The joint-forces culture integrates the external resources and supports resources mainly through two ways. First, it improves the relations amongst the participants of the supply chain by gaining support, promoting cooperation, enhancing the customers' system of value transfer, and adopting an evenly shared benefit strategy. Second, it increases the total value and reduces the total costs for customers. Thus it better satisfies the customers and ultimately builds a sincere and stable relationship with them based on contracts and loyalty and through a comprehensive marketing strategy.

The building of a joint-forces culture has resulted in substantial profits for the Group. How has this happened? The Relay Group, once an old-style SOE and designated as one of the key projects of the national economy in China's first five-year plan, has grown into a successful company with the best electric power equipment and strong market influence. Its sales revenue has increased from 19.2 million yuan in 1984 to 2.88 billion yuan at present, and its profit from 2 million

yuan to 0.25 billion yuan in the same period. In 1984, total investment in the company by the Chinese government totaled 12 million
yuan, while the market value of the Group is now worth more than
3 billion yuan. This represents an increase of over 267 times in the
past 17 years. A main reason for these great achievements lies in
the joint-forces culture of the Xuchang Relay Group.

The core competitiveness of the Group is based on its core products.
Over time, the quality of the products and the level of its technology
have constantly improved. Fifteen years ago, the core product of the
Group was relay protection, which now only makes up 3 percent of
the company's total sales revenue. Seven or eight years ago, the
Group's core product became relay protection and automation of the
electric power system. Two or three years ago, the core product concentrated on the automation of the electric power system. At present,
it consists of electric grid technology, and in the future the targeted core
product is information technology solutions for electric power systems.
The constant advancement of the enterprise's core competitiveness has
assured the high-speed development of the Group.

Similarly, its management has been constantly reformed and
improved. Ten years ago, the Group focused on changing the outmoded notions of management associated with China's planned economy. Five to ten years ago, the enterprise concentrated on improving
its management system by adapting it to the market economy. In the
past few years, the Group has promoted the level and efficiency of
management, transforming it into a system of modern enterprise management. Management is a productive force, and the high efficiency
and modernization of its management will guarantee the reasonable
and efficient allocation of resources and quicken its transformation
into modern enterprise management. It will enable the Group to
achieve even greater success in the near future. Management and technology, strongly influencing each other, are two indispensable drivers
of an enterprise's development. The total adoption and strengthening
of the joint forces culture has translated into rapid growth for the
Group. With 23 percent of the total employees in China's machinery
sector, the Group produces 63 percent of the sector's profits. The
Group has become a large-scale key enterprise in China that offers the
largest selection of electrical equipment and products.

Moral Values of the Joint-Forces Culture of the Xuchang Relay Group

Every culture has its own moral values, which constitute the core and
essence of the culture. The joint-forces culture of the Group is based

on the distinct moral principle that gives priority to the value of human beings over the value of things, to collective value over individual value, and to the social value (or "customers' value") over corporate value (or the value of an enterprise).

The Value of Human Beings over the Value of Things

It is a basic moral principle to give priority to human beings by ranking human values above material values in the management of internal human resources and coordination of human relations in the Group.

The Group has established a vigorous and energetic employment policy through the systematic reform of management, distribution, and employment. People are recognized as the most important resources. Employees are regarded as the designers and producers of the product, the providers of the product in the enterprise, and the final motivators for a normal operation of the Group. They are convinced that people are the lifeblood of an enterprise and hold human resources as the most important operational resources. Motivating the personnel's enthusiasm, initiative and creativity lies at the heart for improving the Group's operational activities and efficiency. In order to create a community in which managers and workers share honor and failure, it is of paramount importance to reach a common understanding in the company and enhance the employees' participation in policy decision making and management. Employees are encouraged to become professionals and regard their work in a lifetime career perspective without any social classification and discrimination. In a highly professional spirit, everyone in the Group should constantly try to make innovations, improve efficiency and the quality of work, and perform as perfectly as possible. Moreover, one should improve the skills for managing the resources and prepare oneself for further development of the Group. In sum, people always come first. The Group tries to take care of them and create the most favorable conditions in order to meet the needs for full development and the raising of values for the people.

Collective Value over Individual Value and
Overall Value over Partial Value

As Chinese enterprises have faced increasing competition in a big market, the external environment has become even more complicated and unstable for them, and technological innovation and customers' demand have changed rapidly. Thus, in order to survive and develop, a company has to be flexible and adaptable. Moreover, horizontal cooperation within the organizations has been extended and intensified as never before with the result that the technological and productive processes have become highly organized. Therefore, compared to the situation in the early 1990s, both the external and the internal business environment have been considerably transformed.

In order to meet the demands of this transformation, the Xuchang Relay Group has been advocating the joint-forces culture and has learned crucial lessons. It gathered that the efficiency of the Group has been affected by numerous factors such as scattered allocation of resources, redundancy of product development, overextended periods of developing the products, low investment-income ratio, low success ratio of projects, high cost of after-sale service, waste of human and financial resources, and unclear accountability for rights and responsibilities between the enterprise as a whole and its individual branches.

As a case in point, the repeated development of products has not only caused direct and indirect economic loss, but has also tended to breed a "chicken head culture," according to which a company chooses to strive to be number one in a mediocre or "hen" environment rather than to be number two or "the tail of a phoenix" in a challenging environment. With such an overbearing and arrogant culture, the company cuts off its contacts with the outside world and generates petty peasant ideology and individualistic heroism, which necessarily leads to the erosion of its organization.

Another example concerns the issue of self-centeredness of business divisions. It results from management problems between the headquarters of the enterprise and its individual branches, restraining the healthy operation of the group. If corporate culture is based on personal and partial interests alone without unifying values of collaboration, it is inefficient in its operation, hardly appealing in the long run and even leading to corporate failure. Therefore, for many years, the president of Henan Xuchang Relay Group, Wang Jinian, has strictly rejected a chicken head culture. Instead, he has advocated a joint-forces culture and the priority of collective values over individual values, and of overall value over partial value.

According to the Xuchang Relay Group, the priority of collective values over individual values involves three dimensions. First, regarding its relationship with the government, the Group emphasizes the goal of making the industry the largest, best, and the strongest in the market in order to ensure the value of the state-owned capital. Second, concerning its relationship with the workforce, the Group strives to continuously improve the conditions for each employee to bring his or her initiative and creativity into full play. The employees must possess a "spirit of camaraderie," in which each individual's interests are linked to the performance of the enterprise. Individuals should be enabled to express their potential within the Group, develop their abilities, and realize individual value while pursuing the interests of the collective (Robbins 1997, 5). Rights and responsibilities should be united, while opposing egoism and the chicken head culture, which can only weaken the cohesion of the enterprise and the commitment to hard work, impairing the company to meet the demand of the modern market economy.

Social Value (or "Customers' Value") over Corporate Value (or the Value of the Enterprise)

The provision of high-quality products and services for the society is the basis of the existence and social responsibility of the enterprise, which is embodied in the notion of "social value." Going even further than the recognition that the customers ultimately control the destiny of the enterprise and determine its profitability, the Xuchang Relay Group has initiated a unique concept of "Customers' Value First" in the belief that the creation of value for the customers is its raison d'être. In its mission statement the Group clearly states its goal of "enabling our customer to fully enjoy the high reliability and high technology of our equipment." In order to fulfill this mission, President Jinian Wang further defined four aspects of the Group's customer-oriented mission. First, the customer is the Group's God, with the customer's demands always coming first. It is the Group's objective to propel the customers forward with optimal products and services. Second, the Group is always honored when customers visit and make any demands on the Group. Third, uttering any complaint to customers is equivalent to digging the Group's own grave. Never shall anyone in the Group argue with them. The Group always takes its customers' interests and demands into account in order to improve and perfect the Group. Fourth, it is the Group's lifetime pursuit to satisfy its customers. Therefore, it strives for perfect quality of products without any defects and for perfect service without any complaints. The Group demands that it exceed the customers' expectations. This concept of "Customers' Value First" reflects the will of the Group to survive and a high degree of social responsibility. And, even more, it expresses the ultimate concern for people and humankind (Qiao 1990, 87).

The advocacy and practice of moral values of the joint-forces culture marked the Group's cultural development at a new and higher stage of growth. Such moral values are rooted in the traditions of Chinese culture and attach much weight to the priority of the value of human beings, collective value, and social value. This culture has been advanced in view of new organizational and ethical relationships that are emerging in China's modern enterprises. Just as a state has its distinctive values to support its wealth-creation system, a successful company has a system of values that serves as its pillar of spiritual values. Since enterprises exist in different cultural contexts, they have developed different moral values. For example, American society emphasizes individualism, while Japanese society stresses collectivism. Xuchang Relay Group has achieved a balance between these two different cultural values by retaining their respective strengths while adding to them. Such development of corporate values offers rich experiences for academic investigations (Hampdon-Turner and Trompenaars 1997, 34).

Xuchang Relay Group has achieved remarkable success in the building of a joint-forces culture with core moral values because it was able to create a favorable environment that has been conducive and supportive to the formation and operation of such a culture. As a model of China's SOEs, the Group has built its success, above all, through an exhaustive reform of the three priorities, in line with the functioning of the market, and thereby forming a mutually enforcing chain between rights, responsibilities, and interests. Moreover, the Group has kept introducing new operational concepts such as Economic Value Added (EVA), Key Proficiency Index (KPI), and a mid-period reporting system of work. It has continued to raise the awareness for creating wealth to customers and society and has avoided the cultural inclination of egoism. As a result, the employees feel strongly motivated to maintain and further develop the joint-forces culture.

In addition, the Group has attached great importance to the systematic coordination of values, the building of the joint-forces culture across diverse activities from planning to the business environment, from technology to production and from management to organization and the reform and integrity of research and development. The impact of these efforts can be easily seen across different areas within the Group. As a result of this coordination, customer satisfaction has increased, the Group has achieved significant breakthroughs in research and development of key projects, the time for research and development of new products has been shortened, waste of human resources has been greatly reduced, and sales revenue has substantially increased. The employees of the Group think very highly of fostering the joint-forces culture in their organization.

APPENDIX: XUCHANG (XJ) GROUP CORPORATION

XJ Group Corporation was well-established in 1970 with its headquarters in Xuchang, Henan Province, located in the central part of China. It is a state-owned enterprise (SOE) and a leading electric company of electric equipments design and manufacture in the power industry of China. The total number of employees is 5,000 at the headquarters and 20,000 nationwide. At the present, XJ Group Corporation includes two public companies, namely XJ Electric Corporation and Tianyu Electric Company.

XJ Group Corporation was named "One of the Top 500 Enterprises in Comprehensive Economic Profitability of China" and "One of the Top Enterprises within China Machinery Industry." In 1996, XJ was awarded ISO 9001 Quality Insurance Certificate, first of its sort in the power industry in China.

XJ Group Corporation mainly supplies the whole range of the following electric equipment for power industries:

- Complete range of electric primary and secondary equipment of power industry including each of these:
  - Power generation, transmission, and distribution equipment
  - Automatic control, relay protection, power station, and substation automation systems
  - Power system communication equipment, and so on
- Electrical equipment for railway electrifications
- Power plant construction and consulting services
- Mechanical and digital meters and automatic remote meter reading systems
- Transformers, Circuit breakers, H/L Voltage Switchgears
- Environment protection engineering
- Automatic car parking systems, auto gates and garage doors, traffic barriers
- E-commerce

XJ Group Corporation enjoys 35 percent of the Chinese electric market and their products have been exported to South Asia, Southeast Asia, Africa, Australia, and so on. The total turnover of 2002 is 4,000 Million RMB.

REFERENCES

Hampden-Turner, C. and A. Trompenaars. 1997. *The Seven Cultures of Capitalism.* New York: Currency Doubleday (1993). Chinese version translated by Xu Lianen. Haikou: Hainan Publishing House.

Qiao Farong. 1990. *Corporate Ethical Culture.* Zhengzhou: Henan People's Publishing House.

Robbins, S. P. 1997. *Organizational Behavior: Concepts, Controversies and Applications.* Englewood Cliffs, NJ: Prentice Hall (1996). Chinese version translated by Jianmin Sun et al. Beijing: University of China Press.

CHAPTER 21

Corporate Citizenship Behavior in a Transitional Economy: An Exploratory Study in the People's Republic of China

Hanlong Lu and Chi Kwan Warren Chiu

Charitable donations play a vital role in redistributing wealth in the People's Republic of China. Of the various sources in society, corporate giving is the most important contributing source. As reforms are deepening and state interference diminishing, enterprises are gradually becoming autonomous economic units. This new trend has already brought changes to the existing resource reallocation system, so that resources channeled to charitable causes will have to rely less on centralized administrative initiatives and more on the voluntary citizenship behavior of corporations. Chinese enterprises, especially state-owned enterprises (SOEs), are less compelled to act as state vehicles to provide social goods and services and more pressurized to meet business goals. Many of these enterprises shy away from public welfare donations, leaving a gap in the redistribution system that cannot be filled in this transitional period. Hence a tension exists between the community's expectation that enterprises will continue to act altruistically and the enterprises' desire to be good citizens. How Chinese enterprises can operate according to market principles and at the same time not forfeit their broader social responsibilities is an acid test for reform success in a socialist market economy. The purpose of this study is to identify antecedents of corporate citizenship behavior and its implications for an evolving socialist country.

THE ROLE OF CHINESE ENTERPRISES
IN SOCIETY

Drastic changes have occurred in the legal and social statue of most Chinese enterprises since enactment of the Corporate Law in 1993 and its implementation in 1994. One change made all subsidiaries of the state or provincial industrial bureaus economic entities independent in property ownership, and another established an ownership structure reflecting diversified stakeholders. Now Chinese enterprises are independent units solely responsible for the operation and management of economic activities. However, these changes are likely to bring social disruption because Chinese enterprises are not mere economic organizations but social entities providing from cradle to grave welfare to internal members.[1] The reforms put Chinese enterprises in a dilemma. Should enterprises continue to shoulder a spectrum of social services on behalf of the state or instead to remain competitive in a new business environment? To abrogate these social obligations would jeopardize the existing system that supports social services and would inevitably trigger administrative and social reforms, including changes in the state's governing role and a reshuffling of social and political forces.

In the pre-reform era, the Chinese economy was essentially a centrally planned system. Enterprises served as an extended arm of the state, performing an all-purpose role in managing, pacifying, and controlling functions in society.[2] This arrangement enabled the state to control all of the means of production and production outcomes. Under instructions, SOEs produced goods and services, and consumed a great portion of them, for the benefit of society.

Under a centrally planned redistribution system, resources spent on social services are consumable items. Social services often are not purchased but instead, a substantial portion of them is provided directly by enterprises. For example, SOEs run schools, offer medical services, provide housing benefits, and organize cultural and leisure activities for internal members. In this sense, a SOE is analogous to a microcosm of the whole society, aiming to satisfying internal members' needs.[3] Through administrative instructions and political mobilization, the state obtained from SOEs what was needed to accomplish its target of delivering social services to society. Enterprise leaders and employees collaborated and embraced these obligatory social responsibilities. After all, the resources spent on these social services belonged to the state and were, therefore, solely at the state's discretion.

After the reforms, the organizational climate of Chinese enterprises changed a great deal. In the face of keen competition in the market, enterprises found the need to be separated from the state and so ceased to be "bookkeepers." Today enterprises are evolving from state subsidiaries into autonomous entities with full legal status, primarily responsible for the management of economic activities.

Like other market driven organizations, contemporary Chinese enterprises set goals to maximize profit, an entirely legal and acceptable motive in the present social and economic climate. However, profit maximization should not be the only justification of their existences. While they repay social obligations by paying taxes, enterprises can certainly do more than merely fulfilling this legal obligation. For instance, progressive enterprises often conduct business in ways that produce social benefits to the communities in which they operate. Organizations, especially large ones, care about their social image and status in society. Through giving to society, community amenities are enhanced and their spirit revitalized; in return, enterprises can promote a positive image and earn goodwill in the community.

Participating in social service seems to be an option for enterprises, but it is actually practically required and socially expected. However, the concept of social contribution is fundamentally different under the market economy than it is under the planned economy. In a planned economy, provision of social services is done through an internal transfer of resources, and the beneficiaries are mainly employees of the enterprises. In contrast, social contribution made under a market economy depends mainly on voluntary corporate citizenship behavior motivated by altruistic values. The beneficiaries include everyone who has needs in society. Social contribution, is, thus no longer an outcome of state policies and instructions. At this transitional stage of reform, the new state apparatus and the emerging altruistic values of society interact to affect corporate citizenship behavior.

Corporate Behavior: Three Arrangements of Exchange

Modern social economic theorists suggest that human transaction behaviors can be classified into three kinds: market exchange, reciprocity and redistribution of social resources.[4] The nature and underlying arrangements of the three differ from one another. Market exchange is based on the principle of equity, and competition is the key to a successful transaction. The medium of exchange is money, and profit is the ultimate aim of the transaction. Reciprocity, in contrast, is not based on making money. It is motivated by a sense of social responsibility and moral obligation. The transaction is enacted to satisfy the mutual interests of a donor and a donee. The donee receives material support, and the donor, in return, obtains recognition and self-gratification. The transaction brings trust and builds human connectivity in the community. The third kind of exchange is redistribution of social resources, an arrangement to reallocate resources from one party to another. The effectiveness of such an arrangement rests upon the use of power. If the act of exercising power is perceived to be legitimate, the transaction fosters loyalty and submission to the redistributing authority. Generally speaking, market transaction is best for economic activities, while in the realm of social services, a combination of reciprocity and redistribution is deemed appropriate.

In the pre-reform era, the redistribution arrangement played a dominant role. Under the centralized planned economy, the state organized production activities, distributed sales, and redistributed goods and services. Administrative bureaus monitored their subsidiary providers of social services through a many-layered hierarchy, with procedures and sets of rules. They were wholly owned and managed by the state as were other state bureaus. These state-sponsored social service providers were notoriously bureaucratic, inefficient and unable to compete with non-state service providers in the market. Hierarchy and regulations embedded in a bureaucracy created huge transactional costs and a cumbersome way of getting things done. Like other state bureaus, these units emphasized meeting political targets. This focus tends to foster short-term behavior with little attention to cost.

What is more important, the reliance on the redistribution system has already prevented the reciprocity arrangement from operating effectively. The demand for social services is increasing. Unfortunately, the state can do little to meet the growing demand through existing redistribution arrangements. A gap persists between resources delivered through the redistribution arrangements and rising social needs. The state can provide a safety net to meet only basic needs. Some needs the state cannot meet nor are they satisfied in the market. Nor will relying on taxation narrow this gap, which is widening because the state cannot effectively mobilize work units to deliver social goods and services. Hence the effectiveness of redistribution of resources has been diminished under the current market-oriented economy.

In view of this, the Chinese government is eager to learn from some successful examples. One model is to outsource social services to outside vendors, a strategy that could build up a market arrangement for social services. New organizations have been set up to provide social services. Because they will be managed according to market rules, these organizations exhibit some of the characteristics of a typical profit-seeking organization. One trait that sets them apart from other organizations is that the return to investment is not considered "profit" but "surplus" and, hence, cannot be distributed to property owners or employees of the organizations. These organizations are therefore called "nonprofit" making organizations. The Chinese government needs to enact laws and regulations to ensure the surplus obtained will not be treated as profit but channeled for the development of future services. However, this nonprofit requirement, if operated under a pure market exchange arrangement, may cause enterprises to be less enthusiastic about making social contributions.

Besides a pure market exchange arrangement, provision of social services can be based on a reciprocity arrangement. Reciprocity is an exchange, not for "fame" and "gains," but for social exchange among community members. To maintain harmonious relationships and to actualize oneself through giving are important outcomes sought after by many in society. Although Confucianism, one of the dominant philosophies in China, does not highly regard human transactions motivated by self-seeking behavior, it does not condemn all forms of material transactions either. Indeed, because Confucius believes that the exchange of gifts promotes human relationships, and that it is improper for anyone to receive but not also to give, a reciprocal transaction seems materialistic but equitable, conforming to his rules of etiquette (*Li*). In sum, Confucius' ideas encourage reciprocity of deeds. Further, reciprocity goes beyond exchanging tangible things, and covers passions, friendship, goodwill, and honor. Thus, reciprocity is rooted deeply in Chinese culture, and it is instrumental for citizenship behavior nowadays.

These three arrangements are important to any enterprise because enterprises are not mere economic entities detached from society. Market forces are affecting how these enterprises operate but many, especially SOEs, are still under the influence of the existing redistribution system. There are factors affecting enterprises' corporate citizenship behavior. First, enterprises are now cultivating the sense of corporate citizenship behavior. Second, enterprises, caring about their public images, would like to earn goodwill from the general public. This is particularly essential for foreign or private owned enterprises, because they need to legitimize their presence as a profit-seeking entity in a socialist country. Giving to the community can project a caring image and indirectly enhance legitimacy. These factors lead to a reciprocal arrangement between enterprises and society. Enterprises will continue to operate in an environment where their giving behavior is affected by a host of other factors like the market, the existing redistributing system, and a sentiment of reciprocity in Chinese society.

All these factors interact with one another, resulting in a unique motive of behaving altruistically.

There has been a proliferation of enterprises of different ownership types since the enterprise reform. Their unique background, operation modes, and legacies have a different equation in terms of corporate citizenship behavior. Examining the factors leading to corporate giving, separately and jointly, allows us to understand how China is undergoing transformation in her economic and social systems. To achieve this aim, this paper reports the findings of a study conducted among major enterprises in Shanghai. The findings enable us to understand more about corporate citizenship behavior in the transitional economy in the People's Republic of China.

DEVELOPMENT OF CORPORATE CITIZENSHIP BEHAVIORS: PROSPECT AND REFLECTION

This research was started in February 2000. Based on a large-scale survey in Shanghai, the results give a snapshot of the situation and problems of enterprises making public welfare donations in Shanghai. As the largest economic centre in China and taking the opportunity of the opening up of Pudong, Shanghai has become an important window for market-oriented reform in China and its development toward international market integration. Shanghai leads the whole country with regard to changes in economic system and structure. Reform and opening up have caused enterprises in Shanghai to diversify and prosper together. The Chinese market economy needs enterprises to take an active role in the development of social services. However, will Chinese enterprises actually respond to this call? What models and practices will best enable Chinese enterprises to participate in social services? What should be done to the government, Chinese enterprises and charitable organizations so that together they better serve the development of social services?

In the survey, we asked enterprise representatives whether their enterprises would make donations to public welfare activities in future. Of the 503 enterprises, only 16 (10 are solely SOE's) clearly stated that they would not make any donations. The main reason is lack of economic capability. This accounts for 3.2 percent of the total number. About one-fourth (25.6 percent) of the enterprises gave ambiguous answers, saying, "It is hard to tell." This attitude is particularly common in private and foreign investment enterprises, accounting for over 30 percent of the total number. 71.2 percent of the enterprises stated that they would make donations to public welfare activities (see table 21.1).

Table 21.1 Intention to make donation of different enterprises (in Shanghai in 2000)

Classification of Units (No. of Enterprises)	Whether or Not Will Make Donations in Future (%)				
	Will Make Donations			It is Hard to Tell	Will not Make Donations
	Have Already Established/ Are Establishing Institutions	Have Already Drawn Up/Are Drawing Up Plans	Not Going to Draw Up Any Plan/ Institutions		
Total no. of enterprises in the survey (503)	24.9	19.7	26.6	25.6	3.2
Unit Donation Records:					
1. Had never made any donation (38)	5.3	5.3	21.1	50.0	18.4
2. Had made donations (465)	20.9	26.5	27.1	23.7	1.9
3. Had not made any donation in 1999 (168)	10.7	15.5	17.9	48.2	7.7
4. Had made donations in 1999 (335)	31.9	21.8	31.0	14.3	0.9
Different Economic Ownerships:					
1. Wholly state-owned (196)	30.6	16.8	26.5	20.9	5.1
2. Collective ownership (38)	13.2	28.9	26.3	28.9	26
3. Joint companies (38)	26.3	18.4	36.8	18.4	0
4. Stock companies (61)	32.8	16.4	27.9	21.3	1.6
5. Private enterprises (6)	16.7	16.7	33.3	33.3	0
6. Solely owned by foreign enterprises (38)	21.1	31.6	13.2	31.6	2.6
7. Sino-foreign joint venture (106)	17.9	19.8	23.6	36.8	1.9
8. Foreign–foreign cooperation (14)	14.3	28.6	50.0	7.1	0
9. Others (6)	0	0	33.3	50.0	16.7
Enterprises with Foreign Investment (145)	20.0	24.1	21.4	32.4	2.1
1. Mainly managed by China (46)	23.9	10.9	41.3	23.9	0
2. Mainly managed by foreign investors (99)	18.2	30.3	12.2	36.4	3.0

Enterprises planning to make donations can be generally divided into three categories. The first type of enterprises, which accounts for one-third (34.9 percent) of the total, has already made donation activities an integral part of the organization or is in a process of institutionalizing these corporate citizenship behaviors. Actions to be taken to institutionalize these activities include establishing special departments and recruiting professional staff members to manage donation activities. Enterprises of the second type do not have special departments or professional staff to handle charitable activities, but they have already planned to make contributions or are planning to participate for the next round. This accounts for less than one-third (27.7 percent) of the total number. The third type of enterprises indicates that they have not done anything to institutionalize charitable activities, and they have no intention to contribute in the future. The last category of enterprises accounts for a little more than one-third (37.4 percent) of the total number of enterprises sampled in this survey. Apparently, among these three types, the most established one is the first type. The third type is not receptive to the notion of corporate citizenship behavior.

What is noteworthy is that enterprises that institutionalize donations are SOEs or stock limited companies with shares owned by the state. Enterprises that have already made, or are making donations, are solely owned by foreign investment. Enterprises that "proceed without any plan" are mostly Sino-foreign cooperation companies, joint venture, or privately owned companies. Thus, findings show that successful SOEs and stock companies with shares owned by the state are, and will be, the key contributors to public welfare donations. Enterprises solely owned by foreign investments are also a reliable source of donations. The other new forms of enterprise, such as general Sino-foreign joint venture or cooperation enterprises, joint-venture economic organizations, and privately owned economic organizations are the final category that has to be motivated and converted to be good corporate citizens. In what follows, we provide some reflections on the results of this survey from the perspective of social policy.

Strengthening the Consciousness for Donation in Enterprises under the Market Economy

Economic capability is, of course, the basis for enterprises to make public welfare donations. However, to cultivate a receptive norm is also very important. Research reveals that the main reason a donation market has not been formed in China is the lack of awareness in enterprises about making donations. When the economic system is undergoing changes, this lack of awareness is unavoidable. For a long time, under the system of planned economy, all resources were controlled by the government; it is natural to think that the development of public welfare activities is the responsibility of the government. This is a duty of the government that cannot be shifted under the redistribution system. Enterprises in China have been making public welfare donations under the system of redistribution to help the poor and the old, and to develop culture and education. However, under the planned economy, such donations were part of the redistribution; they were, in fact, assistance made within the government system. Very often, they were the result of administrative arrangements and political mobilization. Under these circumstances, donations made by enterprises were basically not autonomous actions.

In a society under the market economy system, enterprises are independent production autonomies as well as independent members of society. Supporting public welfare is another means of repayment to society by the enterprises in addition to paying tax and authorizing the government to handle social affairs for them. Under a mature market economy system, enterprises make donations in the form of mutual beneficial exchanges. This is an important supplement to the market exchange and redistribution systems. Since this form allows more autonomy in making donations, enterprises donate money and products and gain honor, reputation, relationships, and self-gratification. Therefore, to enterprises, this is investing capital into society. It can also bring with it various "outputs," including economic rewards. To change the way enterprises in China define their donations to society from organizations undergoing passive redistribution to autonomies actively participating in mutually beneficial exchanges will involve a very important process of change of concept.

Forming an Arrangement that Encourages Donations

Research also reveals that the absence of a concept of making donations in enterprises in China is related to both the internal and external conditions of the enterprises. On the one hand, SOEs are still undergoing reform; they are still not fully freed from the system of redistribution. The independent economic entities and complete social status of state-owned and stock companies owned by the state have not yet been formed. Identification with and integration into the local Chinese society by foreign investment enterprises have not really been completed yet. It is natural that they are not as enthusiastic about making donations in China as they are in their own countries. Only the large multinational corporations (MNCs) and enterprises owned by patriotic Chinese will pay more attention to making public welfare donations. From the survey, we also found that the donation prospects of foreign investment enterprises have much to do with whether the internal management is governed by Chinese or foreign executives. If the management of the foreign investment enterprises is Chinese, it tends to be willing to make donations but will not promise to have any plan or establish any system. It is believed that these Chinese management personnel have to take the attitude of the foreign owners and the interest of the enterprises into consideration. If the foreign investment enterprises are mainly managed by foreigners, they will be more positive and active in planning for donations. However, they will also pay less attention to institutionalizing donation (see information about foreign investment enterprises in table 21.1).

Widely adopted by other countries, providing certain favorable conditions for donations is an effective policy to encourage donations. China clearly adopted this policy in its taxation laws in 1993.[5] However, from the results of the survey, it can be seen that not many enterprises are aware of and are making use of this policy. The Inland Revenue Department and public welfare organizations should strengthen promotion, services, and communication with enterprises. According to the experience of developed countries, the encouragement for tax avoidance/exemption is particularly effective to promote a positive attitude toward donations in enterprises of medium size. China has to create a tax exemption policy for funds that make donations and participate in other social welfare activities. The mass media not only have to be enthusiastic in reporting public welfare donations, they also need to have social and legal knowledge related to this field, so that they can make promotion, educate and guide the whole of society, and thus encourage it to form an arrangement to encourage the making of donations.

Setting Standard and Making Regulations for Acts of Donations

Donations made by enterprises in China are mostly self-initiated, random, incidental, and nonstandardized. The Law of the People's Republic of China on Donations for Public Welfare (hereinafter referred to as the Law of Donations) promulgated in 1999, in effect for less than four years, is still being tested. At the time of writing, many implementing regulations still need to be improved. The enterprises making donations, the public welfare organizations receiving the donations and the government departments responsible for managing the social organizations are working together to facilitate standardization and institutionalization in this area. In this survey, some enterprises gave positive suggestions concerning some of the existing problems. To sum up, there are three issues that are worth paying attention to.

First, according to Article 4 of the Law of Donations in China, "donation shall be made voluntarily and gratis. Any allocation of donations by compulsion or in disguised form shall be prohibited." The enterprises are also required to "stress self-initiative in donating money or manpower according to their capability." Some enterprises reflected that "Many organisations come to request a sponsor. If we refuse to be one, we have to give them reasons. Most of them make requests under the name of the municipal government so as to pressurise us to participate." An expatriate staff of a foreign investment enterprise stated straight forwardly, "It is reasonable to make public welfare donations within our capability. However, making forced allocation or allocations in disguise of donations is very repulsive." Thus, forced allocations really exist in donations. Government departments and public welfare organizations must abide by the regulations when organizing donation activities.

Second, the sponsors request knowledge about the site, use, and management of the donations, where the donations have gone, and how they are used and managed. According to the Law of Donations, "the donor may conclude agreement with the donee on matters of the type, quality, quantity and purpose of the property to be donated. The donor shall have the right to decide on the quantity, purpose and form of donation" (Article 12). Article 21 stipulates that, "the donor shall have the right to inquire about the use and control of the donated property and put forward his comments and suggestions. The donee shall give truthful answers to the donor's inquiries." However, in practice, formal and credible institutions have not yet been formed. Thus, some sponsors receive no information on the uses and outcomes of their donations. Additionally, they do not have adequate procedures for inquiring about these issues. Many note the initial enthusiasm when donations are made and the virtual lack of followup afterward. This negatively impacts future donations. The government departments concerned must strengthen their supervision and expedite the establishment of formal and credible institutions.

Third, enterprises tend to make donations for specific needs. They request that the parties that have needs be publicized so that they can freely target their donations to particular causes. Some suggested that "those that need donations can have their needs publicised through the mass media so that enterprises with the capability and willingness to make donations can know about them and make a choice in making donations." "Disorganisation and practices that give too much burden to enterprises must be stopped." These comments reflect that the donation practice in China is not yet well established. As a result, enterprises that make donations lack confidence in doing so. There is, therefore, a pressing need to strengthen the organization of various kinds of public welfare funds.

Develop Social Organizations, Make the Intermediary Organization Perfect, and Strongly Develop the Organization and Service Functions of Foundations

Under the market economy system, individuals and enterprises usually express their goodwill to society through various foundations. These foundations have the professional function of repaying society, integrating resources, and expressing ideals. At present, the economic and sociopolitical development of China favors these foundations to enter a boom stage. To establish systems of company funds and foundations can benefit the long-term development of enterprises. It can also help the enterprises to coordinate their relations with various segments of society and thus help the enterprises achieve social status corresponding with their economic standing.

Establishment of funds or foundations is an important means for enterprises to position themselves in society. Because it is also a successful way to combine economic resources and social resources, it is the institutional choice of mature and large enterprises. At present, the laws in China have no provision for enterprises to establish foundations. However, since funds of enterprises do not belong to any independent one and are not controlled by the Law of Society Registration, they can usually be formed by the decision of the board of directors. Professional foundations are needed to integrate the use of existing variety funds to make good their effects. Therefore, various foundations in China will be important intermediary organizations to liaise the funds of enterprises and donations made by individual enterprises and public welfare organizations. Through these foundations, the wishes of different organizations to repay society can be collected, their resources can be integrated, and their ideals can be realized. To this end, the government should provide necessary legal protection to enterprises establishing funds and various kinds of foundations. In addition, postsecondary educational institutions will actively train more professionals to manage public welfare and charity organizations.

The purpose of this essay is to understand the present situation and problems of donations made by Chinese enterprises for public welfare. Our findings suggest that there is a need to strengthen the mutual understanding and communication between enterprises and nonprofit making organizations and cultivate the social awareness of enterprises. The Chinese government is urged to strengthen standardization, use enterprise resources, and help the development of various kinds of public welfare foundations supported by enterprises. China needs to prepare for the establishment of various kinds of public welfare foundations, suitable for the needs of China, focusing on organization, institution, policy and regulations, and thus help enterprises to better shoulder their responsibility of corporate citizens thus achieving integrated status as members of society.

Notes

We are indebted to Shanghai City Pudong District Social Development Foundation for providing funding for this research and the Municipal Social and Economic Investigation Team of the Bureau of Statistics in Shanghai City for helping us to conduct the survey. This research was also funded by a research grant (Project B-Q416) from the Hong Kong Polytechnic University.

1. Keith Goodall and Malcolm Warner examined human resource management practices in China and concluded that there is strong evidence of institutional and organizational continuity in the so-called iron rice-bowl practices among Chinese enterprises. "Human resources in Sino-foreign joint ventures: Selected case studies in Shanghai, compared with Beijing," *The International Journal of Human Resource Management*, 8:5, October 1997, 569–594.

2. A. Walder, *Communist Neo-Traditionalism: Work and Authority in Chinese Industry*. Berkeley: University of California Press, 1986; Lu Feng. Danwei: A Special Form of Organisation, *Social Science in China*, Vol. X, No. 3, Sept. 1989, 100–122; Bian Yanjie. *Work and Inequality in Urban China*. Albany, NY: State University of New York Press, 1994; and Xiaobo Lu and Elizabeth Perry. *Danwei: The Changing Chinese Workplace in Historical and Comparative Perspectives*. Armonk, NY: M.E Sharpe Publication Company, 1997.

3. In some aspects, this microcosm resembles what is called a "Clan Culture" proposed by Daniel R. Dension and Aneil K. Mishra, where organizations are characterized by this focus on taking care of employees. "Toward a Theory of Organisational Culture and Effectiveness," *Organisation Science*, 6:2, March–April 1995, 204–223.

4. Turner, Jonathan H. 1986. *The Structure of Sociological Theories* (1986). Chinese version in: Fan Weida and Lu Hanlong. *The Theories of Modern Western Society: Part 3—Exchange Theory.* Tianjin: Tianjin Publication Company.

5. Regulations relating to exemption from tax for donations allow for deductions up to 30 percent of the amount of taxable (personal) income and deductions up to 3 percent of the amount of taxable (business) income.

CHAPTER 22

The Corporation's
Evolving Personality

Lynn Sharp Paine

If the value shift we see in many companies around the world cannot be wholly explained in purely financial terms, can a better explanation be provided? A more satisfactory account begins with an appreciation for a subtle but striking development in what has sometimes been called the "personality" of the corporation—the pattern of attributes thought to define its essential nature. This change in the character of the corporation has affected how companies are thought about, what's expected of them, and how they are evaluated. Seen in broad historical context, this development is nothing short of revolutionary, though its gradual nature, unfolding across the last century, has somewhat obscured its significance.

This development, which has picked up momentum in recent decades, explains why the notion that ethics pays has gained plausibility in recent years—and also why this maxim is nonetheless an inadequate guide for companies that aspire to positions of leadership in today's world. According to the Millennium Poll on Corporate Social Responsibility, a 1999 survey of more than 25,000 individuals across 23 countries on 6 continents, 2 in 3 people say that companies should go beyond their traditional functions of making a profit, paying taxes, creating jobs, and obeying the law.[1] Parallel but even more striking results emerged from an August 2000 survey in the United States.[2] Some 95 percent of these respondents said that companies should sometimes forgo some profit for the sake of making things better for their workers and communities. Although, as with almost any survey research, we could quibble about methodologies, response bias, and other issues, it is noteworthy that both groups of respondents evidently expect companies to exercise moral judgment in carrying out their activities.

A GLANCE AT HISTORY

In attributing a capacity for moral judgment to the corporation, these respondents go against an orthodoxy whose lineage is both long and venerable. The doctrine of corporate amorality has ancient roots in corporate law, and it has played a central role in the thinking of many economists and management theorists up to this day. This doctrine found perhaps its most colorful expression in the comment of an eighteenth-century English jurist who railed at the corporation for lacking either "pants to kick" or "a soul to damn."*

Though forcefully put, the thought itself was not original. In a seminal legal case decided early in the preceding century, another eminent English jurist, Sir Edward Coke, had declared that corporations, because they had no souls, could neither commit treason nor be outlawed or excommunicated.* Coke was writing about a hospital, a charitable corporation, in an era when most business corporations, apart from trade guilds, were bodies set up under royal charters to develop foreign trade and colonies.* In fact, the corporate form came to be used extensively for business in England only in the latter part of the nineteenth century.

To Coke, and to many who came before him, it made no sense to attribute moral responsibility to a corporation. How could such a manifestly "artificial" and "intangible" entity be a moral agent? That it could not seemed self-evident. The logic had been spelled out almost four centuries earlier by Pope Innocent IV, to whom the "fiction theory" of the corporation is sometimes attributed.* After wrestling with the problem of punishment for ecclesiastical corporations, the Pope concluded that the exercise was more or less futile. Unlike a real person, he reasoned, a corporation has neither a body nor a soul to experience the pain of punishment. And therefore, as merely a "fictional person," a corporation was by its very nature an unsuitable subject for punishment or excommunication.*

The fiction theory, shorn of its overt religious origins, was carried forward and reaffirmed in 1819 by the U.S. Supreme Court in the well-known case of *Dartmouth College v. Woodward*.* Although this case concerned a charitable corporation, business corporations were by this time gaining popularity in the United States, where some 350 were established between 1783 and 1801.* Even so, the business corporation was thought of mainly as an agency of government chartered to build bridges, turnpikes, canals, and the like. In exchange for meeting such public needs, it was granted certain special privileges and immunities, the specific nature of which would change and evolve over time.

In *Dartmouth College*, Chief Justice John Marshall described the corporation as "an artificial being, invisible, intangible, and existing only in contemplation of law."* As such, he wrote, a corporation could possess only those properties conferred by its charter of creation. Among these were "immortality" and "individuality," as well as others necessary to carry out the purpose for which it was created. Needless to say, moral personality was not included—nor could it have been, given the "artificial" or "fictional" status ascribed to the corporation. By their very nature, fictional entities lack the attributes necessary for moral standing, or so it was reasoned. Indeed, Marshall declared in another case that, as an "invisible, intangible, and artificial being," a corporation was "certainly not a citizen" under the Constitution.*

In the late nineteenth century, the fiction theory underwent a makeover reflecting the changing times. With the proliferation of "general incorporation statutes," beginning around mid-century, the government's role in forming corporations receded into the background. Under these statutes, corporations could be formed without a special charter from a state legislature.* By 1875, special charters had become largely a thing of the past, and virtually anyone could form a corporation simply by filing the appropriate forms and paying the required fee.* Many did so: The latter half of the century saw a phenomenal increase in the number of incorporations across the United States. A similar expansion occurred in England as freedom of incorporation took hold and the joint stock company, with the advantage of limited liability, became a form available as of common right.* These open policies on corporate formation lent credence to the new idea that the corporation was not, as Marshall had declared, a creature of the state with only those powers conferred by its charter, but a creature of private agreement.*

The new conception of the corporation as a fictional umbrella for a private association of shareholders strengthened the argument against government control over corporations and enlarged their sphere of authority. Nevertheless, the corporation's moral status, or lack thereof, remained unchanged. By reaffirming the corporation's fictional nature, the new approach negated the possibility that the corporation could have an identity separate from the identities of the individual shareholders comprising it. Nor could the corporation have either a moral personality or any responsibilities beyond those of its shareholders viewed as individuals. Besides, as a mere instrument, a corporation could hardly be evaluated in moral terms.

Of course, not everyone bought into the idea of the corporation as a fiction. By the dawn of the twentieth century, with the spectacular growth of corporations in the United States and Europe, academics on both sides of the Atlantic had begun to challenge this characterization. They insisted that the corporation was a "natural" or "real" entity, thereby drawing attention to the sociological fact of growing corporate power and influence as seen in the great railroad and manufacturing corporations as well as the immensely powerful oil trusts of the time.

The natural entity theory found an audience among both critics and supporters of the corporation's growing influence. Critics saw it as justifying their concerns about increasingly large concentrations of capital and its impact on community life. Supporters, on the other hand, saw it as legitimating new rights for corporations and enhancing the authority of officers and directors in relation to shareholders.

The theory squared neatly with a variety of legal doctrines being applied to corporations by the end of the nineteenth century. By that time, the corporation's capacity to sue and be sued, its freedom of contract, and its right to certain constitutional protections were well established in the United States. For legal purposes, the corporation had been declared a citizen, contrary to Justice Marshall's earlier insistence that this was not the case. Moreover, U.S. law had unequivocally embraced the doctrine of limited shareholder liability. Shareholders were now safely shielded from personal accountability for the corporation's debts and other liabilities incurred by corporations in carrying out their activities. At the same time, the law prohibited shareholders from managing the corporation's day-to-day affairs and precluded them from challenging the board of directors' business decisions except in cases involving willful misconduct.*

These developments, which strengthened the corporation's legal personality and diminished the role of shareholders, made it increasingly awkward to describe the corporation as a fiction or to think of it as a purely private contractual arrangement among a group of investors. Indeed, the very term "corporation" took on two usages, sometimes referring collectively to the body of shareholders and at other times referring to those with authority to act on the corporation's behalf.

Although the natural entity theory might have provided a platform for a distinctive idea of corporate, as opposed to individual, morality, it did not develop in that direction.* Instead, discussions of the corporation's personality trailed off into a morass of confusion over such abstruse matters as whether the corporate "person" was really a "person."* By the 1930s, legal academics had largely abandoned this line of thinking, and talk of the corporation's personality faded. However, the natural entity theory had by then done its practical work of legitimating large-scale enterprise in the eyes of the law.* The corporation had attained sufficient stature to be counted among the ranks of society's essential institutions. According to one leading authority on corporations writing at the time, "It was apparent to any thoughtful observer that the American corporation had ceased to be a private business device and had become an institution."*

The "institutional" view of the corporation thus moved into the mainstream and became the dominant framework for legal thinking. With this move came suggestions that the corporation, as such, had responsibilities not just to stockholders but to other parties as well— a position that would seem to imply a moral personality for the corporation. Noting a seeming shift in public opinion, a leading U.S. legal theorist speculated in 1932, ". . . a sense of social responsibility toward employees, consumers, and the general public [might some-day] come to be regarded as the appropriate attitude to be adopted by those who are engaged in business."* However, it would take several more decades for this sense to become widespread. Even in 1958, an opponent of the social responsibility movement called it still "young and rather unassuming" but dangerous enough to portend trouble should it gain momentum.*

Meanwhile, the fiction theory of the corporation had not entirely died off. In certain economic circles, this old bottle was being filled with new wine. Rejecting ideas of corporate entities and seemingly oblivious to the legal developments noted earlier, these thinkers offered up a new blend of private contracts as the essence of the corporation. According to the model that eventually emerged, the corporation was not merely a private agreement among investors but a series of private agreements among providers of production inputs.* Injected with new vitality, the fiction theory was propelled into prominence again in the 1960s and 1970s.

Unlike the English jurist who had seen in the corporation's fictional nature a cause for frustration, the theory's new proponents viewed it as a shield against the period's increasingly strident calls for corporate responsibility.* "Only people can have responsibilities," wrote a leading economist in 1971, in a coolly reasoned argument against corporate social responsibility.* Because corporations are only "artificial persons," he postulated, they can have only "artificial responsibilities."

According to this line of reasoning, advocates of corporate social responsibility are guilty of a grave mistake of metaphysics. By virtue of companies' very nature as legal fictions, they cannot have responsibilities to their employees, customers, or the communities in which they operate—or so the argument ran.

This argument, with its eerie echoes of Sir Edward Coke and even Pope Innocent IV, can only ring hollow to the contemporary ear. The size and influence of today's corporations far exceed anything even remotely imaginable to the authors and early proponents of the corporate fiction doctrine. Yet even today, some lawyers and economists insist that the corporation is merely a "legal fiction," implying that it is not a proper subject of moral assessment. They argue that companies are only amoral instruments of commerce, extensions of their shareholders' property rights. Echoing the centuries-old view, they argue that moral responsibilities can attach only to individual human beings and that it therefore makes no sense to speak of such things in relation to corporations.

Of course, such metaphysical niceties did not prevent the survey respondents mentioned earlier from calling on companies to set a higher ethical standard. Nor have they stopped millions of employees, customers, investors, communities, and concerned citizens around the world from making moral judgments about the behavior of the companies they deal with.

Indeed, as the size and importance of corporations have increased, so has the general propensity to view their activities through a moral lens. We can hardly avoid asking such basic moral questions as: How do companies affect society, and in what ways are their activities beneficial or harmful? Are the benefits they provide sufficient to justify the rights and privileges they enjoy? Do companies respect the rights of others? Is their behavior consistent with basic ethical norms? Given the legal history just referred to, it may seem ironic that people today sometimes seem more inclined to focus their moral concerns on corporate behavior than on individual behavior in private life. The tendency, though, is understandable, given the extensive role played by companies in society today.

THEORY VERSUS PRACTICE

While theorists build models of "fictional" companies operating in a world that is presumed to be morally inert, managers of real companies in the world as it is must deal with moral concerns on a regular basis. As (numerous) examples show, companies today are assumed to be moral agents with a capacity for moral judgment, and they are routinely dealt with, discussed, and judged as such. (Consider) how Salomon's constituencies reacted when management disclosed the bond traders' misdeeds—customers, creditors, investors, and employees alike began to separate themselves from the firm. As one CEO of a client company explained to a Salomon manager, "We know that you personally are ethical, but I can't go to the board and recommend Salomon. You understand that."*

Or consider the criticisms lodged against Shell. Unless a capacity for moral judgment is assumed, it makes no sense to take Shell to task for harming the environment or failing to promote human rights in Nigeria. Similarly, if corporations were entirely amoral, it would be absurd for employees to feel gratitude to Sealed Air for treating them fairly. The same goes for customers who would trust HDFC with their deposits on the basis of its past behavior. All these reactions—blaming, shunning, gratitude, trust—presuppose that companies are proper objects of moral assessment and concern.

The extent to which companies have come to be seen as moral actors is evident from the daily media. Moral controversies, allegations of misconduct, stories of moral leadership—these have all become as much a part of the daily business news as reports on profits, economic trends, and corporate mergers. The amount of such coverage varies, but hardly a day goes by that the front page of the *Wall Street Journal* doesn't include at least one such story.

On one presumably average news day in September 2000, for instance, the *Journal*'s left-hand lead article explored the fairness of the arbitration agreements that some mortgage companies were requiring their customers to sign.* Another lead article in the right-hand column examined safety concerns related to a McDonnell Douglas jet. Short summaries in the second and third columns pointed readers to other stories inside the paper about intellectual property piracy, antitrust issues in Europe, the safety of a new drug, a safety-driven tire recall, protests against unfair fuel prices in Europe, and the appointment of a new tobacco company executive. The summary noted that the new executive, unlike his predecessor, was well versed in regulatory matters and willing to discuss smoking safety with officials of the World Trade Organization (WTO). On that same day, the front page of the paper's second section featured one article about credit card scams in E-business and another about corporate espionage that focused on the rise in computer theft among high-tech rivals seeking competitive intelligence.

When innocent people are injured by corporate activities, moral questions are rarely far behind. Consider the controversy that began in August 2000 when Bridgestone/Firestone, the U.S. subsidiary of Japan's Bridgestone Corp., recalled some 6.5 million tires in the United States. Most had been mounted as original equipment on the Explorer, a popular sport utility vehicle made by Ford Motor Company. Faced with a growing number of accidents apparently triggered when the treads of certain tires pulled away from their rims, Ford and Bridgestone/Firestone together determined that a recall was the only way to prevent further incidents. At the time, tire-related accidents had been linked to 250 injuries and 88 deaths in the United States and at least 51 deaths in various countries in Latin America, the Middle East, and Southeast Asia.*

Issues of corporate responsibility moved to center stage and front pages almost overnight. How long had the companies known about the risks? Why hadn't they said anything earlier? Who was accountable for decisions that had been endangering the lives of unknown people around the world? How culpable were the companies? When subsequent disclosures revealed that both Ford and Bridgestone/Firestone officials had known about the risk of tread separation for some time prior to the recall, consumer trust in the Firestone brand weakened further. One study published less than a month after the recall began reported a drop in consumer trust of 39 percent in Asia-Pacific, 47 percent in South America, and 14 percent in Africa.* A *Newsweek* poll in early September found that more than 80 percent of U.S. respondents said that Bridgestone/Firestone was responsible, either principally or equally with Ford, for failing to warn consumers about the dangers of rollover accidents associated with the tires.*

These judgments took their toll on both companies. Sales of Ford Explorers stalled, and sales of Firestone tires plummeted as distributors and customers began defecting to other suppliers. Bridgestone's credit and investment ratings were downgraded. Injured parties lined up to sue. Congress called for public hearings, with the chairman of one Senate committee declaring that both Ford and Bridgestone/ Firestone had breached their moral obligation to the public in failing to disclose the tire safety issues when they first learned about them. Both companies' stock took a pounding, but Bridgestone was particularly hard hit and fell by more than 50 percent in the month following the recall.*

The 2001 collapse of Enron elicited similar reactions and sentiments. Wall Street analysts claimed to have been misled by the company, and employees who lost their jobs and life savings said they had been betrayed. A conservative political columnist declared that "indignation" was the proper attitude toward Enron's behavior. Other observers described the conduct of Enron and Arthur Andersen, the company's accountant, as "a serious breach in corporate integrity," "a pervasive breakdown in ethics and corporate governance," and a "failure to maintain the ethical standards . . . fundamental to the American economic system."*

What are we to make of this discrepancy between theory and practice? Are all these parties mistaken in treating companies as proper objects of moral assessment? Certainly the injured parties, the general public, government officials, and company executives all speak as if culpability, responsibility, and trust were relevant concepts. Have they not yet realized that a corporation is nothing more than a convenient instrument for conducting business, an "artificial entity" and, as such, inherently amoral? And what about the journalists and commentators at the *Wall Street Journal*, the *Financial Times*, *Business Week*, and other business publications that report on moral aspects of business activity? Perhaps they, too, are mistaken in applying the concepts and categories of moral discourse to companies and their conduct.

Some, like the economist mentioned earlier, have taken this point of view. Presented with moral criticisms of corporate behavior, they refer back to essentialist arguments rooted in traditional theories about the corporation's true nature. The imagery varies—machines, instruments, soulless persons—but the conclusions seldom do. "Corporations are machines. . . . Not being human, not having feelings, corporations do not have morals," says one commentator, adding, "To ask corporate executives to behave in a morally defensible manner is absurd. Corporations, and the people within them, are not subject to moral behavior."* Another states, ". . . the large organization is amoral. It is, perhaps, the most important technological invention of our time, but it is only a tool and it has no intent."* Still other writers assert, "[C]orporations have no concept of inherent right and wrong because they are exclusively goal-directed."*

But such essentialist arguments miss the point. Regardless of traditional thinking and practice, more and more people today are calling for something new. To someone wronged or injured by a company's behavior, the doctrine of corporate amorality is cold comfort. Rooted in medieval ideas about entities and ensoulment, it is a doctrine that has outlived its time. As so often happens in the practical and professional sciences, practice has outpaced theory. And this is the central point. While many theorists have devoted themselves to refining the traditional orthodoxies, the world has changed dramatically. In today's society, the doctrine of corporate amorality is no longer tenable.

NOTES

This chapter, an excerpt from the author's book *Value Shift: Why Companies Must Merge Social and Financial Imperatives to Achieve Superior Performance* (McGraw-Hill, 2003), outlines the history of the corporate amorality doctrine and presents evidence of its displacement by the premise of moral personality. The management implications of this evolution are spelled out in *Value Shift*. Detailed references (*) are omitted in this excerpt.

1. "The Millennium Poll on Corporate Social Responsibility," executive briefing, conducted by Environics International, Ltd., in cooperation with the Prince of Wales Business Leaders Forum and the Conference Board, 1999. Website: http://www.environicsinternational.com/news_archives/MPExecBrief.pdf (March 5, 2002).
2. Aaron Bernstein, "Too Much Corporate Power?" *Business Week*, September 11, 2000, 149.

CHAPTER 23

Corporate Ethics in Germany: A Republican View and Its Practical Consequences

Horst Steinmann

INTRODUCTION: THE ACTUAL SITUATION

Germany's economic order, the so-called Soziale Marktwirtschaft (social market economy), was introduced in 1949. Its founding fathers, the ORDO-liberalists, stressed from the very beginning not only the advantages of the market (as compared to centrally planned economies) for an efficient allocation of resources, for prosperity and growth of the economy, but also underscored at the same time the necessity of embedding the economic system and its (normative) institutions into a broader political order with social justice as one of its important objectives. They regarded it primarily as (one important) task of the (democratic) *state* to find and implement an *acceptable balance* between *economic* prerequisites for efficiency and *social* demands, and to readjust this balance, if necessary, to new conditions. As a consequence highly sophisticated regulations emerged over the last 50 years or so, aimed at protecting different stakeholders of the corporation. "Labor law" and an equally significant and complicated "social law" are but two important results of this development, each with its own jurisdiction, and with institutional arrangements never really understood or accepted by other capitalist countries, like code-termination of workers on the shop floor (*"Betriebsrat"* or workers' council) and within the *"Aufsichtsrat"* (board of directors) as the institution which controls the *"Vorstand"* (top management). It is this specific historical background together with an ever accelerating process of globalization that gave reason for a highly controversial debate about the necessity and extent of *deregulation* and its social consequences. Two (interdependent) aspects of this debate are of importance here.

One, the *national aspect*, is the necessity to strengthen the international competitiveness of German enterprises by removing legal barriers to entrepreneurial freedom. Can and will management use this enlarged freedom in a socially responsible and responsive way, or is it likely that our system degenerates to what the former German chancellor, Helmut Schmidt, has called "turbo-capitalism"? The second, the *international aspect*, culminates in the expectation that big corporations should take part in the global process of building up step-by-step a world (economic) order based on universal economic and social standards, which reconcile (fair) competition with social justice, thereby contributing to world peace. It was the former president of our republic, Roman Herzog (1999) who stressed this second point when he outlined eight maxims for a successful world internal politics (*Weltinnenpolitik*) at the world economic forum in Davos in 1999, quite in line with the similar and well-known initiative of UN Secretary-General Kofi Annan for a "global compact."

In what follows I argue, that both these aspects are systematically related to the idea of corporate ethics. It is then an empirical question to find out how German management thinks about and reacts to these new ethical challenges. Since there are no reliable and generalizable research results so far I shall draw more on cases and occasional information to underline my impression that corporate ethics may slowly gain in importance in Germany, though not yet accepted to a significant degree by German managers, let alone the relevant academic fields, like economics or business administration.

This hope is, of course, partly due to my trusting in a culture of reason as opposed to a culture where power and force is the dominant instrument for inducing and coordinating individual actions. In such a culture of reason (which grew out of the Age of Enlightenment) there is, I hold, a good *chance* that what is reasonable will become real, at least in the long run; drawbacks are, of course, always possible.

Corporate Ethics: A Republican Concept

There are two actual practical initiatives in Germany that demonstrate the search for a broader understanding of corporate responsibility in our country. One carries the label "corporate citizenship," the other "corporate ethics."

The four most important federations of industry and trade in Germany (BDI, DIHT, BDA, ZDH) launched a campaign in 2000 called "Freedom and Responsibility," where corporations can apply every year for an award for such corporate activities that contribute to the solution of any (important) problem of society.

The second activity was initiated by the "German Business Ethics Network" (founded in 1993), in the form of an "Award for Corporate Ethics." It is intended to honor companies that have voluntarily committed themselves to seriously contribute to the solution of those conflicts with corporate stakeholders, which resulted (or may result) from its corporate strategy. This long-term commitment must have been made official and public as an integral part of corporate policy; moreover credible steps and organizational provisions must have already been undertaken to realize it.

There are two important differences between these two concepts, differences which are directly related to the question of what they can contribute to the solution of the two problems mentioned at the outset.

First, corporate citizenship—at least in the (narrow) sense underlying the campaign of the German industry—is not systematically focused on and related to corporate strategy (as is, by definition, corporate ethics); it is, instead, intended to contribute on an ad-hoc basis to the solution of any problem of society, which is regarded by (top)management to be worthwhile treating. In other words: the corporation is looked at here first of all as a (proactive) *civil citizen*, as many other organizations of society are, and not in its capacity as an *economic actor*, which is the *conceptual* starting point of corporate ethics. The concept of corporate citizenship, thus, neglects what is the most important characteristic of modern societies (and which counts for their relatively greater efficiency as compared to traditional societies), namely *systems differentiation*. Systems differentiation results from the application of specific *codes* that determine (in principle) the *kind of rationality* of each subsystem. The dominant code of the economic system is "money" as opposed to the political system where "power" is central; its dominant rationality is *profit maximization*.

From this we conclude the *second* point: Since corporate citizenship views the corporation as a civil citizen (instead of as an economic actor) it can only be understood, like corporate philanthropy, as a (*highly*) *laudable* activity, which ultimately remains, in content and scope, at the discretion of management. Thus, contrary to corporate ethics, it lacks the quality of a specific long-term self-commitment in the sense of a (moral) *obligation* toward society or the public interest. To have it otherwise would either mean that the idea *contradicts* the dominant code of the economic system; or it is would mean to *neglect systems differentiation* altogether, which is certainly not the intention of the German protagonists of the idea of corporate citizenship.

Understood this way the idea of corporate citizenship, though laudable, carries with it a *specific deficit* in so far as it cannot unfold, contrary to the idea of corporate ethics, any conceptual power (and thus practical relevance) to make a *systematic* contribution to the solution of the two problems of public interest, which are of relevance here, that is, to improve the competitiveness of the German economy and to help keep up world peace. This would require better clarifying and specifying of its *normative content* and to link it *conceptually* to what is usually called *public interest* (or common welfare). It is the notion of corporate ethics, understood as a *republican* concept, which is *constructed* in such a way that it can take care of these questions.

According to the idea of the republic, going back to the ancient Greeks and Romans and brought to political life again and further developed by the French Revolution (Rousseau 1762) we have to distinguish, as is well known, the notion of the "*volonté de tous*" (as an empirical concept) from the "*volonté générale*" (as the legitimizing principle of the republic). If we reinterpret the "volonté générale" as a *procedural and discursive* (political) concept (Petersen 1996, 194, with reference to Habermas' theory of communicative action), we can take up at this point the proposal of certain German philosophers of the so-called school of Methodological Constructivism to introduce the notion of "peace" as a "de-transcendental" concept (Lorenzen 1987, 238). It is de-transcendental in the sense that it is derived not from any kind of transcendental reasoning (as it is the case with Kant, see Habermas 2001) but from a long-lasting and trustworthy (bewährt) *pragmatic experience* within our own culture, and this with respect to the question of how to arrive at successful resolutions of conflicts and coordination of actions. We learned, as *participators* in practical political processes of conflict resolution, that exchanging and scrutinizing *arguments* to find out what could count and be accepted as "good reasons" will make, in general, for a more stable coordination of common actions than the use of power in its multifaceted forms. Peace, as introduced here, is thus a *pragmatic category* (for this pragmatic approach see Kambartel 1998; Schneider 1994).

Peaceful conflict resolutions are then to be characterized by a *general free consensus* (Lorenzen 1987), based on the insight (*Einsicht*) in the better argument, as a (possible) result of argumentative processes. This notion of "peace" (as a procedural expression of the public interest) conceptually connects "freedom" (of free and equal individuals) with "responsibility" (for the public interest).

And from here we can arrive at a *republican notion*[1] *of corporate ethics*. It is in the public interest, so the argument goes, to *grant* entrepreneurial freedom and the license to operate a private corporation because this helps to organize economic processes (more) efficiently than in centrally planned economies; and economic efficiency reduces scarcity of goods and thus the probability of conflicts, thereby *indirectly* contributing to peace. Entrepreneurial freedom can, therefore, be regarded as a *necessary condition* for peaceful coordination of actions. That it is not at the same time a *sufficient condition* is due to side effects of managerial actions which may—as a matter of experience—cause serious conflicts and may thus threaten peace *within* and *between* societies. In so far as law *alone* is not able to provide for peaceful resolutions of such conflicts in complex societies (which proves more and more to be the case) this task falls back, at least partially, to those loci where entrepreneurial actions are taken, that is in our context: the corporation. In order to *fully* legitimize entrepreneurial freedom it is, therefore, necessary that corporations take responsibility, not for any arbitrary problem of society, as is the case with the idea of corporate citizenship, but exactly for those conflicts that arise out of their corporate strategy and that may threaten peace.

It is, thus, reasonable to understand the license to operate a private company as being granted by law not unconditionally but under the "provisio of peace": it should be regarded as part of (top) management's duties and liabilities to *avoid or peacefully resolve* such conflicts with stakeholders which (may) result out of corporate strategy.

Understood this way, corporate ethics has the task *to support the law* (as the original protector of peace in constitutional states) in three ways (Steinmann and Löhr 1994, 117): (1) to *apply* (relevant parts of) existing law; (2) to *supplement* the law where necessary, that is, where legal provisions for conflict resolutions do not yet exist, because conflicts have not been foreseen or because there is no legislator (yet) as is the case today for the world as a whole; (3) to *further develop* the law by criticizing it in so far as it may threaten peace in society (unfair rules of competition, discrimination practices, etc.).

Understood this way, corporate ethics can help to continually legitimize corporate actions and thus to contribute to the solution of the two problems mentioned earlier. In what follows, I show how this could be the case, using two practical cases from Germany.

Two Practical Cases

Corporate Ethics and Corporate Competitiveness: The Case of VW

As mentioned in the introduction there are strong demands in Germany for deregulation in view of globalization and international competition. The existing rules of "labor law" and "social law" are especially under attack. Labor law does not sufficiently allow, so the critics say, for specific tailor-made agreements between management and the workers *on the level of the corporation*; according to existing law conflicts between employers and employees about wages, working conditions, and so on must be solved, at least to a large extent, by collective bargaining *on the level of industry (Flächentarifvertrag)*. The mechanism behind is that of *countervailing power*, both parties (employers associations and trade unions) have the ultimate right to go on "strike" if no compromise is reached.

It is generally accepted that this system had great advantages for both parties during the first decennia after World War II when a totally destroyed economy had to be rebuilt quickly and when exceptional growth rates of the economy were the rule. Under these conditions conflicts of interest could be solved in a *generalized* way, without taking into account the specific economic situation of individual companies. Employees got equal pay for equal work; and for employers great parts of working conditions were taken out of (national) competition. As a consequence, strikes were comparatively seldom in Germany in those years; social peace was regarded to be an important competitive advantage of our country.

Globalization is now turning these advantages into disadvantages, and this not only for the parties of collective bargaining, but for the country as a whole. More flexibility is required to react to the specific requirements of a branch.

But to shift collective bargaining procedures to the level of the corporation, though probably *economically rational* under conditions of globalization, may become a serious threat to (internal) *social peace*, namely if the concept of countervailing power will still remain the *dominant* idea for conflict resolution. The outcome of the bargaining process then depends on the given *distribution of power*; each change here will cause new conflicts, and peace will remain notoriously unstable.

It is in view of this situation that I argue that ethics at the level of the corporation must gain in importance in Germany. This is especially true when we take into account that globalization may require, at least in the short run, serious *sacrifices*. Only if we provide in our institutions for a good chance to reach a *fair distribution* of these sacrifices, we can hope that the German economy will regain and strengthen its competitive advantage in the long run. It was the case of Volkswagen (VW), which demonstrated convincingly that corporate ethics can become a powerful means to cope with the challenges of globalization.

VW was in a serious economic situation in 1993–1994. Some 30,000 workers, it was said, had to be released to lower fixed cost and to reach the break-even-point again. This was, one can imagine, a nightmare not only for the workers, but also for the whole region of the city of Wolfsburg. Management and the workers council together started creative investigations to find suitable alternatives to mass release. A whole package of measures was agreed upon: general reduction of salaries and wages according to social criteria, redistribution of work with a corresponding reduction of individual work hours, regional mobility of workers, flexibility in working time, new rules for sabbaticals, early retirement for elder workers to give the younger employees with families a better chance, training for requalification, and so on.

Peter Hartz, the HR-manager of VW, characterized the agreement by the slogan "success by consensus" (1996). What he meant was just the paradigmatic change in industrial relations already mentioned, namely from (countervailing) power and *compromise* to fair and just solutions based on *consensus* of all parties involved. "Justice as fairness" proved to be an important basis for economic success in this case. It is for this fundamental change that the VW-case raised much attention in the media and in political circles in Germany.

Obviously, the VW case is an example of what we mean by corporate ethics. It opens a new perspective for the relationship between capital and labor, management and employees, with far-reaching consequences for our understanding of the (big) private enterprise. Instead of starting cooperation between both parties with the *individualistic* assumption of fundamentally incompatible interests, which had to be compromised temporarily on a contractual basis, to make cooperation possible at all, the vision is that of corporate governance (structures), which rests on some fundamental rules of justice and peace. Instead of management inducing cooperation via *socio-technical* financial incentive systems (alone), thereby relying primarily on *extrinsic motivation* of workers, the VW case revealed that there is another powerful source of competitive advantage, namely *ethical considerations* where *individual subjectivity is transcended* by both parties and where management relies to a large extent on *intrinsic motivation.*

It goes without saying that this *vision* of the enterprise as a both economically and, in a specific sense, ethically oriented value-creating community must have consequences for the *income* of all participants: sharing the fruits of cooperation in one form or the other, for example, by profit sharing, would be an integral part of a *fair distribution* of the value added. Of course, to change corporate culture toward such requirements of corporate ethics may take some time.

Corporate Ethics and Global Peace: The Case of Otto-Versand

Using corporate ethics as a *means* to rebuild and strengthen the economic position of the corporation has, of course, its limits. How much burden and what sacrifices will the people shoulder in the name of national competitiveness before political conflicts will arise and the internal peace be seriously threatened? This question relates to the limited capacity of *national* initiatives to secure peace, a problem well-known from the debate about globalization: delimited national economies escape, at least partially, the regulative power of national law. This points to the second problem mentioned in the introduction, namely the necessity to harmonize, in the name of peace, the normative basis of the world economy, at least in the long run. It is here that corporate ethics may play an important role again. I will demonstrate this thesis by referring to another German case, namely the activities of Otto-Versand Hamburg for ethical sourcing.

The fundamental conflict that is of importance here is well-known from various initiatives (e.g., Kofi Annan's proposal for a "Global Compact" of 1999). Kofi Annan has referred in his address to the "Universal Declaration of Human Rights," to the International Labor Organization's (ILO)'s "Declaration of Fundamental Principles and Rights at Work" and to the "Rio Declaration of the UN Conference on Environment and Development" (1992).

It is for *ethical reasons* that a number of governments of highly developed Western countries push for a worldwide acceptance of these normative rules, considered to be universally valid (which is, of course, sometimes questioned). On the other hand, governments of developing countries argue that this would threaten the competitive advantage of their national *economies*, and they are afraid that developed countries may close their markets for the products of those countries that do not comply with such rules. Up to now political initiatives of different countries and international organizations did not succeed to come to a general agreement, for example, within the World Trade Organization (WTO). So, the existing normative "disequilibria" are a continuous threat to world peace since they can be used to exploit those countries that try to comply with the rules. It is in this situation that multinational corporations (MNCs) may help to develop step by step a consensus about a worldwide web of normative rules. This is, in fact, the intention of Annan's initiative mentioned earlier.

Quite a few of well-known big German multinationals have decided to support these initiatives. Moreover, there are other, even medium-sized, companies that have taken concrete steps to realize (part of) the program of sustainable development. One of them is Otto-Versand Hamburg, the world's largest company in mail order business, with 51 foreign affiliates in 20 countries on 3 continents.

It was the owner and CEO of this company, Dr. Otto, who took the initiative to redirect the strategy and the management system of the company toward the principle of sustainable development in its threefold form: *economic, ecological, and social sustainability.* It is said that his basic motivation for this step came from the Christian message of the Bible.

Otto-Versand was the first and only German enterprise that was asked in 1996 by the Council on Economic Priorities to bring in its expertise and to start different pilot projects to implement the SA 8000 and, moreover, to have the results certified by an independent authority. The social standards that are relevant here are those of the ILO, mentioned earlier; they are well known: no child work, minimum wages as required by law, a maximum of 48 working hours per week, no forced labor, and so on. Otto-Versand made all these standards an integral part of corporate policy via a "Code of Conduct." And it took three steps ("strategies") to make them effective:

1. *The strategy of commitment*: All suppliers were asked to commit and comply with the social minimum standards; they were asked to participate in training activities (workshops) and to agree to subsequent controls in their production facilities and those of subcontractors; offenses were sanctioned.
2. *The strategy of superior initiative*: The company is ready to participate in the development of a worldwide system to implement and certify social standards according to the principles of the SA 8000. This system is intended to enable suppliers and subcontractors step by step to take ultimate responsibility for implementing and certifying the social standards agreed upon.
3. *The strategy of accompanying activities*: Otto-Versand fosters all kinds of social cooperation with and between innovative

organizations whose activities are directed toward the implementation of social standards in third world countries. It helps
to set up projects for sustainable development, which take into
account equally social and ecological aspects.

Today the Department of Environmental and Social Affairs at
Otto-Versand is responsible for all measures of implementing, auditing,
and (outside) certifying social standards. It reports directly to the
board of directors. Two times a year it carries out social audits (together
with ecological audits). It evaluates the results and makes suggestions
for improving the strategies mentioned earlier. Internal reports are
handed over to the board two times a year. After approval they are the
basis for the public report. This was published for the first time in
2000, together with the environmental report. This practice corresponds with the policy of other German multinationals. In line with
the idea of sustainable development it slowly becomes good practice
today to address three stakeholders in the annual public reports of
corporations: shareholders, employees, and the environment ("triple
bottom line"). This kind of report makes allowance for a central and
indispensable element of corporate ethics, namely to open corporate
activities to *public critics* as a basis, not primarily for *reputation
management*, but for *corporate legitimacy*.

The case of Otto-Versand Hamburg shows how *private* companies
operating on an international scale can contribute, at least to a certain
extent, to the *public* task of establishing a global order of world peace.
This can be done *directly* by reducing or solving conflicts with main
stakeholders (strategy one earlier) or *indirectly* by working together
with other organizations like nongovernmental organizations (NGOs),
international organizations, or states in order to form a web of rules,
which should govern corporate behavior (strategies two and three as
seen earlier). Following the third strategy, Otto-Versand is now seriously trying to gain support of the "German Federation of Retailers";
there is a good chance that this powerful organization will join the
initiative.

The problem remains, of course, that a few swallows do not make
a summer. What is needed today is a broad worldwide movement for
corporate ethics as Kofi Annan has envisaged in his "compact for the
new century."

Unfortunately most German professors of economics and business
administration refuse to contribute to such a change because they still
hang on to a *positivistic* ideal of social sciences with its dogma of *value
neutrality*. To give up this deep-rooted dogma takes time. Moreover,

there remains a serious theoretical problem to be solved, namely how to integrate corporate ethics into the theory of management. How will the classical managerial functions of planning, organizing, staffing, directing, and control (and their interaction) be afflicted by the demand to orient corporate actions not only toward effectiveness and efficiency but simultaneously toward corporate ethics? As a consequence, and more than before, to successfully handle dilemma situations will become an integral part of management and management theory.

NOTE

1. The notion "republican view" is not meant to relate to any political party, but refers to the notion of the "republic" well known in political philosophy since the ancient Greeks.

REFERENCES

Habermas, J. 2001. *Kommunikatives Handeln und detranszendentalisierte Vernunft*. Stuttgart: Reclam.

Hartz, P. 1996. Unternehmerisches Handeln und Mitbestimmung im Wandel—Erfolg durch Konsens. In: Bertelsmann-Stiftung and Hans Böckler-Stiftung (eds.), *Unternehmensleitbild und Unternehmensverfassung*. Gütersloh: Gütersloher Verlagshaus Gerd Mohn, 87–105.

Herzog, R. 1999. Für eine globale Verantwortungsgemeinschaft. *Frankfurter Allgemeine Zeitung*, No. 24, January 29, 8.

Kambartel, F. 1998. Vernunft: Kriterium oder Kultur? Zur Definierbarkeit des Vernünftigen. In: H. Steinmann and A.G. Scherer (eds.), *Zwischen Universalismus und Relativismus*. Stuttgart: Suhrkamp Taschenbuch Wissenschaft, 88–105.

Lorenzen, P. 1987. *Lehrbuch der konstruktiven Wissenschaftstheorie*. Mannheim: BI-Wissenschaftsverlag.

Petersen, T. 1996. *Individuelle Freiheit und allgemeiner Wille*. Tübingen: Mohr-Siebeck.

Rousseau, J.-J. 1762. *Du contrat social*. Amsterdam (Paris: Union Générale d'Éditions, 1973).

Schneider, H. J. 1994. Ethisches Argumentieren. In: H. Hastedt and E. Martens (eds.), *Ethik. Ein Grundkurs*. Reinbeck bei Hamburg: Rowohlt, 13–47.

Steinmann, H. and A. Löhr. 1994. *Grundlagen der Unternehmensethik*. Second edition. Stuttgart: C.E. Poeschel.

Business Ethics and Corporate Governance in the King II Report: Light from the Tip of a Dark Continent?

Deon Rossouw

INTRODUCTION

Corporate governance enjoyed unprecedented attention around the globe over the last decade. There are various reasons for its recent prominence. These reasons are very context-specific. In some (mostly developed economy) contexts its prominence was driven by the agency problem (Collier and Roberts 2001, 67) and investor activism (Rossouw 2002, 137), whilst in other (mostly developing economy) contexts it was driven by the desire to attract foreign investment and to gain national and international legitimacy (Chernoff 1999, 2).

This essay focuses on the relationship between corporate governance and business ethics from a developing country perspective. More specifically, it will look at a recent development in South Africa where the Second Report on Corporate Governance for South Africa (IOD 2002), also known as the King II Report, gave particular prominence to business ethics. The motivation for its emphasis on business ethics as well as its guidelines for the governance of ethics will be explored and, in closing, also critically reviewed.

The King II Report on Corporate Governance for South Africa

The King II Report on Corporate Governance for South Africa 2002, named after the chairperson of the committee who drafted the report, Judge Mervyn King, is the successor code to the King Report on Corporate Governance for South Africa 1994 (IOD 1994).

The King II Report not only opts for an inclusive stakeholder approach (referred to as a "participative corporate governance system" in the report, p. 7), but also assigns responsibility for the governance of ethics to the board of directors. In a section of the report titled, "Integrated Sustainability Reporting," it discusses the responsibilities of the board of directors with regard to the social, ethical, and environmental performance of the corporation. The report makes it clear that the social, ethical, and environmental performance of the corporation crucially determines whether the corporation will be able to sustain its financial performance. By social performance the report implies the moral obligations of corporations toward social transformation issues such as black economic empowerment and human capital development, by ethical performance it refers to the standards of corporate behavior or integrity, and by environmental performance it alludes to the obligation to protect the natural ecology. This detailed and explicit emphasis on social, ethical, and environmental obligations has been hailed as a "world first" for corporate governance reports (KPMG 2001).

A close reading of the King II Report reveals that the report is informed by the contemporary theoretical discourse on corporations and their moral obligations. The view of the corporation that underlies the report is one that contradicts Friedman's idea (1970) that corporations have no other moral obligations than making profits for their shareholders. It rather supports French's view (1979) that corporations can and should be regarded as moral actors. Like Evan and Freeman (1993) and Goodpaster (1991), it contends that corporations have moral obligations to a wide range of stakeholders.

This stakeholder notion of the corporation is reflected in the report's option for an inclusive stakeholder approach as well as in its recommendation that the board of directors should take responsibility for the governance of ethics. The following considerations are explicitly mentioned in the report as motivations for the inclusive model of corporate governance that the King II Report opted for:

- Sustainability
- License to operate

- Social power
- Good corporate citizenship
- Societal values
- Corporate reputation

Each of these motivations are subsequently discussed in some more detail.

Sustainability

The thinking behind the King II Report's commitment to an inclusive stakeholder approach seems to be guided by the ideal of corporations with "sustained business success and steady, long-term growth in shareowner value" (IOD 2002, 8). Stakeholders are defined in the report as "those upon whose co-operation and creativity it [the corporation] depends for its survival and prosperity" (p. 98). This implies that the ideal of sustainability can only be achieved when a company succeeds in gaining and retaining the support of its various stakeholders. Their ongoing support of the company will ultimately determine whether it will be able to continue as an "ongoing concern." The dependence of companies upon their stakeholders is formally recognized in the King II Report through its recommendation that boards of companies engage regularly with stakeholders. The report advises boards to identify their key stakeholders and determine what expectations these stakeholders have of the company. Boards should also give an account of how they have catered for the interests of these key stakeholder groups and then disclose regularly to these groups how the company has acted in their mutual best interest.

License to Operate

The King II Report further recognizes that a company needs more than legal approval to continue its operations. It also needs to be legitimized by its stakeholders and the communities in which it is operating. The ongoing process of being legitimized by its stakeholders, is referred to as the company's "license to operate" (IOD 2002, 8). The licence to operate is earned through responsible behavior that demonstrates to its stakeholders that the company's existence is to the mutual benefit of the company and its stakeholders. According to the King II Report, the stakeholders from whom the company receives its license to operate includes, amongst others, groups like the state, investigative media, ethical pressure groups, consumers, employees, and communities. In order to secure its license to operate, the report recommends that boards of companies engage regularly with these stakeholder groups.

Social Power

A further motivation for the inclusive stakeholder approach adopted by the King II Report is based upon the social power and influence of corporations in society. The report recognizes the fact that modern corporations often have a more immediate presence and a more immediate impact on citizens than the state. They often determine, to a greater extent than the state, the quality of individual and community life. This increased social power and influence of corporations yields added responsibilities for the boards of companies. Although not explicitly stated, the King II Report hints that if boards of companies do not take explicit charge of the added responsibilities that go with their social power, they will either be forced by the state to take that responsibility, or they will have to bear the brunt of the resentment of special interest groups, the media, or local communities. The report therefore opts for a proactive approach where boards of directors willingly take responsibility for their social impact and engage with their stakeholders in order to ensure that the interests of all who are affected by the operations of the company are being catered to and cared for. In this regard the report sounds a warning to boards that "in the age of electronic information and activism no company can escape the adverse consequences of poor governance" (IOD 2002, 10).

Good Corporate Citizenship

The option for an inclusive stakeholder approach is also motivated by claiming that it is imperative for companies to act as good corporate citizens within society. Good corporate citizenship does not only entail respecting laws and human rights and refraining from discrimination and exploitation, but also entails strengthening and developing the societies in which companies operate. This implies that companies should become involved in the most pertinent developmental issues in the contexts where they operate. Those issues that have a direct bearing on the success of companies should be addressed specifically. Within the South African context the report identifies at least three such areas that should figure prominently as part of the social responsibility of companies. They are as follows:

- *Black Economic Empowerment*: The inclusion of black people in the mainstream of economic activity in order to facilitate a more equitable distribution of wealth. Affirmative action is considered an important aspect of this process.
- *Health*: HIV/AIDS is singled out as a challenge since "current indications show that over 20 percent of South Africa's economically active population will be directly affected within the next five years" (IOD 2002, 109).
- *Human development*: The development of human capital is considered a high priority, not only because of educational deficits caused by Apartheid, but also because enterprises are in need of well-educated and trained employees.

The commitment to good corporate citizenship advocated in the King II Report thus stems from the conviction that strong sustainable companies require strong sustainable societies to survive and prosper. This is evident when the report justifies its option for an inclusive approach to corporate governance in contrast to an exclusively shareowner approach by stating that "any company's long term commercial success is inextricably linked to the sustainable development of the social and economic communities within which it operates" (IOD 2002, 98). Constructive responses to these developmental needs of the society require that companies should form partnerships with communities, local and national governments, and other stakeholders in order to be effective. Once more the report implies that this responsibility for good corporate citizenship lies with the board of directors.

Societal Values

A further motivation provided to justify an inclusive stakeholder approach revolves around the societal value system within which corporate governance is being designed and practiced. Underlying this motivation is the assumption that there is no one universally valid corporate governance system. To the contrary, corporate governance systems should reflect the uniqueness of the societies in which they originate. Specific reference is made to a value system that Africans across the African continent embrace. This African value system is sometimes captured under the term "*Ubuntu*," which signifies a commitment to coexistence, consensus, and consultation (IOD 2002, 19; also see Shonhiwa 2001a and 2001b, 19). By affirming these African values the report seems to suggest that corporate governance systems of African countries should reflect this value orientation. Such an orientation would render an exclusive focus on shareholders' interest undesirable, as it would fly in the face of values such as coexistence, consensus, and consultation.

Corporate Reputation

A final motivation for the King II Report's inclusive stakeholder approach is based upon the importance of corporate reputation. This argument is based on the obligation of directors to protect company assets. These assets do not only include physical assets, but also the symbolic assets of companies. Prominent among the symbolic assets is the reputation of the company as it not only impacts on its market valuation, but also on its ability to attract investment, clients, and talented staff. Reputation is described in the report as "a function of stakeholder perception of a company's integrity and efficiency" (IOD 2002, 98). By implication this means that boards need to engage regularly with stakeholders in order to gauge what their current perceptions of the company are.

Unlike the previous five arguments that all maintained a balance between the interests of the company and those of its stakeholders, the last argument is merely concerned about the company's reputation in order to protect its own assets. Despite its lesser focus on the interests of stakeholders, it nevertheless serves as a motivation for adopting an inclusive stakeholder approach to corporate governance.

The six arguments just discussed all double as a justification for the report's recommendation that the board should take responsibility for the governance of ethics. It seems that the authors of the report assumed that board commitment to an inclusive stakeholder corporate governance system automatically also implies that the board should take responsibility for translating that commitment into a system that will ensure that all employees of the company honor this commitment to serve the best interest of all stakeholders.

The report recommends that boards implement a best practice model for the governance of ethics that consists of the following aspects:

- Determining stakeholders' perceptions and expectations of the company
- Codifying the ethical standards of the company
- Institutionalizing ethics on the strategic and system levels of the company

- Monitoring ethics performance
- Communication and training on ethics
- Rewarding ethical conduct and/or disciplining unethical conduct
- Providing safe systems for reporting unethical or risky behavior
- Accounting and auditing ethics performance
- Disclosing ethics performance to stakeholders

Farsighted or Futile?

The King II Report's inclusive stakeholder approach combined with its recommendations on the governance of ethics discussed earlier extends these two dimensions much further than most other corporate governance reports around the globe. The question that I want to pose and answer in this concluding part of the paper is whether the corporate governance model proposed by the King II Report is farsighted and should therefore be taken seriously in at least other developing economies, or whether it is a futile approach that does not deserve serious attention.

The main argument for the futility of the King II Report's approach to corporate governance most probably is the one that states that the purpose of developing good corporate governance in developing economies is to enable companies "to compete for capital in a global market" (Chernoff 1999, 2). In order to compete successfully for capital, developing countries need to simulate the corporate governance systems and approaches of those developed economies where capital is most likely to come from. In the case of Africa that means that the Western-style corporate governance models and practices of the United States and the European Union need to be adopted. Because institutional investors from that part of the world are comfortable with and prefer the corporate governance standards of their home countries, they will be more likely to invest in economies where they see the same corporate governance standards being adhered to. Since the existing corporate governance models in at least the Anglo-American world are premised upon an exclusive shareholder approach, the King II Report's option for an inclusive stakeholder approach might not be palatable to Western institutional investors. It might therefore be suggested that the King II Report's approach to corporate governance defeats the purpose of the exercise and is therefore an exercise in futility.

This argument is flawed in a number of ways and contradicts recent findings in comparative corporate governance research. In concluding this paper, this argument is dismissed by exposing three flaws in it.

The *first flaw* in the earlier argument relates to the implied notion that there is a universally accepted best standard of corporate governance. This flies in the face of evidence that shows that corporate governance is always context-specific. It is also emphasized in the Organization for Economic Cooperation and Development (OECD) guidelines for corporate governance, where one of the guiding principles states that "International guidelines must recognize the international differences in governance systems" (Berglöf and von Thadden 2000, 300; OECD 1999, 10). The distinction between market and control models of corporate governance emphasizes why corporate governance models need to differ according to the context in which they apply. Table 24.1 highlights the differences between the two models.

The table demonstrates that the institutional landscapes differ considerably between the two models. Whereas the market model (which is typical of the Anglo-American context) is characterized by companies that are widely owned, the control model (which is more typical of developing economies) is characterized by concentrated ownership by families, banks, and the state. Similarly the market model is characterized by high takeover activity, whilst takeovers are relatively limited in the control model. These differences between the two models suggest that corporate governance systems designed for contexts with widely owned companies and active takeover markets could hardly be appropriate and relevant for contexts with concentrated ownership of companies and limited takeover markets.

This is confirmed by recent comparative corporate governance research that indicates that the widely held firm with dispersed

Table 24.1 Differences between the Market Model and the Control Model

Market Model	*Control Model*
Shareholder Environment	**Shareholder Environment**
• Dispersed ownership	• Concentrated ownership
• Sophisticated institutional investment	• Family, bank, and public finance
Capital Market Liquidity	**Capital Market Liquidity**
• Active private equity market	• Underdeveloped new issue market
• Active takeover market	• Limited takeover market

Source: Adapted from KPMG 2001.

shareholders is a rare phenomenon outside the Anglo-American world (Berglöf and von Thadden 2000, 277; Sarkar and Sarkar 2000, 161). It therefore does not surprise that Halpern, despite his stated preference for market model corporate governance systems, concludes that "the market-based system [of corporate governance] is not a viable alternative [for developing countries] in the short or medium term" (Halpern 2000, 3).

Admitting differences like the ones mentioned earlier should not, however, amount to admitting that good corporate governance is only possible within market model contexts. Good corporate governance is possible within both, even though the models themselves differ in many important respects. What matters is not the form of the corporate governance system, but whether it is true to the core values of good corporate governance, namely fairness, accountability, responsibility, and transparency.

The *second flaw* in this argument is the suggestion that good corporate governance systems need to be exclusively shareholder-orientated. There are both solid empirical and theoretical grounds for believing that an inclusive stakeholder approach can be as effective as an exclusive shareholder approach. The empirical evidence is provided by inclusive stakeholder corporate governance systems in developed countries with strong economies like Germany, France, and Japan. In these countries at least employees are included in the corporate governance systems without adverse effects on corporate performance (Jenkins-Ferrett 2001, 24).

The theoretical ground for an inclusive stakeholder approach is provided by the investment-argument advocated by Etzioni (1998) and others (Berglöf and von Thadden 2000, 287–289). The investment argument is based upon the belief that investors should be rewarded for their investment in companies. This reward is not only in the form of benefits that accrue to them, but also the right to have a voice in the governance of the companies in which they have invested. This right to voice is described by Etzioni (1998, 683) as being "entitled to form a relationship with the users of their resources to help ensure that the usage will be in line with their interests and values." In the case of shareholders this right to voice is exercised by voting for the appointment or removal of directors responsible for directing and controlling the companies they have invested in.

If investment is defined as "the outlay of money, time or other resources, in something that offers (promises) a profitable return" (Etzioni 1998, 682), then other stakeholders should also be considered as investors. Employees, for example, can be regarded as investors, since they have committed their talents and energy to the firm. This is especially true in the case of long-serving employees who have been asked to make sacrifices to help a company survive or to reach higher targets. In similar fashion other stakeholder groups like local communities and creditors can also be regarded as investors and should therefore be equally entitled to benefits and voice.

A *third flaw* in the argument under discussion relates to its neglect of the specific conditions that often prevail in developing economies. By insisting that corporate governance systems of developed economies should also apply in developing economies, it neglects important social differences between the two contexts. In developing economies, companies often need to take on responsibilities that are not normally considered the responsibility of companies in developed economies. In order to ensure stable and strong communities in which they can operate, companies in developing economies need to involve themselves in matters such as eradicating backlogs in education, training, health care, and so on, developing human capital, and resourcing and reinforcing the legal system and its enforcing mechanisms. Attending effectively to these and other social and developmental needs requires a wider corporate governance agenda than in developed economies where the same responsibilities either do not exist or where it can be delegated to the state or organs of civil society. Neglecting these issues of crucial importance to developing countries could in fact constitute poor corporate governance as it might be considered a lack of corporate vision and control by the board of a company. Such lack of vision can ultimately undermine the steady growth in value of shareholder (and stakeholder) investments and the long term sustainability of the corporation itself.

REFERENCES

Berglöf, E. and E. von Thadden. 2000. The Changing Corporate Governance Paradigm. In: S. S. Cohen and G. Boyd (eds.), *Corporate Governance and Globalization*. Cheltenham: Edward Elgar, 275–306.

Chernoff, J. 1999. World Bank and OECD Push Rules for Developing Countries. *Pensions and Investments*, 27(13), 2–3.

Collier, J. and J. Robberts. 2001. An Ethic for Corporate Governance? *Business Ethics Quarterly*, 11(1), 67–71.

Etzioni, A. 1998. A Communitarian Note on Stakeholder Theory. *Business Ethics Quarterly*, 8, 679–691.

Evan, W. M. and R. E. Freeman. 1993. A Stakeholder Theory of the Modern Corporation: Kantian Capitalism. In: T. L. Beauchamp and N. E. Bowie (eds.), *Ethical Theory and Business*. Englewood Cliffs, NJ: Prentice Hall, 75–84.

French, P. A. 1979. The Corporation as Moral Person. *American Philosophical Quarterly*, 3, 201–215.

Friedman, M. 1970. The Social Responsibility of Business Is to Increase Its Profits. *New York Times Magazine*, September 13; 32–33, 122–126.

Goodpaster, K. E. 1991. Business Ethics and Stakeholder Analysis. *Business Ethics Quarterly*, 1(1), 53–73.

Halpern, P. J. N. 2000. Systemic Perspectives on Corporate Governance Systems. In: S. S. Cohen and G. Boyd (eds.), *Corporate Governance and Globalization*. Cheltenham: Edward Elgar, 1–58.

IOD. 1994. *King Report on Corporate Governance*. Johannesburg: Institute of Directors.

IOD. 2002. *King Report on Corporate Governance for South Africa 2002*. Johannesburg: Institute of Directors.

Jenkins-Ferrett, K. C. 2001. How Directors View Corporate Governance in Their Day-to-day Operations. Aberystwyth: University of Wales (Unpublished MBA dissertation).

KPMG. 2001. *Corporate Governance 2001 in South Africa*. Johannesburg: KPMG.

OECD. 1999. *Principles of Corporate Governance*. Paris: OECD Publications.

Rossouw, D. 2002. *Business Ethics in Africa*. Cape Town: Oxford University Press.

Sarkar, J. and S. Sarkar. 2000. Large Shareholder Activism in Corporate Governance in Developing Countries: Evidence from India. *International Review of Finance*, 1(3), 161–195.

Shonhiwa, S. 2001a. African Imperatives and Transformation Leadership. *Directorship*, March, 4–5.

———. 2001b. African Values for Business. *Financial Mail*, May 19, 4.

CHAPTER 25

"Global Corporate Citizenship" for a Globalization with a Human Face

Urs Baerlocher

Modern societies are highly complex organizations that are based to a large degree on division of labor and whose individual members are bound together in a relationship of mutual dependence. To ensure that there is a maximum level of synergy—or at least a minimum amount of friction, the various players in the theatre of society tacitly expect that everyone by and large observes the rules.

It is of course true to say that companies do their best to achieve maximum profits; if they did not do so, then sooner or later they would go out of business. Generally speaking, however, companies do *not* seek to maximize profits at any social or ecological price; anyone who asserts the contrary is suggesting that those who have ultimate responsibility for their companies are severely lacking either in intelligence or in basic common sense. I do not dispute that there is always going to be the occasional "rotten apple," but one should not conclude from one speck of mold that the whole basket of apples is going to be tainted.

The overwhelming majority of reputable corporations behave as responsible members of the community, in the sense of "corporate citizenship." It is therefore in the interest of the majority of enterprises to promote greater transparency—this will reveal which companies live up to the standards that legitimize the operations of a global corporation and will exert public pressure on those which do not live up to expectations. The "naming and shaming" process should then be confined to the "rotten apples" and should not simply round up the *usual suspects* by casting a net over all multinational corporations (MNCs).

Defining "Corporate Citizens" and "Corporate Citizenship"

As with all difficult issues, it is always a good idea to set out by first defining one's terms. For this I refer to the definition of "citizenship" given in the *Encyclopaedia Britannica*:

> the relationship between an individual and a state in which an individual owes allegiance to that state and in turn is entitled to its protection. Citizenship implies the status of freedom with accompanying responsibilities. Citizens have certain rights, duties, and responsibilities that are denied or only partially extended to aliens and other noncitizens residing in a country . . .

But what does this mean in concrete terms? Let us extrapolate the concept to a MNC for a moment and say that

- a corporation owes allegiance (or, let us say loyalty) to the state in which it is engaged and in turn is entitled to its protection; and
- corporations have certain rights, duties, and responsibilities.

For a truly relevant and practical interpretation of the "Global Corporate Citizenship" concept, four principal conditions are necessary in my view:

- Clear societal division of responsibility
- Shared values
- Good governance
- Willingness of the different players in civil society to cooperate

Division of Labor and Responsibility

No one in a society is responsible for everything: no one has sweeping rights and no one is beholden for all the duties of society. Experience shows that a nation's economic and societal success—crucial for the public welfare of a society—is at its greatest if there is both a clear division of labor and responsibility between the different members of civil society and a common understanding with regard to shared values and the overall goals of society—including a fair equilibrium of duties and rights.

National and multinational companies have specific and fairly clearly defined "duties and responsibilities" in society's division of labor. To provide goods and services that succeed in meeting effective customer demands and can be sold at prices that are competitive and in the best interest of the corporation is among the most important. The goods and services that are sold provide society with different kinds of value added. In the case of pharmaceuticals, they prevent premature death and disability, accelerate cure, or alleviate the symptoms of diseases for which there is so far no cure. Being a successful pharmaceutical corporation therefore not only means being profitable, but also raising the quality of life of sick people, avoiding costly hospitalization for patients, and enabling people to go back to normal working lives instead of being bedridden.

It is not only a *right* of a corporation to strive to be as profitable as possible; I firmly believe that it is a part of its social responsibility and its duty within the framework of its corporate citizenship to be as profitable as possible. Sustained profitability resulting from sustained competitiveness on global markets is the precondition for a corporation to assume sustained responsibility toward society as a whole—that is, to be a good corporate citizen. All societies in the world are best served by successful enterprises because only they can offer a sustainable basis for

- providing goods and services of high quality;
- keeping, hiring, and competitively remunerating employees;
- paying taxes; and
- being a good corporate citizen by contributing toward pension and insurance systems and other social purposes.

In this era of globalization it is as true as ever to say that every effort to exert a sustainable and responsible influence on the shaping of the economy and the behavior of the people operating in that economy must observe a sense of economic propriety. In business terms, anything that goes against the principles of economic propriety cannot be correct from a *corporate citizenship point of view*.

I want to emphasize this point because many people still believe that there is a necessary trade-off between good economic performance and good corporate citizenship. This would be a false assumption. No doubt the management of a corporation is under an obligation to satisfy the shareholder—after all, it is the shareholder who owns the company. But there is equally no doubt that they are beholden to other stakeholders, including the communities in which they operate and the citizens who live there. Anyone who invests and wants to attract the best people in the job market for his company needs favorable conditions in which to operate, and this means at least the certainty of law, fairness in the way people live and work together in society, and a social climate that is favorable to business. For this reason, any intelligently managed company will include the expectations of society in its business considerations and decisions. There is therefore no question of either one or the other in choosing between a corporate behavior that is guided by a sense of responsibility out of a concern for public welfare and business behavior that is driven by the profit motive. For sustainable corporate success and for a successful civil society that derives its success from harmony and cooperation, both are essential.

The specific responsibilities of a corporation differ from those of other players in the same society, for example, the state, trade unions, nongovernmental organizations (NGOs), or the church. In a perfect world, every individual player in civil society contributes to the common good by fulfilling its specific core responsibility in the best and most cost-effective manner. The synergies created by the division of labor and specialization would allow for the highest level of national welfare.

Shared Values and Aspirations

As societies flourish, most members *share a basic set of common values.* Everywhere in the world, people accept a certain framework of standards for living together without conflict and for settling differences of interest without violence. These are mostly norms that have served for thousands of years as a compass to guide humankind in all their different forms of culture and religion. Whether we read Lao-tse, the Gospels, the Koran or Hindu writings, we find similar views on what is considered good and correct human behavior and on what constitutes a meaningful human existence. There is no reason to call these views into question in this age of globalization. The Golden Rule is one such universal value, either in its passive interpretation (Book of Tobit 4:15) or even in its active interpretation (Matthew 7:12). Observance of this rule would be sufficient to earn both individual and corporate actions a seal of approval, leaving most contemporary criticism without foundation. Another significant value to be shared is "Good Governance."

Good Governance

In order to assume the responsibility of being a "good corporate citizen," a corporation, like all other players in civil society, needs first and foremost a framework of good governance. Good governance is the *protection* to which *a corporation*—like all other members of a society—*is entitled*. Good governance relies on empowerment and cooperation and political institutions acting as partners, catalysts, and facilitators for sustainable development. The main responsibilities are to get the fundamentals right by

- establishing a clearly defined legal framework that provides stability and predictability as well as procedures for the peaceful solution of conflicts;
- maintaining a nondistorting policy environment for all players in civil society;
- investing in basic social services and infrastructure;
- caring for the vulnerable; and
- protecting the environment.

Good governance is an absolute precondition for sustainable economic and social development. As all empirical data show that economic growth is the single most important contributor for the alleviation of poverty and economic empowerment of lower-income groups, it is obvious that national governments must act as a facilitating and enabling factor for economic development. MNCs—within a framework of good governance—are seen by the United Nations as a leading vehicle for the achievement of economic stability and prosperity in developing nations because they stimulate economic growth and improve the international competitiveness of recipient countries (United Nations, *The World Investment Report*, New York 1994).

As rapid economic growth does not automatically translate into sustainable improvements in living standards and social conditions for the broad base of the public, the benefits for the poor depend to a large extent on a government's ability to strike a balance between giving incentives for improved and merit-based economic performance and protecting the vulnerable by appropriate safety nets. The taxes paid and other contributions made by the private sector provide the public sector with the resources to run the state and finance redistributive social policy programs.

WILLINGNESS TO COOPERATE AMONG THE DIFFERENT PLAYERS IN CIVIL SOCIETY

In today's world, there is another precondition for sustained profitability resulting from sustained competitiveness in global markets: *social acceptance.* To strive for sustainable success and social acceptance, a corporation will have to do more than just perform economically. It will have to be economically successful in a socially and environmentally compatible way, that is, to keep its house in the best order. This again means that it will strive to have good social, ecological, and other standards in its work and follow these standards in the countries in which it is active. Excellent companies strive for leadership in these areas as much as they strive for economic leadership.

But how can leadership in the context of Global Corporate Citizenship be operationalized? Who sets the standards and with what legitimacy? These are questions that companies cannot answer for themselves in isolation. But who should the discussion partners be for a consensus-oriented dialogue? In this respect, life is often made difficult for MNCs because the management has to deal with hundreds of stakeholder groups, which turn to these companies with thousands of different lists of demands.

To establish the parameters of responsible Global Corporate Citizenship, the international community has taken a major step forward in the last 18 months: consensus has been reached on a clearly formulated and largely undisputed core catalogue of social, ecological and political standards. This core catalogue was presented in the form of the UN Global Compact by Kofi Annan, Secretary-General of the United Nations (see www.unglobalcompact.com). The UN Global Compact is based on the conviction that weaving universal values into the fabric of global markets will help advance broad societal goals while securing open markets. The UN Global Compact calls for the observance of nine principles, two of which relate to human rights, four to working conditions, and three to environmental protection.

Questions, nevertheless, remain open. Any serious entrepreneur will tell us that while profits may be essential for long-term existence, they must not be achieved *at any social and ecological price*. But what "price" is acceptable in terms of business ethics? What deviations from that which is regarded in Germany today, for example, as a legitimate quality of social, ecological, or other standards are relevant in terms of business ethics to employment conditions in a developing country? In concrete terms, if the indicator for the cleanliness of the Rhine is the successful reintroduction of the salmon, is a comparable indicator then also applicable for investments in the Ganges or the Yellow River? Or is observance of the relevant local laws sufficient to be considered legitimate? If two extremes have to be weighed one against the other, is there anything like a proper balance in ecological terms?

And what about pay and social benefits? Whereas clear-cut judgments are passed relatively quickly in cases of "unpaid prison work in the prisons of countries under despotic rule," it is much more difficult to evaluate differences in salaries, wages, and social benefits. Differences in pay per se are no evidence of differences in moral standards. The principle of "equal pay for equal work" is a legitimate one when women are compared with men, foreigners with indigenous workers, or other equally qualified groups *within the same company.* Owing to enormous differences, for example, in the cost of living, productivity, and other factors, Swiss salaries cannot be taken as a standard of comparison when assessing the legitimate pay levels of workers in a developing country in Africa. Like must be compared with like; in other words, differences in productivity and in parity of purchasing power play an important role. For poor countries with high unemployment and underemployment, an old moral demand has to be called to mind: the duty to pay "living wages" that guarantee a basic level of subsistence.

Contrary behavior may be among the customs practiced in a far-off developing country, but companies that wish to be regarded as respectable "Global Corporate Citizens" cannot afford to adapt to the local rules of play and adopt that old adage "when in Rome do as the Romans do." Efforts to adapt to local practices in a social setting of poverty lose all legitimacy when they deviate from what *as a matter of principle* is considered to be proper by those in positions of corporate responsibility. To make excuses by referring to the deficits of others has no credibility: Power to act is rarely an absolute power, nor does it have to be. Responsibility is also borne by those who only have indirect or minimal power to exert influence.

Getting the Right Balance as a "Good Corporate Citizen"

Wherever several objectives are being pursued within the same time frame with the same available resources, conflicts of interest arise. Those in positions of responsibility are then faced with the issue of how to ensure that everything is properly proportioned to ensure that the various corporate and societal objectives can dovetail into concrete entrepreneurial action. To find the right balance and to form it into sustainable entrepreneurial action is at the heart of good quality management, which companies are already seeking to achieve in terms of both business ethics and technical objectives.

Toward an Enhanced Definition of Corporate Citizenship

Corporate citizenship does not normally include philanthropy or charitable activities. And yet, some corporations have decided to support philanthropic activities. NOVARTIS has done so for more than

20 years. After all, history does not just happen, it is made. This means that individuals may not remain passive in the face of a state of affairs that they find intolerable. Our philanthropic commitment is based on the conviction that those who have more resources at their disposal also have, in an unwritten social contract, a moral obligation over and above payrolls, social welfare contributions, and taxes.

Philanthropic activities respond to problems that cannot be fully or adequately solved by market mechanisms and allow a company to directly return something to the needy section of society, to those who cannot benefit from labor markets and who fall through the net of public social support. One such example are the leprosy patients for whom we donate Multiple Drug Therapy in cooperation with the World Health Organization and others. Apart from this, NOVARTIS has for 20 years been involved in development policy and assistance programs that have saved thousands of lives, cured tens of thousands of patients, and benefited millions of small farmers throughout the world (see www.novartisfoundation.com).

It is in the interest of companies to be guided not only by their own individual and short-term self-interest, but also by respect for the common good and the needs of the less fortunate—for this reason, it is an entirely rational decision for a company to strive after responsible corporate citizenship.

If all the players in civil society—politicians, entrepreneurs, researchers, and others—assume their specific responsibilities as local and global citizens with the highest possible standards, and if all institutional players in civil society—be they political parties, corporations, NGOs, or others—cooperate in a constructive manner, the synergism created is likely to allow for a bright economic, and therefore social, and therefore political, future. But it will not come about automatically, as Karl Popper notes:

> The future is wide open. It depends on us—on all of us. It depends on what we and many other people do and intend to do—now, tomorrow and the day after tomorrow. And what we do and intend to do depends on our philosophy; and on our desires, aspirations and fears. It depends on how we view the world; and how we perceive the wide-open possibilities of the future. This represents a major responsibility on the part of us all.[1]

NOTE

1. K. R. Popper, Freiheit und intellektuelle Verantwortung. In: *Alles Leben ist Problemlösen. Über Erkenntnis, Geschichte und Politik.* Sixth edition. Edited by K. R. Popper. Munich: Piper, 1995, 239.

NOTES ON CONTRIBUTORS

Urs Baerlocher, Dr., is a member of the Executive Committee of Novartis, Basle, Switzerland, and among other responsibilities, in charge of Social Corporate Responsibility, International Relations, and Legal Affairs.

George G. Brenkert is Professor of Business Ethics at Georgetown University, Washington D.C., United States, and editor-in-chief of the *Business Ethics Quarterly*.

Chi Kwan Warren Chiu is Professor in the Department of Management at the Hong Kong Polytechnic University, Hong Kong, China.

Jane Collier is Senior Research Associate at the Judge Institute of Management Studies, University of Cambridge, and Fellow and Director of Studies in Economics and Management at Lucy Cavendish College, United Kingdom.

Richard T. De George is University Distinguished Professor in the Department of Philosophy and Co-Director of the International Center for Ethics in Business at the University of Kansas, Lawrence, Kansas, United States, and former President of the International Society of Business, Economics, and Ethics (ISBEE; 1996–2000).

Georges Enderle is Arthur and Mary O'Neil Professor of International Business Ethics at the Mendoza College of Business, University of Notre Dame (Indiana, USA), and former President of the International Society of Business, Economics, and Ethics (ISBEE; 2001–2004). Before joining the faculty at Notre Dame in 1992, he was doing research and teaching in the field of business ethics in Europe over ten years and was co-founder of the European Business Ethics Network (EBEN). Since 1994 he has been involved in numerous research and teaching activities in China, particularly at the China Europe International Business School in Shanghai. His has authored and edited 18 books and over 100 articles. He co-chaired the Second World Congress of Business, Economics, and Ethics in 2000 in São Paulo, Brazil, and the subsequent Congress 2004 in Melbourne, Australia. His publications include *Improving Globalization* (2004), Business Students Focus on Ethics (2000), *International Business Ethics: Challenges and Approaches* (1999; in Chinese 2003), *Handlungsorientierte Wirtschaftsethik* (Action-oriented Business Ethics, 1993; in Chinese 2002), *Lexikon der Wirtschaftsethik* (Encyclopedia of Business Ethics, 1993; in Portuguese 1997 and Chinese 2001), and *People in Corporations: Ethical Responsibilities and Corporate Effectiveness* (1990).

Huizhu Gao is Professor at Shanghai Normal University, Shanghai, China.

Zhenping Hu is Professor at the Center for Deng Xiaoping' Theories Studies, Shanghai Academy of Social Sciences, Shanghai, China.

Kaifeng Huang, is Director of the Youth Academic Cooperation Center, Shanghai Academy of Social Sciences, Shanghai, China.

Peter Koslowski, Dr. Dr. h. c., former Director of the Hannover Institute of Philosophical Research, Germany, is Professor of Philosophy at the Free University Amsterdam in Amsterdam, the Netherlands.

Kit-Chun Joanna K. C. Lam is Professor in the Department of Economics, Hong Kong Baptist University, and Guest Professor at the Centre for Business Ethics, Shanghai Academy of Social Sciences, China.

Lanfen Li is Professor at the College of Business Administration, Suzhou University, Suzhou, China.

Hanlong Lu, Dean of the Faculty of Social Development Studies, is Professor and Director of the Institute of Sociology at the Shanghai Academy of Social Sciences, Shanghai, China.

Xiaohe Lu is Professor at the Institute of Philosophy and Executive Director of the Centre for Business Ethics, Shanghai Academy of Social Sciences (SASS), China. She is the author of over 60 articles on business ethics including the following in English: Business Ethics in China, On Economic and Ethical Value, Globalized Economy and Orientation of Corporations in China, Ethical Issues in the Globalization of the Knowledge Economy, and On Business Ethics in China: Its Characteristics, Dilemmas, and Trends. She authored Out of Jungle (1999) and co-edited Developing Business Ethics in China (Chinese version, 2003) and two book series: New Studies on Business Ethics (7 volumes, 2002), Translation Book Series on Business Ethics (5 volumes, 2001-2003). She co-founded the Centre for Business Ethics of SASS in 1999, organized many conferences on business ethics for the Centre, including the "International Conference on Developing Business Ethics in China" (2002), and created the "International Series Forum on Business Ethics" in 2003. She is Council Member of the China Association of Ethics (2000–2008) and Member of the Executive Committee of the International Society of Business, Economics, and Ethics (2001-2008).

Koichi Matsuoka is Professor of Economics and Regional Development at the Faculty of Policy Studies, University of Shimane, Shimane-Ken, Japan.

Yukimasa Nagayasu is Professor of Economics and Social System Theory at Reitaku University and Research Center for Moral Science of the Institute of Moralogy (Moral Science), Tokyo, Japan.

Lynn Sharp Paine is John G. McLean Professor of Business Administration at Harvard Business School, United States.

Farong Qiao is Professor at the Center for Ethics and Morality Construction, Renmin University of China, and Professor and Director of the Research Center for Business Ethics, Henan Institute of Finance and Economics, Henan, China.

Deon Rossouw is Professor and Head of the Philosophy Department at the University of Pretoria, South Africa, and President of the International Society of Business, Economics, and Ethics (ISBEE; 2005–2008).

Horst Steinmann, Dr. Dres. h. c., is Professor Emeritus of Business Administration at the University of Erlangen, Nuremberg, Germany, Member of the Executive Committee of the European Business Ethics Network (EBEN; 1986–1992), and Founder and former President of the German Business Ethics Network (DNWE; 1993–2000).

Xiaoxi Wang is Professor of Ethics and Dean of the School of Politics and Administration at Nanjing Normal University, Nanjing, China.

Zeying Wang is Professor at the Institute for Ethics, Hunan Normal University, Changsha, Hunan, China.

Dajian Xu is Professor at Shanghai University of Finance and Economics, Shanghai, China.

Jianwen Yang is Professor, Vice Director of the Institute of National Economics and Vice Director of the Centre for Business Ethics, Shanghai Academy of Social Sciences, Shanghai, China.

Xiuyi Zhao is Professor of Philosophy, East China Normal University, Shanghai, China.

Xiuhua Zhou is Chairperson of the Board of Dazhong Transportation Group, Shanghai, China.

Zhongzhi Zhou is Professor at the College of Law and Politics and Director of the Center of Business Ethics at Shanghai Normal University, Shanghai, China.

Yiting Zhu is Professor of Philosophy at East China Normal University, Shanghai, China.

Name Index

Subject Index

Printed in the United States
76075LV00002BA/343-426

9 781403 972538